MW00412124

OCCUPATIONAL HAZARDS

OCCUPATIONAL HAZARDS

*Sex, Business, and HIV
in Post-Mao China*

Elanah Uretsky

Stanford University Press
Stanford, California

Stanford University Press
Stanford, California

© 2016 by the Board of Trustees of the Leland Stanford Junior University.
All rights reserved.

No part of this book may be reproduced or transmitted in any form or by any
means, electronic or mechanical, including photocopying and recording, or in any
information storage or retrieval system without the prior written permission of
Stanford University Press.

Printed in the United States of America on acid-free, archival-quality paper

Library of Congress Cataloging-in-Publication Data

Uretsky, Elanah, 1969– author.
Occupational hazards : sex, business, and HIV in post-Mao China / Elanah Uretsky.
   pages   cm
   Includes bibliographical references and index.
   ISBN 978-0-8047-9576-0 (cloth : alk. paper)
   ISBN 978-0-8047-9753-5 (pbk. : alk. paper)
   1. HIV infections—Social aspects—China. 2. Businessmen—Sexual behavior—
China. 3. China—Officials and employees—Sexual behavior. 4. Social networks—
China. 5. Masculinity—China. I. Title.
RA643.86.C6U74 2015
362.19697′9200951—dc23

                                                                        2015018701

ISBN 978-0-8047-9756-6 (electronic)

for Lucille Munion Rubin, M.D.

Contents

Illustrations

Acknowledgments

THE FRONT COVER OF THIS BOOK BEARS MY NAME AS
author, but in no manner is it the product of one person's effort.
Countless individuals and organizations in the United States and China generously supported the completion of this project.

Long-term field research anywhere can be a daunting and isolating experience, not to mention in an area at the margins of the world. From the first
day I arrived, the people of Ruili welcomed me with open arms, even half-
joking at one point that I should be appointed as the city's first honorary citizen (*rongyu shimin*) since honoring Chen Xiangmei, the widow of the Flying
Tigers commander, Claire Chennault, with that title. Many friends in Ruili
told me it must not be easy to come so far to such a remote area for such a long
time. Their friendship and warmth made it seamless. These people were not
only research subjects; they became close friends who enriched my own life. I
especially need to thank the four men who acted as my teachers and my protectors while I was living in Ruili. The close intimate friendship among these
men and their generosity toward me taught me so much about what it means
to be a Chinese man. Thank you so much for allowing me to become part of
your close network of friends. I have tried to portray both the people of Ruili
and the place itself in a way that does justice to the trust and confidence they
placed in me. This book would not have been possible without their support.

There are a number of people and institutions in China who have also provided me with continuous support and friendship. I was hosted by Yunnan

University while conducting the original fieldwork for this book. Their Foreign Affairs Office helped me navigate the initial intricacies of life as a foreigner in a remote Chinese city. My academic advisor at the time, Yang Hui, from the Department of Anthropology, gave me support in the field and insights into life in Dehong Prefecture and the Jingpo community that she gained from experience with her late husband Wang Zhusheng. Zhao Jie also generously shared important lessons on gender in China from a local perspective in Yunnan. I am also indebted to the foreign NGO community in Kunming. Kellie Wilson and Kate Wedgewood, who worked for Save the Children UK at the time of my research, instilled a level of trust in me and my research that opened up the initial doors for me in Ruili. Grace Hafner and Ted Nierras also lent a great amount of support and collegiality to me while I was in the field.

I was equally fortunate in Beijing to be embraced by a community rich in intellectual stimulation as well as friendship and support for my project. Jing Jun welcomed me into the anthropological community and mentored me in Beijing as well as reminding me that I needed to master a repertoire of karaoke songs to conduct successful research on men in China. Weng Naiqun gave me further intellectual stimulation and introduced me to the intricacies of doing research in a minority community in rural Yunnan. I am also grateful to the many people living with HIV and AIDS in Beijing, as well as members of the medical and public health communities and local NGOs working to combat HIV/AIDS, for embracing me and my work. Their courage and tenacity in the face of such challenges is a testament to their character. I also benefited from a vibrant expatriate community in Beijing. Billy Stewart's support and belief in this project was as invaluable to me as he was to the initial response to China's HIV epidemic. Elisabeth Rosenthal's coverage on the front page of the *New York Times* of the Henan blood scandals provided a lot of inspiration, and she was also extremely generous early on in opening up many doors for me into the community of HIV researchers and activists in Beijing.

I have benefited from many communities in the United States, beginning with an extremely supportive and engaged group of scholars from Columbia University and Harvard University who helped to guide this project. Richard Parker's humanistic approach to studying the HIV epidemic has been an inspiration to my own inquiry into the subject in China. His support for my project and gentle reminders throughout my research and writing helped to keep me focused. The lessons I learned from Lesley Sharp through her teaching and her unflagging encouragement have been invaluable. I also thank Jennifer Hirsch for her careful reading of drafts and reminders that I need to think outside the confines of China studies. I owe immeasurable gratitude to Arthur Kleinman for his support throughout this project. I first began thinking about HIV in China during Arthur's Deep China course in the fall of 1999. His continued input has been important to framing this project within the context of China. Tony Saich also offered invaluable feedback on drafts as well as an amazing amount of support for the ideas I was developing. I have benefited tremendously from the knowledge he has acquired during his forty years of experience in China. Gary Dowsett also extended invaluable lessons during the early stages of this project, always offering helpful and supportive feedback on theory and process.

A community of friends and colleagues in Boston, where I lived as a graduate student, continue to offer unwavering support. I exchanged experiences, thoughts, and methodological queries with Kasumi Yamashita, Sarah Wagner, and Katrina Moore, who conducted simultaneous fieldwork for their projects in Saõ Paulo, Srebrenica, and Tokyo. I am also extremely fortunate to have the friendship and support of Nicole Newendorp and Elizabeth Remick, who are always there to answer questions and show me the way. The input I have received from Kate Mason on several chapters was invaluable for pushing them forward. Manduhai Buyandelgeriyn and Paul Festa also contributed necessary feedback on earlier drafts of my work. Matthew Kohrman is an incredible source of intellectual and moral support. Matthew and his family lived in Kunming while I was conducting fieldwork in Ruili and always invited me over when I visited Kunming. I was focused on studying Chinese men, but Matthew urged me to pay close attention to the border. This added a necessary perspective that helped this project reach its potential.

I began drafting this book as a National Institute of Mental Health (NIMH) Postdoctoral Fellow at the Center for Interdisciplinary Research on AIDS (CIRA) at Yale University, where I got initial feedback from colleagues and mentors that included Kim Blankenship, who has given me never-ending support, and Peg Weeks, as well as Ted White, Jhumka Gupta, and Elizabeth Reed. My time at Yale was enriched by Jeannette Ickovics, who directed the program, and Jon Atherton, who was responsible for its careful administration. More recently, I have received the support of a wonderful set of colleagues from the departments of global health and anthropology and the Elliott School of International Affairs at George Washington University. I am lucky to be part of a vibrant community of China scholars at GW, notably Ed McCord, who has furnished gentle yet constant support in my writing this book. Bruce Dickson and David Shambaugh have also given sound advice on my book-writing process. In the Department of Anthropology, Barbra Miller has been a constant source of support, and I have Christina Fink, at the Elliott School, to thank for feedback on material related to Burma. And Charlotte Byram in the Department of Global Health made available an immense amount of support in preparing the final manuscript for submission. Any remaining errors and shortcomings in the book, however, are my sole responsibility.

Financial support for this book has come from several sources along the way. The initial research and writing for the project was made possible by the generous support of a Ruth L. Kirschstein National Research Service Award Individual Fellowship from the National Institutes of Mental Health (F31 MH069075–03). I received additional fieldwork support from the Sasakawa Young Leaders Fellowship Fund. Two Weatherhead Fellows Program Training Grants from the Weatherhead East Asian Institute at Columbia University allowed me to do the initial work to set up this project. Summer Faculty Research support from the Sigur Center for Asian Studies at George Washington University also allowed me to return to China to keep my data current as I was completing this book. I am most grateful for this financial support.

At Stanford University Press, I would like to thank Michelle Lipinski for her support and expediency in handling this project. She identified two external reviewers who supplied critical and encouraging feedback that helped me complete the aims of this book. Nora Spiegel and Tim Roberts provided additional editorial support that helped to complete this book.

I owe the greatest amount of debt and gratitude to members of my family, who believed in me and have supported my endeavors in China for many years. My mother, Dr. Lucille Munion Rubin, who had a vague interest in Chinese artifacts that decorated my home as a child, inspired my initial interest in China. It is unfortunate that I was never able to share my passion, knowledge, and experiences in China with her since she passed away before my first trip to China in 1993. Without her support, however, that trip and my subsequent career would not have been possible. For this reason, I dedicate the book to her memory. Finally, I owe an unimaginable amount of gratitude to my husband, Stewart Uretsky, who has been an emotional anchor in life and throughout this project. His confidence in me when I lost confidence in myself, as well as his tolerance and patience throughout this entire project, have helped me realize my goal. He and our two wonderful daughters, Maya and Anya, are constant reminders of why it is important to take a break from work now and then. They are for me an endless source of laughter and entertainment. I am forever indebted for the unconditional love and support they give me, as well as the joy and humor they bring into my life every day, without which I would have not completed this book.

OCCUPATIONAL HAZARDS

Introduction

*An Epidemic at the Margins of Governance
and Governmentality*

IN DECEMBER 2012, CHINA'S INCOMING PRESIDENT, XI
Jinping, announced a set of austerity measures that would form the
basis of his trademark crusade against official corruption. He began with
restrictions on the lavish banquets that are characteristic of political relations
in contemporary Chinese society. Government officials and businessmen
in post-Mao China have grown to rely on banquets replete with expensive
alcohol, cigarettes, and food (often followed by some sort of female-centered
entertainment, which can include the services of a commercial sex worker)
to pave the way to success in a market economy that operates under the guise
of a Leninist bureaucracy. Xi told party officials to limit themselves to "four
dishes and a soup" (*sige cai yige tang*) when entertaining guests. He extended
his reach to smoking shortly before Chinese New Year 2014, with the
announcement of a policy prohibiting government officials from smoking in
public and using public funds to buy cigarettes. Xi's policies, which struck at
the very heart of the informal mechanisms that have become central to party
politics in China, aimed to limit corruption. But those same policies could
have formed the basis of an aggressive public health campaign because they
restricted officials from engaging in practices that rely on excessive eating,
drinking, smoking, and even commercial sex, which all have the potential to
place people at risk for the types of chronic diseases, and sexually transmitted
infections, including HIV, that have been ravaging the Chinese populace for
the past twenty-five years.

This book examines the unintended public health consequences of the ritual practices of *yingchou* that incite the lavish banquets Xi Jinping has targeted with his austerity measures. Anyone who has ever tried to accomplish anything in cooperation with a Chinese partner in China knows what *yingchou* is even if they have never heard the term. It is the requisite eating, drinking, smoking, and entertainment, which can include offers of commercial sex, that a Chinese host expects their guests to engage in as a means for establishing a relationship and initiating communication. *Yingchou* has had a huge impact on how governance is conducted in China. These behaviors have become essential for establishing and maintaining the personalistic relations, known as *guanxi*, that are necessary for political and economic success in post-Mao China. Avoiding these activities poses an inherent risk to success for China's rising elite, but they are seldom recognized for their association with serious public health risks.

Standard public health paradigms frame the ritual practices related to *yingchou* as individual behaviors that can be changed through standard behavioral interventions. But in China, where eating, drinking, smoking, and commercial sex are part of a singular ritual practice used to develop and maintain important social and professional relationships, these are all collective behaviors that have become a "dominant discursive trend" (Rabinow 1996: 7) in governing the distribution of state-controlled resources under a plan of market reforms. China's new market economy created a contradictory environment where state-controlled resources, normally rewarded on the basis of trust and loyalty to the state, must now be made available to private entrepreneurs who do not work for the direct benefit of the state. *Yingchou* is employed as an informal mechanism for demonstrating the trust, respect, and loyalty necessary for governing distribution of China's state-controlled resources. And although these practices have helped China's market economy grow within its Leninist political system, they have had some unintended consequences on its public health situation. Rates of chronic disease from smoking, drinking, and eating exploded following implementation of Deng Xiaoping's economic reform measures in the 1980s (Bazzano et al. 2007, Chen et al. 2005, Cochrane et al. 2003, Gu et al. 2009, Hao et al. 2004, He et al. 2005, Lam et al. 1997, Wang et al. 2007, Yang et al. 2008). Sexually transmitted infections (STIs) also rebounded in the 1980s after their declared eradication in the 1960s (Beyrer 2003, Chen et al. 2000, Chen et al. 2007, Cohen 1996, 2000, Gil 1996). And a nascent HIV epidemic emerged in the late 1980s. This book focuses on the sexual aspect of *yingchou* and approaches it as a traditional masculine practice motivated by a need to find an alternative way to conduct governance, rather than simply as an individual behavior. Sex for these men, in other words, is work, and not merely a way to satisfy an individual desire. Addressing the problems that result from these sexual encounters will require examining them through a sociocultural and politico-economic lens that will reframe how we look at public health risk within this context.

My focus on the sexual practices inherent to *yingchou* stemmed from an interest in China's HIV epidemic. When I arrived in China in the summer of 2002 to explore possible topics for research on the HIV epidemic, one-third of the patients under treatment for HIV/AIDS in Beijing at the time were homosexual men.[1] Many people in the international community of HIV/AIDS experts thought this might represent a turning point in China's epidemic to make it mimic the early epidemic in the United States. I later learned that even though one-third of the people who sought treatment for HIV/AIDS in China at the time were gay men, there were scores of other men around the country who were at risk for infection but not willing to come forward, whether for testing or treatment. At the time, a national AIDS hotline was flooded with calls from businessmen and government officials who had visited female commercial sex workers and subsequently learned about the potential risk incurred through such behavior. Many of these men exhibited what one prominent Chinese AIDS researcher later called "AIDS Panic" (Cao 2004). Afraid they could have contracted HIV, these men frantically called the hotline to ask the attendant if she could diagnose them over the phone, since approaching their local anti-epidemic station[2] would be politically risky if they were suspected of illegal behavior, or worse yet found to be HIV-positive. This of course was not possible; they would need an HIV test to determine their serologic status.[3]

The men who called this hotline were not alone. Nationally, men who travel and engage in business entertaining (*yingchou*) fuel China's burgeoning commercial sex industry, placing them at higher risk for sexually transmitted infections, including HIV, than any other class of men in China (Parish et al. 2003, Parish and Pan 2004). Despite these statistics, the epidemiologic paradigms that govern HIV prevention and intervention strategies in China neglect these men in their efforts. The global HIV narrative is dominated by epidemiologic paradigms that associate risk for infection with individually motivated behaviors. But the narrative becomes much more complex when forces outside an individual's control compel them into such behavior. In this book, I show that China's HIV epidemic is not solely the result of epidemiologic transmission patterns but one that fundamentally occurs at the intersection of everyday practices of governance, which are often informal, and the contrasting mode of self-censoring that many men simultaneously exhibit to support the type of government rationality or governmentality (Foucault 1991) that helps to sustain party legitimacy and traditional masculine performance. This has resulted in a standard set of competing discourses that daily pose serious risks to the men involved in governing China because even though they are unofficially obligated to eat, drink, smoke, and solicit commercial sex as a way of achieving political and economic success, they must simultaneously cover up any evidence of such behavior to uphold the moral principles of their official duties and the party that supports their livelihood. This type of juxtaposition, caused by the competing discourses between informal governance and formal governmentality in post-Mao China, has become even more acute under Xi Jinping's anti-corruption campaign. Large restaurants and entertainment venues previously supported by government patrons have closed down, and sales of luxury brands of alcohol have plummeted.[4] But government officials find alternative ways to fulfill their unofficial needs, widening the gap between governance and governmentality that has shaped the HIV epidemic in China. So, while this is a book that highlights the HIV epidemic in China, it is not about HIV/AIDS per se. HIV in this book acts rather as a lens to understand the significant impact that everyday practices of informal governance, founded in elite masculine tradition, can have on the lives of those who engage in its processes. It answers questions about HIV in China that can inform public health practice around the epidemic, but it also explains the masculine processes that drive the political bargaining that has characterized party politics in the post-Mao era. This cultural analysis, which sits at the nexus of public policy and public health, will also contribute to our knowledge and understanding of global health by offering valuable insights into the mechanisms that are responsible for both the emergence and the resolution of global pandemics in China.

I begin with the story of a government official who engaged in *yingchou* as a way to build his own career to demonstrate the unintended consequences everyday practices of governance can have on individual lives and public health in China.

Turning AIDS on Its Head

When I first met Wang Yantao in 2003, he had already been diagnosed with AIDS and his wife also knew she was HIV-positive as a result of having sex with her husband. Wang lived in an area made infamous by its many injection drug users, commercial sex workers, and the HIV epidemic, but neither he nor his wife fit the profile of someone typically perceived as "at risk" for infection. Neither had ever injected drugs, and she had never sold sex. In fact, they were middle-class people who both worked in stable, secure government jobs. Wang was young and quickly climbing up the local ladder of officialdom. They had a young daughter who was pretty and cunning, and they had also just built a new house. Such success did not come easily though. Wang had to work hard to reach the point where he could build such a nice house at such a young age. Work in this case often came in the form of the many nights he spent away from home attending banquets with colleagues and superiors, drinking and smoking heavily with them, and accompanying them to the local karaoke and disco clubs where they could eat, drink, sing, and dance in the company of a female hostess who could also provide sexual services for an extra fee. Wang sometimes made it home after a long night of entertainment but other times woke up the following morning next to a young woman he had never met before.

Wang Yantao's HIV status is certainly not surprising to anyone familiar with even the most basic epidemiology of HIV/AIDS. After all, he displayed the classic risk profile of a man who engages in repeated unprotected sex with commercial sex workers. He could have used a condom to protect himself, his wife, and his other sexual partners, but he didn't know he was putting himself or others at risk for a deadly virus. In fact, he had little knowledge about HIV or AIDS before he was diagnosed with the full-blown disease. There were very few HIV prevention messages and programs at the time in the remote area of China where he lived. Those that did exist were mostly targeted at the young women who sold sex to Wang and his colleagues. Sex workers, considered at high risk for HIV infection, are more common targets for HIV prevention programs looking to have a large measurable impact on the epidemic. Wang, who such programs consider a "client of a sex worker," may not have responded to standard public health messages anyway, for his repeated visits to commercial sex workers were not prompted by the individual behavioral patterns that public health programs typically target, but rather by his quest for the professional success that allowed him to build his house. From his perspective, Wang was engaging *yingchou*, which had become an unofficially required duty of his work as a rising government official. Not doing so would have threatened his political status. Any public health model used to prevent Wang from infecting himself or his sexual partners would have aimed at helping him avert some sort of *biological risk*. But Wang was much more concerned about averting the *social risks* (Hirsch et al. 2010) he could have incurred by not engaging in these behaviors. To him, he was not infected simply because he had unprotected sex with a sex worker but because he was seeking the success that lies at the nexus of masculinity, male sexual culture, and governance in China. The response for a man like this must also consider the role that local socially, culturally, and politically constructed meanings play in promoting the behaviors related to a disease like HIV (Parker 1991, Vance 1991), rather than simply following epidemiologic pathways of causation.

It may seem odd to begin a book on HIV/AIDS—an epidemic so rigidly defined by global discourses of risk, vulnerability, and stigma caused by inequalities of wealth, gender, race, and sexuality (Carrillo 2002, Gutmann 2007, Padilla 2007, Parker 1999, Farmer 1992)—with the story of a man like Wang Yantao, who has access to power and privilege. Men like Wang are considered to be among the arbiters of power and wealth. Theories of structural violence attribute HIV infections to the actions of such men but do not include them among the narratives of a disease that has been painted as the purview of marginalized groups of injection drug users, female commercial sex workers, and men who have sex with men. But these very same men shape and control the institutional and social structures that foster inequalities and create the vulnerabilities we so desperately want to address. Including them in the narrative is an important piece of transforming our inquiries about HIV/AIDS into an effective tool for designing public policy by offering explanations behind the processes implicit in distributing power (Parker and Aggleton 2002, Courtenay 2000).

The story of Wang Yantao also defies the epidemiologic narrative of China's HIV epidemic. HIV in China was initially associated with injection drug users.[5] It was later globally recognized because of a localized epidemic among people who sold blood plasma in central China, but the official epidemiologic narrative of HIV in China is still categorized according to traditional risk categories. Statistics show that the epidemic is now primarily transmitted through sexual contact (both homosexual and heterosexual), but this mode of transmission is most readily associated with commercial sex workers and men who have sex with men (MSM),[6] categories of people who fit neatly into public health paradigms, and not someone like Wang who, despite his behavior, is not considered at-risk (Lu et al. 2008, Sanderson 2007, Patton 2002). (See Fig. I.1.)

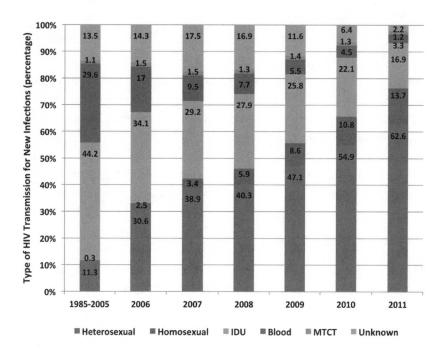

FIGURE I.1   Type of HIV Transmission for New Infections in China by Year,
1985–2011.
SOURCE: Ministry of Health of the People's Republic of China. 2012. China AIDS Response
Progress Report.

The risk of HIV to men like Wang Yantao is not evident in official statistics because men like him lie outside the standard public health definitions of
"risk" that would qualify them for inclusion in HIV prevention programs. But
these men fuel the demand for commercial sex and have shaped the unique
pattern of China's HIV epidemic. Indeed, the foreign director of an international HIV/AIDS prevention program in China once looked at me and said
"you don't work on AIDS" because my work focused on a group of men who
fall outside the standard paradigms that framed her work. In order to properly respond to the HIV epidemic in China, we must turn AIDS on its head by
challenging paradigms in public health and social science that dictate a singular focus on marginalized populations as a way of addressing vulnerability to
HIV infection. Neglecting the role that men like Wang Yantao play in the HIV
epidemic neglects a large proportion of the people at risk for HIV in China
and also reifies a focus on marginalized populations that has unintentionally

placed an undue burden on vulnerable members of society who are assigned the blame for infection (de Zalduondo 1991). Consequently, this book employs an unusual turn in anthropologic inquiry by "studying up" (Nader 1974) to offer an analysis that lets us understand how structures of power in China create vulnerability for both the men who control power and their more socially vulnerable partners (Lynch, Brouard, and Visser 2010, Mane and Aggleton 2001), who are implicated by the elite masculine practices that govern bureaucratic operation in post-Mao China. This requires further understanding of how governance is conducted in post-Mao China and also of the masculine practices often used to govern.

The Crack Between Governance and Governmentality in China

Governance, or the act of governing, refers to the methods governing bodies use to make decisions. Global discourse encourages a movement toward "good governance," that relies on standard policies and procedures to make decisions. This promotes transparency and accountability among policy makers and makes information available for policy analysis (North 1990, Heimke and Levitsy 2005, Tsai 2007, Howell 2004a, Nonini 2008). This type of governance, however, is an ideal that often cannot be achieved in the face of the complex cultural models that can influence how public officials make decisions (Jing 2011).

In China, for example, governance is often conducted outside the official halls of government and instead is influenced by activities that take place in top-tier restaurants, karaoke clubs, massage parlors, and saunas (see Photo 1.1). The shared and unwritten code that government officials (usually male) use to communicate and conduct government outside officially sanctioned channels offers alternative ways for achieving state and societal goals, which serve as an influential force in governance in China and other transitional socialist economies (Wedel et al. 2005, Tsai 2007, Heimke and Levitsy 2005, Howell 2004a, Chan 1983, Oi 1985, Pye 1981, Walder 1995).

One need look no further than official state visits to witness the importance of these cultural institutions. Photos of Richard Nixon or Bill Clinton sharing a toast with Zhou Enlai or Jiang Zemin are equally hailed as those in the official greeting halls because of the influence informal ritual practices have over building the official relationships that are so integral to governance in China. Even the groundbreaking climate change agreement signed between

PHOTO I.1 Hua Yi Tianlun Water World is located in downtown Beijing.
The sign outside the club states, "the club is an ideal place for your business,
negotiation, personal leisure, health preserving and health care." Photo by author.

Barak Obama and Xi Jinping in 2014 was announced in the newspapers with
a photo of the two men toasting each other at a banquet in the Great Hall of
the People (*renmin dahui tang*) rather than with a picture of a handshake, a
signing ceremony, or some other gesture more representative of major diplo-
matic accomplishments.

   Informal mechanisms of governance, performed through *yingchou*, however, are not the only forces working on men's sexual practices in China.
These modes of governance inherently undermine the formal bureaucratic
rationality of the state and as such are officially proscribed in China. Nevertheless, government officials and party members responsible for protecting
the state's legitimacy and moral integrity through formal bureaucratic means
also face informal expectations to engage in the very practices and behaviors
that are prohibited for them. This inherent contradiction between the informal practices of governance that are unofficially required to climb the ladders
of economic and political success in China and the governmental rationality,
or governmentality as Foucault (1991) called it, leaves men in a void that is

inaccessible to standard HIV prevention campaigns, which depend on public health messages targeted at certain individuals who can be associated with high-risk behaviors. Examining the lives of men like Wang Yantao demonstrates the cracks (de Carteau 1984) opened up by this divergence between governance and governmentality and the effects these cracks can have on both individual lives and the surrounding society.

Wang Yantao was a government official, a man responsible for establishing virtue in government and society by carrying out Communist Party policy and guarding China's official moral and social code (Shirk 1982). This prohibited him from engaging in activities that involved commercial sex. At the same time, however, the sociocultural structure that influenced his success within the local political milieu was dependent on informal practices that included sex work. Wang and others told me they were expected to engage in the eating, drinking, and entertaining that occupied many of their days and nights as a means for demonstrating loyalty to their superiors. The many businessmen I met also told me about their own engagement in similar practices of *yingchou* with government officials who controlled many of the resources, permits, and licenses that were so crucial to their success. Official proscription of these activities, however, left them in a liminal space defined by the competing discourses between their political and social lives.

Gendering Men

My examination of these competing discourses between governance and governmentality in China reaches beyond the institutional mechanisms of bureaucracy, into the masculine social mechanisms that have become integrated into Chinese decision-making processes. Consequently, much of the discussion in this book focuses on masculinity, its role in governing post-Mao China, and its effect on the spread of sexually transmitted infections in China, including HIV.

Gender is frequently recognized as a category that is influential in the spread of HIV but, when employed for the purposes of public health inquiries, is usually framed as a measurable variable associated with risk rather than as a social category useful for explaining how the epidemic spreads (Courtenay 2000). This is particularly true in the case of men. Most HIV research on men focuses on the individual behaviors that classify them as "clients" of sex workers. But there is little effort to examine the broader experiences of these men, who do not identify as clients, to understand how their true identity shapes their desire or need to solicit the services of a sex worker. This has placed us at a huge disadvantage for responding to diseases that occur along gendered cleavages. In an epidemic where men are seen as both the origin and the solution of the problem, though (Foreman 1999), it is important to understand the socially and culturally constructed set of values and beliefs that inform masculinity and ultimately guide men's everyday practices. This helps to place men's "risk-taking behaviors" into a context that can explain the social origins behind behavior that may be perceived as irrational from an epidemiologic perspective (Brown, Sorrell, and Raffaelli 2005, Connell 2000, Cornwall and Lindesfarne 1994, Morrell 1998).

Recognizing the relational aspects of gender will help relax the tension exerted by the dichotomy of the "female victim" and her "male perpetrator" and allow inquiry into the question of how a woman's often more powerful male partner became infected (Connell 2002, 2005, Cornwall 1997, Dworkin 2005, Campbell 1995, Harrison et al. 2006). The first step in achieving this goal is to realize that men are "engendered and engendering beings" (Gutmann 2007). Such inquiries help us move beyond the behavioral factors commonly discussed in HIV prevention literature, which limit our views of men as "clients of sex workers" to a place where we can access men's lives by learning what it means to be a man (Bernstein 2001, Gutmann 1996). Recognizing the role that men play in spreading HIV also requires accounting for local contextual factors that define maleness rather than relying on simple "categories of maleness" (Dowsett 2001, Gutmann 1997b, Carrigan, Connell, and Lee 1985). Constructions of masculinity are context-specific and subject not only to sociocultural and politico-economic factors but also to historic disruption that can challenge men's abilities to achieve local requirements of masculinity (Carrillo 2002, Gutmann 2007, Padilla 2007, Parker 1999, Connell 1995, Jobson 2010). In addition, we need to consider the effect of hegemonic ideals on our understanding of masculinity (Gutmann 1996, Carrigan, Connell, and Lee 1985, Connell and Messerschmidt 2005). In this book, I develop a "class-specific form of masculinity" (Connell 1995) related to sex and the important roles that power, nationalist ideology, the free market, and marriage play in construction of the elite forms of masculinity that government officials and wealthy businessmen adhere to in China. Such discussion will permit greater understanding of how masculinity can influence HIV transmission in China.[7]

China's Local Sexual Culture

Discussions of masculinity also commonly incur rhetoric around sexuality because the two are so often associated with one another in a dialectical space that confounds sexual prowess with hegemonic forms of masculinity. The local form of masculinity I describe in this book does not readily associate maleness with sexual prowess but is one that adheres to the cultural model that guides men's sexual practices and determines patterns of HIV transmission in China (Patton 1985, Parker 1987).

Gilbert Herdt defines sexual culture as:

> A consensual model of cultural ideas about sexual behavior in a group. Such a cognitive model involves a world-view of norms, values, beliefs, and meaning regarding the nature and purpose of sexual encounters. It also involves an affective model of emotional states and moral guidelines to institutionalize what is felt to be "normal, natural, necessary, or approved" in a community of actors .(Herdt 1997: 10)

Discourse around contemporary sexual culture in post-Mao China is often framed in terms of a "sexual revolution" (Zhang 2011) that has occurred as a result of the importation of Western values that incited a shift away from sexual austerity following implementation of Deng Xiaoping's economic reform measures. But China is actually home to its own rich sexual culture that is seen as an essential part of health and social structure. Taoist tradition views the bodily fluids emitted and exchanged during sex as a crucial part of the natural universe needed for maintaining the balance of *yin* and *yang* energy within the body, an integral measure of primordial mortality (Furth 1994, Micollier 2004). Taoist manuals on social conduct provided common guidance for practices of health and hygiene to people in imperial China, including proper sexual technique (Henriot [1997] 2001, Hershatter 1997, Ruan 1991).

Confucian moral code also recognized the centrality of eroticism to social life. To Confucius, though, eroticism represented an excess that could disrupt the domestic order, which was also believed to be a major determinant for state order in imperial China. Confucius thus relegated conduct of extraneous erotic behavior to spaces outside the home as a means for maintaining cosmic, and hence state, order (Micollier 2004, Bauman 1998). Government officials traditionally chose wives who were worthy of their kinship network, mothering their heirs, and gaining access to the economic resources of their lineage. A wife was also chosen for her ability to support her husband's political and social status, without concern for love. She was not, however, associated with provision of erotic pleasure, which a man could seek elsewhere.

Extramarital relations with minor wives or lovers bestowed a certain amount of status on a man and could also furnish him with love from a woman (Brownell and Wasserstrom 2002, Furth 1988, Sommer 1997, 2000). Traditional social mores guiding sexual practices also extended into the more casual realm of courtesans and prostitutes. Elite men, who typically hailed from a class of educated literati during China's late imperial era were partially socialized through their interaction with courtesan women, who primarily served in entertainment roles but could also offer sexual services.

China's newly emergent market economy has engendered a new class of elite men who are defined by money rather than scholarship. Many of these men lived through a period of tight political controls where sexuality was suppressed. The relaxation of political controls that has accompanied market reforms created a space where Chinese men can once again realize the sexual privileges historically accorded to them. This has led to the rise of a contemporary class of Chinese men who often identify as "Confucianists" (rujia) and feel entitled to relations with women who play various social and sexual roles in their lives. This surge of sexuality that we are now noticing is thus a result of a sudden emerging space that has allowed men to once again realize the entitlements available within their own sexual culture, and not a revolution toward a foreign sexual culture. I thus rely primarily on historical context to frame discussion of male sexuality in post-Mao China, which sets precedent for a rich sexual culture well before any Western incursion. An examination of sex also incurs discussion about private and individual lives. This leads to questions about whether people can develop private lives and express their individual desires within a society still ruled by a socialist bureaucracy that prioritizes the state over the individual. Private expression is thus forced to negotiate with the power of the state over individuals.

The Relationship Between Sex and Work in China

In most instances, particularly those related to HIV, sexual behavior is associated with an individually motivated desire. Most of the men I discuss in this book, however, mention that their engagement in sexual relations outside of marriage is often prompted by a need to fulfill expectations for informal duties related to work. As a result, I examine masculine practice, including the related sexual practice, as a part of work—an association that I argue will require redefinition of the term *sex work* in the Chinese context.

The sexual practices of elite men in Asia are often described within the context of work (Hoang 2015, 2014, Otis 2012), yet sex work is still closely associated with women. The "sex work" agenda has grown out of human rights discourse, which promotes a need to increase the legitimacy of women involved in the industry and protect them from exploitation and consequently vulnerability to HIV infection (Prestage and Perkins 1994). But the term *sex work* still focuses on the individual rather than the broader social structures that create vulnerability to HIV infection. This continued focus on identity results in a situation where mention of the term conjures up images of vulnerable and marginalized women but neglects the role of the men who prompt the exchange. As a result, commercial sex workers legitimated by their new discursive identity are still marginalized because these women are seen as "vectors of HIV infection" (de Zalduondo 1991, Grosz 1994, Linge and Porter 1997, Parker and Aggleton 2002).

I take a novel approach to the term *sex work* by looking at sex not only as the professional purview of women but also as a professional requirement for men that helps to create gendered structures of vulnerability (Uretsky 2015). Realizing the dialectical nature of sex work in China is, I believe, important for adapting the global discourse of HIV prevention to this local context. The men I interviewed for this project buy sex as a means of fulfilling a duty related to their job or career, transforming sex into work for both women and men in China. Effective use of the term *sex work* for targeting HIV prevention in this context should thus consider not only the sale of sex but also how an actor uses sex in their everyday conduct of affairs (Uretsky 2015). This may even require us to reconsider the definition of work in China and ask questions about what work is, what types of activities and responsibilities are involved in work, and where work takes place.

Fieldsites

The effects that the interaction of governance, governmentality, and masculine practice have on the HIV epidemic in China came to life for me partially because of the fieldsite I chose for my research. From October 2003 until March 2006, I conducted a total of eighteen months of ethnographic research on male sexual culture, masculinity, and HIV/AIDS in urban China. This fieldwork was supplemented by periodic visits back to the field between 2008 and 2011. I spent most of that time in the small remote city of Ruili, located in Dehong Prefecture in western Yunnan Province adjacent to the Burmese[8] border (Map I.1).

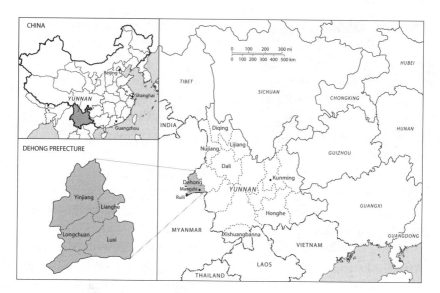

MAP I.1 Dehong Prefecture.

Ruili is akin to the ground zero of China's HIV epidemic, the first place in China to experience a concentrated epidemic. Epidemiologists discovered the HIV epidemic in Ruili in 1989 among 146 injection drug users from ethnic minority communities (primarily Jingpo and Dai). The local epidemic in Dehong Prefecture remains one of the largest epidemics in China and continues to be fueled by drugs smuggled over the border from Burma.[9] My close proximity to the border helped me appreciate how involvement of the masculine practices I ascribe to the informal modes of governance conducted in post-Mao China are not only linked to the spread of STIs and HIV but also related to the rise of HIV in this remote area because of the strategic role the region plays in the development of China's economy.

My understanding of these complex political, social, and cultural dynamics within the realm of public health was also clarified through the few months I spent conducting fieldwork in Beijing, which acts as China's political hub and also as the administrative center for its HIV epidemic. This fieldwork was preceded by two preliminary visits to Beijing and Yunnan during the summers of 2001 and 2002, which helped acquaint me with China's HIV epidemic and introduced me to the local and international actors working in response to the situation. Together these two strategic locations offered insight into the complex social, economic, and political connections that help construct male sexual culture in urban China as well as its HIV epidemic (Marcus 1998,

Dowsett 2001). They also allowed me to observe how webs and networks of power at the local, national, and international levels influence HIV transmission in China. I observed life in these sites independently of one another but also considered how their interaction affected the local HIV epidemic in Ruili. I spent most of my time in Ruili, which is a much more manageable and researchable location. It is, however, also home to a set of complex and overlapping local, national, and international flows. This nexus of multiple meanings, stories, and discourses that intersect, overlap, reinforce, and subvert each other has created a geopolitical crossroads that offered me a lens into the motivation behind China's HIV epidemic (Treichler 1999).

Working in Ruili gave me access to a maturing epidemic situation in a country that has not experienced a noticeable prevalence rate.[10] This translated into a local government that was familiar with the effects of HIV/AIDS on its population as well as the needs to prevent and treat the epidemic. As an area that is politically and economically strategic both locally and nationally, Ruili and Dehong Prefecture not only offered a perspective on the specific pattern of HIV that has developed in China but also presented an ideal place to demonstrate the potential for sexual transmission of the virus. Though it is remote, Ruili has a very active cross-border trade industry. Much of the business conducted in the area depends on relations between rising entrepreneurs and local government officials, which are established and maintained through the practices of *yingchou*. Such relations occur throughout China but are difficult to observe in larger, more central locations where the presence of China's bureaucratic panopticon is always felt. But the mountains are high and the emperor is far away (*shan gao di yuan*) in Ruili, so the people (government officials in particular) are often not as restrained in their behavior or speech.[11] This commingling of a relaxed culture with the strong presence of the Han state yielded a perfect microcosm to observe and learn about how the informal modes of governance that have become so pervasive in China are interacting with urban male sexual culture, masculinity, and HIV/AIDS. Overall, this environment allowed me to observe the types of relationships used to negotiate the many political and economic situations that are otherwise kept under cover in China, but still pervasive in the daily operation of business and policy.[12] In Ruili, as I witnessed, these types of relationships that bring men together over food, drink, and sex can be equally as important to establishing a new legal business as they are to operating an illegal business or promoting a new program or policy necessary for HIV prevention. These types of relationships are central to the daily lives of contemporary China's businessmen and government officials but stand apart from any relationship one would associate with HIV risk. Yet when we examine their structure, they are essential to the narrative of HIV in China.

Beijing

Fieldwork in Beijing proved to be a useful contrast to Ruili. This stage of research continued to contribute to my understanding of contemporary trends of masculinity and male sexual culture in urban China, but I was much more dependent on testimonial information because Beijing's sheer size and political significance precluded me from directly observing masculine practices. A city under pressure of the political scrutiny concentrated at the party's center and the social demands of a growing global metropolis offered a closer perspective on the relative impact that China's rigid bureaucratic system has on urban men's use, interpretation, and negotiation of sex. In addition, Beijing's engagement in the global community allowed me to analyze the effects that globalization has on men's networking practices in urban China and ask what role practices of *yingchou* will have on men's behavior as China continues its process of development. Recent economic developments since the institution of Xi Jinping's anti-corruption campaign seem to suggest that *yingchou* is essential to China's economic progress.

Fieldwork in Beijing was also integral to my understanding and analysis of how the intersection of domestic and international politics and actors affects the administration and management of China's HIV epidemic at the local level. From a local epidemic situation in a remote area, I was able to peer up the vertical bureaucratic ladder to see how policies and discourses affect the responses that seem so important at the local level. In Beijing I attended national and international conferences and met with local and international actors who guided the response to China's epidemic and indirectly affected the response I observed at the local level. Juxtaposition of bottom-up and top-down perspectives fostered a rich understanding of how national policy and local politics interact in China; offering insight into the complex sociocultural and politico-economic negotiations that take place between the local, national, and international actors who participate in a particular flow of people, commodities, policies, and ideas that affect the development and administration of China's HIV epidemic.

Methodology

Inquiry into any complex social phenomenon is dependent on understanding not only the individuals involved and their behaviors but also the environmental factors and structures that prompt such behaviors. This involves going to where people live and doing what they do in order to enter the "everyday space of moral processes in a local world" (Kleinman 1999, Watson 1997). Accordingly, my inquiry into the sexual practices of urban men in China looked well beyond the basic questions of who they have sex with, where they have sex, and whether they use a condom. Instead, it delved into the social, cultural, and political dynamics that shape these behaviors. This took me into the traditional places where men seek sex, but also into their homes, places of work, and other various places of leisure.

Specific Research Methodologies

I used standard ethnographic methods to conduct this research. This included participant observation and semistructured open-ended interviews. Participant observation first took me into the karaoke clubs and other entertainment establishments where men typically host and entertain each other. It is difficult to simply be an observer in a Chinese karaoke club, though. I became an active participant in the singing, drinking, and dancing and developed a standard repertoire of songs by the time I completed fieldwork. I also conducted research inside one of Ruili's popular massage parlors by going for regular massages. The female Burmese masseuse who usually performed massage on me became one of my key informants. The most valuable fieldsites, however, were those located outside the entertainment establishments, where I could observe men's "lived experiences." Men invited me to their homes, where I met their wives and children; to their places of work, where I met colleagues; and often out to meals, where I was able to meet other men within their professional and social networks. I also periodically went along on business trips or was taken to see construction of their latest business venture. Spending time with these men allowed me to learn about those aspects of their lives that structure decisions about their sexual relationships. Through this regular interaction, I learned about the "local vocabulary" used to construct masculine identity in urban China as well as the social processes that govern men's lives. Other points of observation included clinics where HIV and STI patients seek treatment as well as the various conferences, meetings, and workshops on HIV/AIDS that I attended in Beijing, Kunming, and Ruili.

Public health research predominantly relies on data collected through quantitative survey research methods that are valued for their validity, reliability, and generalizability across populations. The data for this project were collected through more informal yet structured methods, which offered access to the contextual ethnographic information that informs our understanding of public health risk behaviors. The predominant portion of my data was collected through participant observation and informal conversations with the various men and women I met in Ruili and Beijing. This allowed me to build a comprehensive picture of the daily activities and events that influence their decisions. Scheduling formal interviews would have been difficult at best because success for these men depended on flexibility and impromptu appointments. As a researcher tracing these men's lives, I had to be ready to follow them to wherever they lived or worked. I was often invited, and welcome to accompany, men and women on business trips or on a visit to their ancestral home for a holiday or special occasion. Sometimes they approached me to share certain aspects of their lives that they knew were important to my research. And some of the men in my networks came to consider themselves as teachers who could offer key lessons about masculinity in China. This rather unstructured process originally proved frustrating to a researcher with a research plan, a goal, and a finite amount of time. As with most ethnographic research, however, my efforts finally started to pay off after an initial period of rapport building with the men in my networks. One day I received a call from a wealthy businessman inviting me to attend his mother's sixtieth birthday celebration at their natal family home, which was located 100 kilometers from Ruili. I traveled together with him and his driver in his car, while his wife drove in a second car just in front of us. About ten minutes into the trip, he unexpectedly started telling me about his plans to find a second wife (bao ernai), have another child, and simultaneously maintain the two marital relationships within the boundaries of Chinese law. This represented a turning point in my research process, opening up the door I needed into men's lives.[13]

This and other informal conversations that took place during my research allowed me to piece together a comprehensive picture of men's lives that was constructed from the people living these lives rather than from a set of questions or prompts initiated by an outsider without the proper understanding to lead such a conversation. This subsequently led to a stage in my research where I felt prepared to ask more directed questions that could be used to analyze specific aspects of their lives. After building a foundation of knowledge about urban Chinese men's lives, I designed a set of open-ended questions that I used to conduct more directed semistructured interviews in order to fill in the gaps in information still needed to answer my specific research questions.

Finally, my ethnographic data also draw on textual sources. Popular music and television supplied many cues about how Chinese people view sex in contemporary society. Other media, including newspapers, magazines, and the internet, also provided information on this type of discourse. Data from these types of sources as well as historical sources have been critical to my understanding of how sexual culture is changing in a broader Chinese context.

The Impact of Social Networks

This book describes the role that traditional social networks play in the transmission of disease. These are primarily networks between Chinese people that are important for facilitating transactions in Chinese society, but foreigners operating within this society are also expected to engage in the same type of social networking processes (Yang 2002). The success of this project was thus dependent upon my own ability to build local networks in Ruili. I developed relationships with varying networks of men and women at various status levels and within a number of local cultural contexts. Each relationship I developed offered insight into different aspects of the masculine concerns of politically and economically elite men in China as well as the institutional and sociocultural structures that help to shape their sexual practices.

One network developed through my relationship with the local Bureau of Health. Shortly after arriving in Ruili, I contacted them regarding my research plans and to ask for their assistance in identifying men who could introduce me to the local entertainment venues where men participate in collective activities of eating, drinking, singing, and dancing. That meeting led to an introduction to a young man with little social or political status who had been exposed to a set of experiences that gave him unique access into elite male society in Ruili. His rich knowledge of both public and private life in Ruili made him the perfect guide and key informant to introduce me to men's lives in Ruili. His lessons served as a roadmap for the remainder of my fieldwork, which led me through the social, ethnic, and political structure in Ruili as well as its varied entertainment establishments, including large karaoke clubs, massage parlors, and hair salons.

The second network of men that became integral to my research developed through a random event that is perhaps unique to an ethnographic project. My husband, who accompanied me to Ruili during the initial stages of fieldwork, discovered on arrival that he had lost his Blackberry. Thankfully, it fell out of his pocket while in a friend's car on the way to the airport in Kunming before flying to Dehong Prefecture. The friend of another friend eventually brought the Blackberry down to Ruili with him on a business trip several weeks later. This man was a successful businessmen who lived in Kunming but originally came from Dehong Prefecture and had once worked for the local government.[14] To my husband, who cannot speak Chinese and has trouble remembering Chinese names, this accidental courier affectionately became known between us as Blackberry Man, but I will refer to him as Liu Dun. After telling Liu Dun about my purpose in Ruili, he became very interested in my research and proceeded to introduce me (and my husband) to his network of friends, which included other successful businessmen in Ruili and a host of high-level local government officials. This particular network of men became trusted friends and informants who taught me about the meaning of being a Chinese man with status.

Aside from these two networks of men, I also became friendly with many women in Ruili who both worked for the government and lived as private citizens. Discussions with these women were crucial for my understanding of men's lives in this society. In addition, many of the officials I met through the network of contacts I developed from Liu Dun were also responsible for responding to the local HIV epidemic and taught me valuable lessons about the structure of the local response. A study such as this, aiming to explain public policy, is dependent on observing and interviewing the political elites responsible for designing and implementing that policy. As Susan Greenhalgh (2008) demonstrated in her study of China's birth planning policy, creatively tapping personal networks or working with international organizations engaged in program work can give anthropologists an entrée to political elites and create some unique perspectives on policy making. This was in fact the case for my fieldwork. My understanding of the local situation also benefited from doctors and staff from the local Center for Disease Control (CDC), who were responsible for HIV/AIDS testing and treatment in Ruili, as well as doctors at private health and STI clinics. Unfortunately, little of my understanding of the epidemic in Ruili comes from people living with HIV and AIDS because of an environment that makes it difficult for them to come forth with their identity.

Accessing Data

Accessing data is always a concern for research on sensitive topics and hard-to-reach populations. The primary funder for this project (the National Institute of Mental Health) was particularly concerned about my identity as a foreign woman doing research on men in China. This certainly factored into the outcome of the project, but I think it yielded both advantages and disadvantages. Many people were reluctant to speak to me because of my identity as a foreigner. Ruili has been the subject of many scandalous articles in both Chinese and Western media, a fact that has sullied their reputation domestically and internationally.[15] As the only Westerner in town,[16] I was often suspected of being either an American spy or a journalist. This did hinder access to sex workers. People often asked what news agency I worked for and where my camera and microphone were hidden. And although I did meet Ruili's highest government officials, many other officials (particularly those from the Jingpo community) who were interested in speaking to me were reluctant because they were afraid I was an American spy and could report damaging information about them to either the Chinese or the American government.

In general, I had very little difficulty gaining initial access to the men I met in Ruili. Many people there had never met an American before, and even for those who had, I presented the first opportunity for them to speak to an American and learn about the United States because I am fluent in Chinese and lived there for an extended period of time. My identity as a woman did not hinder my invitation or acceptance into a group of men. In fact, I was often the only woman in a group of men who had gathered to eat, drink, smoke, sing, or play cards. It seemed odd to the men at times because they were unaccustomed to the presence of a woman in their homosocial networks. In fact, they sometimes felt obligated to invite another woman along to make me feel comfortable. Eventually, however, these men learned to accept me as an equal and became comfortable having me in the group because my character as an independent American woman is perhaps more similar to a masculine Chinese character than to that of the average Chinese woman. After spending several months in Ruili, men started telling me they no longer felt as if they were talking to a foreigner when speaking with me. And (for better or worse) many men also told me they felt they were having a conversation with another man when speaking to me. My identity as a woman, or perhaps as an outsider, however, did prevent me from accessing masculine culture beyond a certain point. For one thing, of course, I never witnessed a man engaging in or negotiating for sex. But that was immaterial to my project, which was more concerned with the sociocultural and politico-economic factors motivating sexual practices than with the behavioral aspects of risk. The foundation of my relationships with these men did, nevertheless, pose a limit to the depth of their development. Many of the men I met in Ruili formed relationships based on common business interests, and I was rarely able to access that sensitive aspect of their bonds; I myself did not represent a business opportunity despite their desire to access the U.S. market. In addition, although I was able to participate in the more casual communication used to network and build relationships over food, drink, and song, the more important business aspect of these relationships was strictly reserved for the male partners involved in these ventures. As a result, I was able to maintain a level of curiosity in my male informants for many months because of my novel character as an American woman. But these relationships cooled down once we passed through the process of building up rapport because I was unable to engage in the type of bond these men seek in each other, which is ultimately structured on a male-centered business relationship.

Finally, my identity as a woman did pose further obstacles to the development of deep relationships with government-employed male informants because of the political sensitivities surrounding male-female relationships in a homosocial society that is not accustomed to witnessing men and women together in casual settings. Most male informants who work for the government usually invited another friend along to accompany us to dinner, tea, or any other activity. This protected them from any suspicion of a prohibited type of relationship with a woman. This became an issue for my key informant, who worked for the government but was also often seen with me in public and seen escorting me home late at night after returning from the karaoke clubs. Because he was someone with very low status, his superiors quickly began asking him why he was seen driving through the alleyway where I lived. A fear of threats to his job and the dangers of rumors or questions about his relationship with the American soon limited my contact with him. These obstacles catalyzed more involvement with women during the later stages of my fieldwork. This was something I welcomed because aside from giving me greater entrée into women's perspectives, it also allowed me to retire from the hours of drinking and eating that create bonds between Chinese men and instead participate in the long two-hour facials that serve as a foundation for building social networks among Chinese women.

Access to data and research participants is not only a factor of individual willingness to participate in a study. But in China it is also reliant on political scrutiny over the researcher. In her ethnography of *guanxi* relations, Mayfair Yang (1994) made note of the weight she felt lifted from her shoulders whenever the train left Beijing's central station. Scrutiny over foreign-based researchers in Beijing was very strict when she conducted fieldwork in the late 1980s. Rapid growth and a growing expatriate community has made it difficult for the government to achieve this high level of scrutiny over foreigners living in Beijing in recent years. As a foreign researcher conducting fieldwork in a sensitive area that is important to China's national security, I often felt this type of scrutiny in an area where many Chinese people go to escape government watch. To my surprise, the local government in Ruili was not overly concerned with my access to sensitive information about men's lives. They were much more concerned with the possibility that I might inquire into more sensitive topics that threaten national security, such as relations between local ethnic minority communities or military relations between China and Burma. The local Party Committee assigned someone to monitor my daily actions, and in fact at one point my key informant claimed he was the person assigned to watch me (perhaps that's why they were so forthcoming with an assistant). At the very end of my fieldwork, another close friend who worked for the party also said to me, "You may not know this, but there are people in the government who have always been very suspicious of you and they keep a close eye on you. You may be sitting next to a man who you think is just an old peasant, and in fact he is a member of the National Security Bureau." As a result, I often reflected on Mayfair Yang's thoughts as I waited for the plane to take off from Mangshi (the prefectural capital of Dehong and the closest airport to Ruili) but felt as if scrutiny over my actions decreased the closer I got to the center. Even though this level of scrutiny was always present in my mind, I never felt as if it compromised access to the data I needed to complete my project.

Moral judgment is also one final consideration that must be taken into account in a cross-cultural study of sexuality. The Western religious values that serve as the basis for my own cultural background dictate that men and women should be monogamous and that success should be determined according to merit. But when working to understand a "local world," we must operate within the context of how "moral experience" is defined locally within a "social space that carries cultural, political, and economic specificity" (Kleinman 1999: 365). Many of the things I observed and learned during research for this project are not moral according to my own value system. But "good" is a subjective term often imposed on the moral by a hegemonic discourse of ethics that is foreign to the local context (Kleinman 2006). In a sociocultural environment where such actions are normative, accepted, and necessary for professional success, they can be properly understood and analyzed only if they are allowed to escape any moral judgment subject to foreign value systems.

Summary of Chapters

The following chapters, which are divided into two distinct sections, elucidate on the questions and themes I have raised in this introduction. The first section of the book describes the rituals of *yingchou* and the masculine and sexual cultures that affect and are affected by the informal use of *yingchou* in daily practices of governance in post-Mao China. This begins in Chapter One, which discusses in detail the structure and uses of *yingchou*. The chapter begins a description of how the unique set of sociocultural and politico-economic factors that converge within men's work-related roles and duties makes them vulnerable to STI and HIV infection. The next three chapters explain the patterns of masculinity and male sexuality that influence how *yingchou* is used in post-Mao China. Chapter Two offers an analysis of elite masculinity in contemporary China. I discuss the importance of work, status, family, responsibility, respect, and friends in a man's life. The second part of the chapter examines the relation between love and marriage, and love and sex in contemporary urban China. Chapter Three looks at how people exercise their individual desires (in this case sexual desires) in a society that is still largely controlled by the state. It is often believed that increased development of the economy and the market has been accompanied with greater ability to develop private lives. On the contrary, I illustrate that industrialization and marketization do not always result in the retreat of the state from either private or sexual lives. Finally, in Chapter Four I discuss the importance of tracing and considering sexual networks in our efforts to prevent further sexual spread of HIV in China. Many HIV prevention programs concentrate on commercial sex workers, but the networks of female sexual partners in China include an equal number of casual lovers and minor wives (*xioa laopo*).[17] Urban men in contemporary China are constantly negotiating between a social world that allows them to seek sexual relations outside of marriage and a political world where such practices are officially castigated. These competing demands are satisfied through the development of relationships with various women who serve different sexual and affective roles in a man's life. This chapter examines the cultural scripts used to create sexual networks in China and how they contribute to the dichotomy of risk and behaviors that are associated with HIV transmission.

The second section of the book goes beyond the individual effects of *yingchou* to examine how use of these rituals has affected the HIV epidemic itself. Chapter Five discusses the role that these practices played in the development of China's HIV epidemic in a remote rural region on the Burmese border. The analysis I present in this chapter attributes the unique occurrence of an HIV epidemic in such a remote region to the unique and complex network of cultural, economic, and geopolitical forces that govern the area. The chapter explains how the nexus of local and national interests in economic growth and security supported by this cross-border region, so rich in many lucrative natural resources (including opium), helped to catalyze an HIV epidemic. The chapter ends with discussion of the dominant local discourse of happiness (*kaixin*) that is used to sustain the local economy through protecting the many questionable but lucrative industries that have contributed to their economic growth and stability. Within this environment, I demonstrate that the same networking practices used to foster relations between businessmen and government officials also keep outsiders happy to the point where they are convinced to look away when facing commodities that can promote HIV transmission. Chapter Six brings the discussion forward with examination of how the HIV epidemic is managed and administered within the Chinese context. I discuss the history of the government's response to the epidemic and their stated commitment to prevention and treatment. As I illustrate through an examination of local, international, and grassroots efforts, responding to HIV in China requires careful political coordination at the local, national, and international levels. The concluding chapter of the book highlights the most important lessons learned at all these levels of HIV management and administration in China and demonstrates how they can be used by public policy experts and public health practitioners to improve the HIV prevention and intervention programs implemented in China.

Overall, this ethnography should provide lessons not only to anthropologists hoping to gain an understanding of sexual culture in China but also to global public health experts looking for new ways to respond to disease in China. China represents one of the biggest contributors to many contemporary problems of global health, from emerging infectious diseases to some of the highest rates of chronic disease in the world. The emergence and control of many of these situations are dependent on the modes of governance and governmentality described in these pages.

1 BUILDING *GUANXI*: THE EFFECT ON CHINA'S MALE ELITE

1   The State, Work, and Men's Health

A revolution is not a dinner party.
 —*Mao Tse-Tung, "Report on the Investigation of the Peasant
 Movement in Hunan" (March 1927), Selected Works, Vol. I, p. 28*

I GOT A CALL ON A SATURDAY AFTERNOON IN THE MID-
dle of June 2004 from one of Ruili's high-level officials, who I will call
Leader Zhu, inviting me to dinner the following day. Leader Zhu and I had
become friendly, and we had eaten lunch and dinner together several times. But
this meal would be different because it opened a lens into networking practices
that support China's contemporary political economy and helped me understand both the important role that *guanxi* relations play in post-Mao China as
well as their close relationships with rituals of *yingchou*. It also validated some
of the important lessons I was learning about why men were consuming inordinate amounts of cigarettes, food, alcohol, and commercial sex, which, as I suspected, was not simply a result of increasing access to wealth in the post-Mao
era (Beyrer 2003, Hao et al. 2004, Wang et al. 2007) but a symptom of the close
connection that has developed between work, the state, and men's health.

Leader Zhu, like all the officials in Ruili, knew about my work. But unlike
other officials who were afraid of its ramifications, Zhu understood the importance of such questions around men's roles in spreading HIV for addressing
the local epidemic. Still, Leader Zhu had a responsibility to protect state integrity as a high-level official, which meant exercising extreme discretion over
official improprieties or transgressions in Ruili. Thus, despite a willingness to
help, Leader Zhu was initially reluctant to facilitate, in any way, my access to
that part of official life. Nevertheless Leader Zhu vowed to find a way to help
me and kept this promise with a simple invitation to dinner.

A Day Out in Ruili

Leader Zhu told me to be ready to leave for dinner at three o'clock the next day. A little early for dinner, I thought, but after all, it was a weekend. She arrived at my home the next day with two other women. Together, the four of us drove to a small mountain retreat about twenty minutes outside the city. When we arrived, I learned it would be more than just the four of us for dinner. Several other government officials and employees had arrived before us, and approximately thirty-five people gathered at the retreat by the time dinner was served around six o'clock, including most of Ruili's highest-level officials, heads of several local government bureaus, and some of Ruili's most prominent businesspeople. Guests passed the warm summer day playing cards and mahjong. Most of the restaurants in Ruili provide decks of cards so people can play *zimei dui*[1] while they wait for their meals to arrive. That day as usual, I sat on the side trying to figure out the complicated rules of the game, which is played between two teams of two people each who make paired combinations of cards from two decks, with a goal of amassing eighty-five points. Inevitably someone always tried to explain the complex rules to me in Chinese. But I was never able to understand the many terms specific to card playing, which are not part of my vocabulary in English, let alone Chinese. So, I usually just sat on the side and observed as people dealt and organized their cards, made their pairs, and ultimately came up with the eighty-five points needed to win. Some of the men who arrived before us sat by a lamb roasting over an open pit, lazily smoking cigarettes and sipping *baijiu*, a strong, clear liquor made from rice and sorghum. I spent my time moving between the groups of people, playing cards and mahjong at separate tables covered under bamboo enclosures.

We all moved to the dining area at six o'clock for dinner, which consisted of many dishes made from the lamb that roasted over the open pit all day. Everyone sat around four large round tables organized by gender and political hierarchy. The "head" table on the upper level of the property was reserved for the highest-status men, including the mayor, the male vice party secretaries, and the husband of a female vice party secretary. Some local businessmen sat at the neighboring table. Most of the women sat at two tables situated on a lower level of the property. The segregation helped excuse the women from the excessive male drinking rituals that were about to begin and allowed the men to talk about things that men usually talk about. Several exceptions were made to this order, though, for the wealthy businesswoman who hosted the event, her female assistant, and myself as an honored foreign guest who had a known rapport with local government officials, built through previous demonstrations of respect. We all sat at the head table with the high-level officials. I was originally reluctant to presumptively sit with the men or the high-ranking officials, but every one insisted that I sit with them. They said to me, "You should be sitting with them." And so, I became one of the men for the evening.

We were all happy to see dinner arrive after spending several hours at the retreat consuming nothing but tea and *guazi* (sunflower seeds), but of course, as is customary, the ritual drinking began before the ritual eating. The businesswoman who hosted the event formally commenced the banquet by inviting everyone at the table to *ganbei* or empty a glass of liquor, which remained the same strong *baijiu* the men sipped during the day. This ritual practice continued during the course of dinner, as eating was interspersed with frequent invitations to drink a glass of *baijiu*, which included toasts that demonstrated respect, honor, and gratitude for past and future relations toward a respective partner or partners. Each person at the table got up in turn to toast every individual around the table as well as the collective members seated at the table, beginning from the highest-level official and then moving around the table in order of political or social rank. Every person toasted also reciprocated the favor to everyone else seated around the table, which resulted in an inordinate consumption of strong liquor. People in attendance were also expected to demonstrate their respect and loyalty to those seated at other tables. Many men wandered over to the head table to toast all the high-ranking officials who were present that day. This demonstrated respect and loyalty to the officials. Refusing an invitation to drink was unheard of because it would be tantamount to an insult. Each man was also expected to finish every drop in his glass each time he engaged in a toast, to demonstrate full respect to the person who invited him to drink. Not doing so indicates a person who is not trustworthy in their endeavors.

The atmosphere became a little more casual after dinner as rigid hierarchy broke down and men started playing a traditional Chinese drinking game called *huaquan*, which requires each of two players to throw out between one and five fingers. They each simultaneously yell out the aggregate number of fingers they predict will be thrown out, but in a very animated way accompanied by friendly jests. The player who accurately predicts the number of fingers thrown out wins; the loser drinks a cup of *baijiu*. This scene continued until people started returning to the city around 8:00 p.m. I returned in Vice

Party Secretary Wang's car with him, his driver, and one of the women who arrived earlier in the day. He invited us all to a karaoke bar when we got back to Ruili, but the other woman in the car declined on the pretense that her young son was not feeling well. I continued to take advantage of the opportunities Leader Zhu had offered me that day.

Vice Party Secretary Wang's driver had reserved a private room at the karaoke club where we could sing, dance, drink, and eat snacks. Ten minutes later two of Ruili's high-level officials, and the wealthy businesswoman (and her assistant) who hosted dinner joined us in the room. The businesswoman also called in two girls who worked inside the karaoke club as *sanpei xiaojie* or "three accompaniment misses," girls who accompany men in singing, dancing, and drinking and who can also provide sex.[2] We each, in turn, sang songs that we ordered from the menu on the karaoke machine. Each man, in turn, also politely invited each woman in the room to a slow waltz dance. And we continued to drink out of respect for each other. This type of scripted ritual performance (Fordham 1995) lasted until 11:30 that night, when Vice Party Secretary Wang suddenly announced, "It's time to go home, we have to be at work tomorrow morning at 8:00!" The two young girls were then dismissed, and the wealthy businesswoman assumed her responsibility as hostess and settled up the bill with the club, which included rental fee for the room, drinks, snacks, and the accompaniment services of the two young women.

Leader Zhu's creative assistance that day opened up a complete snapshot into the questions I had come to examine in my research. The banquet, the activities that led up to it, and those that followed were not simply a meal and some recreation, but parts of the complex process of *yingchou* that have become unofficial duties for men (and women) working to achieve economic and political success in post-Mao China. The woman who hosted the banquet was head of the local branch of a provincial Chamber of Commerce, one of many local branches that operate around China.[3] She knew, however, that her success in aiding the success of businesses from her province in Ruili depended on having the personalistic relations imbued in *guanxi* with local government officials, but she lacked the innate connections that constitute such relationships. The day of banqueting, card playing, drinking, and subsequent entertainment she orchestrated helped her build *guanxi* through repeated demonstrations of respect, which represent a marker of loyalty deserving of access to precious state resources in China. That day was also a pivotal moment in my research, demonstrating a need to broaden my inquiry beyond sexual practices, which I learned acted merely as a coda to a much more complex ritual process primarily structured by shared practices of feasting, drinking, and smoking. Certainly HIV and STI infection are directly related to the entertainment and commercial sex activities that often occupy men's time at night, but the meaning behind these practices is embedded in a larger ritual process that can fill their entire day. I then knew I needed to understand why *yingchou* is such an important aspect of the daily lives of urban businessmen and government officials in contemporary China. Much of the answer, as I discovered, revolves around a need to find an alternative means for distributing state-controlled resources in post-Mao China.

Loyalty, the Redistributive Economy, and Adaptation of the Informal Institution of *Guanxi*

Economic resources in China are officially controlled by the state, making distribution dependent on the basis of impersonal loyalties measured objectively through efforts like work output (Walder 1986) rather than simple monetary exchange. Susan Shirk (1982) speaks of a "virtuocracy," which is unlike a meritocracy in that it confers reward and recognition in exchange for loyalty and political virtue rather than on the basis of intellectual or technical merit. This has presented some fundamental challenges to the market-oriented economic system initiated under Deng Xiaoping because its success relies on a different incentive system. Markets typically award access to resources on the basis of an agreed financial exchange. Therein lies the fundamental contradiction between the political philosophy that governs China's bureaucratic system and its current economic model. In 1984 Shirk even questioned whether a Party that keeps itself in power by enforcing virtuocratic standards could continue to exist under an era of economic modernization (Shirk 1984). This has forced government officials to devise new ways for demonstrating the impersonal loyalties expected of China's redistributive economy in order to ensure the success of a market economy within a Leninist political system.

Many entrepreneurs who depend on access to government resources demonstrate impersonal loyalties through public displays of homage to the state. This often translates into attendance at state-sponsored events, which are almost uniformly well attended in China. Many people in the stands at the Beijing Olympics in 2008 attended simply to demonstrate loyalty by showing support for the biggest event ever sponsored by the Chinese state. A good turnout at this and other state-sponsored events underscores the party's strength and their dominant position in society even among the entrepreneurs, who represent an ideal that obviously contradicts state socialism. In Ruili, I often attended government-sponsored events with local businessmen who told me how they are careful to accept invitations to these opulent public performances in order to demonstrate their loyalty and commitment to the state. I attended the fiftieth anniversary celebration of Dehong Prefecture; public celebrations of International Women's Day; government-sponsored celebrations of ethnic minority holidays at the township, county, and prefectural level; and the celebration produced for Ruili's most important holiday, Chinese-Burmese Brotherhood Festival (*zhongmian baobo jie*).[4] Demonstrating this loyalty to the state was an important part of my process of building *guanxi* with the officials who welcomed me and hosted me in the city. But even though these public displays are useful for demonstrating loyalty to the party, distributions from individual government officials require more personal displays of loyalty that help to build strong networks of *guanxi*.

Guanxi: Networking and Relationship Building with Chinese Characteristics

Most people who do business or conduct operations in China, whether Chinese or not, know the value that *guanxi* holds for their success. But what is *guanxi*, and where do you get it? *Guanxi* is founded on the set of dyadic hierarchical relationships that structured Confucian society. These relationships between a ruler and his subjects, a husband and his wife, a father and his son, an older brother and his younger sibling, and friends were structured around demonstrations of filial piety (*xiao*) and humaneness (*ren*), which established valued characteristics of trust, loyalty, and reciprocity between two individuals. The filiality inherent in the system ensures that subordinates demonstrate respect, loyalty, and obedience to their superordinate. *Ren*, which is often translated as humaneness, humanity, love, benevolence, or perfect virtue, stresses the degrees to which one shows their love for another individual and guarantees reciprocity in a relationship. As Mayfair Yang (1994) explains, "once *guanxi* is established between two people, each can ask a favor of the other with the expectation that the debt incurred will be repaid sometime in the future" (1). This occurs because people joined by *guanxi* share a bond imbued with human sentiment (*renji guanxi*) typically characteristic only of close family members. This type of system also created a bureaucracy based on loyalty and implicit trust because the bond between a ruler and his subjects was founded on the same principles as those between close kin (Yang 1994, Yan 1996). These bonds eventually extended to include networks of classmates (*tongxue*), old friends, army buddies, workmates (*tongshi*), people who share their native place of origin (*laoxiang*), and people who share a surname (*tongxing*). These quasi-kin relationships, particularly those based on native place, are founded on a shared characteristic that allow people to form conditions of *ren* and *xiao* that establish a kinlike bond (Nonini 2008, Skinner 1977).

Guanxi discourse was silenced under Mao because he viewed these traditions as an incipient form of corruption. But *guanxi* has once again emerged as an informal institution (Tsai 2007) capable of mediating between state, society, and the market because the personal loyalties characteristic of traditional Chinese authority and patrimonialism are also useful for representing the impersonal loyalties the party usually demands in exchange for state-controlled resources (Nonini 2008, Walder 1986). Consequently, savvy businessmen and government officials have become proficient in the art of building *guanxi*. This is crucial for success in a market economy operated under the guise of a state that believes no one other than cadres indoctrinated in party loyalty should be entrusted with the task of managing the resources required for production (Meisner 1999). Making entrepreneurs dependent on government officials also helps to guarantee that they will do their utmost to maintain state stability as a way of ensuring their continued economic success (Tsai 2007).

Demonstrations of *guanxi* performance have become standard practice for corporate interests needing government approval in post-Mao China because of the trust imbued in these relationships. Mayfair Yang (2002) cites the importance of *guanxi* relationships between businessmen and local government officials for accessing contracts, imports, bank loans, favorable tax incentives, and exemptions from laws and regulations that may hinder successful completion of planned business activities. David Wank's examination of businesses in the southeastern coastal city of Xiamen (1999) also discusses the important role social networks play in developing the markets, trust, and politics that govern private business in China and demonstrates how entrepreneurs draw on existing ties and create new ones to influence local state agents. Personal ties with state agents enhance access to resources and protect the interests of private businessmen. As one of Wank's informants instructed him, "Your market activities depend on the social environment.

If your connections (*guanxi*) with officialdom are good, then your business can develop, but if they are bad then officialdom squeezes you and you can't get anywhere" (4). I learned similar lessons in Ruili. A small businessman who owned a local computer shop struggled to attract customers but knew it was because he lacked *guanxi*. "Some businesses are successful," he told me, "because their owners have previous relationships (*guanxi*) with local government officials and others have money that is useful for establishing such relationships. These people can use their money to take officials out to eat, drink, and have a good time."

Men continuously impressed on me the importance of having good relations or *guanxi* to succeed in business or government. Even my own research was influenced by the *guanxi* I was able to build with local officials. I often benefited from previously existing *guanxi* between a key informant and a local businessman or government official. This gave me entrée into the networks of some of the highest-level and least-accessible local officials. One of these introductions led me to observe how such bonds translate into success among a group of men who were both trusted friends and business partners. The group included two local businessmen who owned casinos and restaurants, a contractor (who formerly worked for the prefectural government), a local businessman who was trying to open a bamboo factory in Ruili at the time of my fieldwork, and a man who held a prefectural-level position in the party. Together they formed a type of quasi-business cooperative of people who operated independently but also depended on each other for success. Their close relationship, which bridged their roles as friends and business partners, often led me to question the distinctions between business and government in China, since the success of the businessmen was clearly dependent on the support they received from the party official. Their success also translated into his material gain. By the time I completed my research, the party official and his wife were decorating their newly purchased condo with the benefit he derived from just supporting but not directly participating in his friends' business ventures. Government officials are prohibited from running businesses. The *guanxi* these men built up over their long relationship, however, meant he could trust that his business partners would never compromise his position. They equally trusted that he would always support their business ventures because they had formed a bond similar to that of brothers (*gemen*). They often instructed me that the only way to do business in China is with friends whom you can trust as *gemen*. Such relationships have become common business practice in China because it is often the case that entrepreneurs can access necessary resources only through such innovative arrangements, which include discreet collaboration with a local official (Tsai 2007).

This has transformed the "art of *guanxi* making" into a necessary part of the cultural habitus (Bourdieu [1980] 1990) that helps to define the structure of China's commercial system in the post-Mao era, which looks very different from a "universalistic" free market despite its characterization as a market-oriented economy (Wank 2000, Hertz 1998). When such behavior began during the beginning of China's market reform era, cigarettes and alcohol were sufficient for gaining favor from government officials. People used to "*yanjiu yanjiu* officials"[5] (Yang 1994). As men amassed wealth in the reform era, cigarettes declined in value, and televisions and other expensive household items eventually became institutionally commodified (Wank 1999, Yang 1994). State employees use the same mechanisms to seek added benefits. Workers who demonstrate loyalty to the party through personal favors performed for their superiors can benefit from distribution of extra noncash resources or career opportunities that are rewarded for maintaining harmony within the enterprise and the state because the measurement of "good performance" is so vague within a virtuocracy. Leaders can define the "virtue" rewarded under such a system in their own way, allowing them to promote those deemed "loyal" and demote those who pose a perceived threat to the leader's success (Lai 1995, Walder 1986, Shirk 1982). Deng Xiaoping had hoped to foster a meritocratic environment after instituting market reforms, but this proved difficult under a Leninist system where virtuocracy was important for maintaining party legitimacy. Under a meritocratic system, the people may want leaders removed if they see little evidence of economic development. Maintaining the virtuocratic system guaranteed that any leader could remain in power so long as he demonstrated loyalty to the party (Shirk 1982). In the current market economy, where a work unit can find legal ways to provide an official with a car and other material goods, the banquets and entertaining that are characteristic of *yingchou* have become the standard vehicles for developing the loyalties necessary in grooming important relationships needed for success. Prior to the Xi era, engaging in such practices was thought a good way to protect officials who were afraid of violating laws or being held accountable for accepting monetary profit but still allow businessmen to demonstrate the loyalty that government officials expect in exchange for state-controlled resources (Sun 2004).

One could argue that staging these performances of state loyalty for *guanxi* building with the government officials who control entrepreneurial success is important at a low-level prefecture that has not yet experienced much economic or social development, but perhaps not as important in more developed cities. But the need to *yingchou* to build *guanxi* is prevalent throughout China in both government and business operations. Scott Kennedy and Deng Guosheng (2010) gathered evidence from a national survey of Chinese corporations that showed the importance of *guanxi* for building trust and accessing approvals and permits companies seek from government officials.[6] John Osburg (2013) discusses the same networking practices among men in Chengdu, and Kate Mason (2011) describes the effect that *guanxi* making through *yingchou* practices has on the operations she observed at the Shenzhen CDC (Center for Disease Control). I also witnessed several examples in Beijing. My apartment in Beijing was located down the block from a large, opulent, multistory karaoke club that opened just as I was moving in. The manager was kind enough to let me attend the opening night celebration, which featured all types of performances and blonde Russian girls lining both sides of the winding grand central staircase leading from a marble-filled foyer to a floor of grand-scale karaoke rooms. When we spoke, I asked him how long it took to build such a large palatial complex. He said, "Building the club was easy; that only took three months." But it took two years of building *guanxi* with local officials and demonstrating the loyalty necessary to obtain the permits and allowances necessary to build and open the club. But even if *guanxi*-based relationships offer the type of trust and loyalty needed to facilitate exchange in China, most government officials and businessmen who, like this karaoke club owner, deal in negotiations for the exchange of state-controlled resources do not have the *guanxi* necessary for their success. Engaging in *yingchou* offers them the opportunity to establish these bonds and regularly reinforce them through the practices of shared drinking, eating, and entertainment that I described at the beginning of this chapter.

Yingchou: The Dominance of a Minor Practice in Men's Lives

Yingchou is a minor ritual that men have used since the Song dynasty (960–1279) to establish and strengthen social relations with each other (*Ci hai* 1979). The shared rituals of eating, drinking, smoking, and female-centered entertainment that characterize *yingchou* were central to socialization of the elite literati class during China's imperial era. The tradition has since evolved into a "series of scripts and patterned expectations" (Fordham 1995: 154) that act as an "adaptive informal institution" (Tsai 2007) to help participants establish the networks of personal relations (*renji guanxi*) that support the patron-clientelism developed in post-Mao China. Most businessmen lack the party connection required to access the state-owned resources necessary for their operations and success.[7] They also often lack the personalistic relationships bound together with human sentiment that offer one the entrée needed to access those resources from outside official state boundaries. *Yingchou* helps them build up the trust and loyalty characteristic of traditional *guanxi* relationships, which can be translated into a demonstration of party loyalty in post-Mao China.

I first heard the term *yingchou* during a visit to Ruili in July 2002. At the time, I met a woman who worked for the local CDC. She invited me to her home for dinner with her mother and son and asked about my work. I told her I planned to return to Ruili in order to conduct research on men. She immediately responded, "Oh, my husband says it's much more difficult to be a man than a woman." When I asked why, she said he complains about constant requirements to *yingchou*. Her husband, incidentally, was not home for dinner because he was out, as she said, doing *yingchou* (*ta zai waibian yingchou*). I constantly heard men and women invoke *yingchou,* and its linguistic kin *jiedai keren* (literally, to host and entertain guests), as explanation for why men could not go home at night and were always so tired. These lamentations transformed *yingchou* into a central focus of my research. I learned that the drinking, eating, smoking, and sex that are so common among contemporary Chinese men are not merely a result of increased access to wealth in post-Mao China, but are closely tied to the rituals that elite men are traditionally entitled to practice.

Feasting and Drinking

Feasting and drinking play an important role in structuring social organization in most societies, but their purpose and format are often unique to the given context. Understanding their social function offers a lens into the role they play in motivating behavior. In China, feasting and drinking rituals indicate social hierarchy and help to construct a particular social and now political world for men (Dietler 2006).[8] *The Book of Rites*, the Confucian text that established standards for social forms, ancient rites, and court ceremonies, described rigid patterns that dictated the order of eating and drinking at state dinners. Proper administration of social ceremony, which established hierarchical structure and secured social solidarity, included standards that dictated the size of the drinking vessel, the spatial positioning or seating of the guests, the order for serving and consuming the drink and food, the number of accompanying dishes, and the quantity of drink served to each guest (Cohen 1974, Dietler 1990, Joffe 1998, Smart 2005). For men who lived in late imperial and Republican-era Shanghai (1648–1949), these rituals provided a means for building the bonds that distinguished them from other classes of society. Such men often attended banquets in courtesan houses, where they could drink, eat, smoke, and joke with male friends in the company of female entertainment. These rituals helped to validate a man's social status and even curry favor with the courtesans who could further raise their position in society (Hershatter 1997).

The feasting and drinking practices that help lubricate relationships in contemporary China are reminiscent of the rituals established in the Confucian texts. Present-day practices still adhere to a rigid social code that prescribes a specific order of who initiates a meal, who receives the first toasts, and who has the privilege to enjoy the most valued parts of the shared meal (Smart 2005). Likewise, the food and drink used during these ritual processes have maintained their historical roles in establishing the necessary social status and bonds of trust that allow Chinese men to negotiate and cooperate with one another. The wealthy businesswoman who hosted the banquet I attended in June 2004 offered the first toast to the mayor of the city. She was similarly the first person to "move her chopsticks" (*dong kuai*) at the banquet. Likewise, the participants at an organized meal between colleagues and business partners will serve themselves only after serving the most valuable and delicious pieces of meat to those who command the most respect at the table. At a meal of fish, the fish head is always presented to the person of highest status at the table. I was once invited to a restaurant specializing in dog meat for a meal hosted for businessmen and government officials. I was able to decipher the political hierarchy of those invited to the meal according to the order of people offered dog paws, the most coveted part of the animal.

The collective rituals of eating so integral to Chinese networking practices are paired with ritual drinking practices structured by China's culture of liquor (*jiu wenhua*), which can vary by region. I always noticed the hierarchical order that structured the toasts offered at banquets I attended in Yunnan, but it was never overtly stated. On the contrary, banqueters in neighboring Guizhou Province rigidly follow a set of rituals put forth at the table. Formal meals in Guizhou are preceded by three small cups of Moutai, the local liquor that is also Guizhou's most famous and successful export (Kazer and Yu 2012). A host at a banquet in Guiyang, capital of Guizhou Province, instructed me that the three cups are required to honor the three essential elements that structure the world (*sancai zhi shuo*)—heaven (*tian*), earth (*di*), and man (*ren*)—before the meal can begin. Only the host can invite all others in attendance to share in those initial three toasts. Once all those elements have been honored, the meal can commence and people can continue honoring each other with toasts in a less structured but still reverent manner.[9]

Drinking alcohol, exchanging a cigarette (*fayan*), or sharing a meal is a deliberate shared activity that demonstrates respect and mutual reciprocity fundamental for validating the close feelings and sentiments (*renqing*) required for a relationship worthy of *guanxi* (Hertz 1998, Yan 1996). Each time a cup is raised, the person inviting someone to a drink precedes the request to empty a glass with words of respect, joy, and perhaps favor. Someone may thank a counterpart for help in the past, ask a person for help in the future securing success or a better position, or wish him or her everlasting joy, youth, beauty, and health for government officials whose positions within the Communist Party prohibit them from seeking the wealth and prosperity (*facai*) often conveyed toward counterparts in China. People rehearsed in the art of toasting become quite animated and humorous. Finally, the person who initiates the toast demonstrates the highest level of respect by announcing to the person being toasted, "For you, I will empty a cup" (*wo wei ni yao gan yibei*). The partner reciprocates this respect by drinking an equal amount of liquor. The base of trust is finally solidified when the two provide evidence of their empty cups. Conversely, refusing the offer of a cigarette or invitation to drink is considered insulting, disrespectful, and a sign of someone who is not willing to engage in mutual exchange (Yan 1996). Those who do not offer cigarettes or invite others to drink are similarly not considered trustworthy. Smoking and drinking in China are shared rituals and not individual behaviors. Someone who takes out a pack of cigarettes offers one to those around him and glasses are usually raised together following a toast inviting others to share in a drink.

Entertainment

The feasting and eating rituals that are central to processes of social networking and hierarchical structuring in many modern societies (Mars and Altman 1987) are distinguished in China by the addition of entertainment that is also integral to the scripted practices making up rituals of *yingchou*. This entertainment, which typically takes place in an establishment that provides female-centered corporeal services, has been used to distinguish the male social elite in both imperial and modern Chinese society. Elite men distinguished themselves through mastery of the Confucian classics during China's imperial era, a distinction that helped to guard the moral and ideological pedigree of the nation. Accepted socialization for these men, who were regularly sequestered in their studies, took place at the homes of courtesan women who were trained in the arts of poetry, song, and dance befitting an elite scholar (Hershatter 1997, Peterson 1979, Xu 1995, Yan 1992, Ch'ü 1965, Leung 2000, Sommer 2000, Micollier 2004, Zamperini 1999). Courtesans served as a marker of "status performance" for these elite men, making their talent and poise inaccessible to men from other classes of society (Sommer 2000). This tradition was especially popular in eighteenth- and nineteenth-century Shanghai, a cosmopolitan metropolis where educated literati competed with domestic and international traders for attention and status. Courtesans were primarily valued for their talents, but men could also request sexual favors from their favorite entertainers (Hershatter 1997, Xu 1995).

Common prostitutes slowly supplanted courtesan women as an affluent consumer society that placed more value on a woman's sexual services than her erudition emerged in a commercializing Shanghai (Henriot [1997] 2001, Hershatter 1997). This led to development of a vibrant cabaret culture that became deeply enmeshed in the political economy of 1920s Shanghai (Field 1999). The cabaret girls who worked in the dance halls accompanied men in song and Western-style social dancing (ballroom and jazz), which was imported from America and Europe after the First World War. These women primarily worked as companions to accompany men in song and dance, but could also be coaxed into providing some "extra" service for a negotiable fee (Field 1999).

A similar culture designed to serve the needs of a modern economic and political elite has reemerged in post-Mao China. The *"yanjiu yanjiu"* Mayfair Yang spoke about in 1980s China is no longer sufficient for cementing *guanxi*.

The stakes are different now, and the *guanxi* machine is now oiled with the bodies of women who serve as mediators providing the glue that finally binds relations (Otis 2012, Yang 2002). Now, Yang says, "The night may start with a banquet for the official(s), then the party may proceed to enjoy women at a dancehall, karaoke bar, or sauna, to be followed sometimes by the host hiring a prostitute to visit the official in his hotel room" (Yang 2002: 466). Consequently, the business entrepreneurs and government officials who make up contemporary elite male society are once again underscoring and protecting their social status through the consumption of female-centered entertainment activities that now take place at saunas, massage parlors, hair washing salons, or disco and karaoke clubs. The modern karaoke club is reminiscent of the cabarets that dotted the landscape of 1920s Shanghai, where businessmen, politicians, sailors, soldiers, adventurers, gamblers, and gangsters enjoyed nights filled with fantasy. These dance halls were similar dark environments where men negotiated sexual eroticism under pressure of strict government censorship (Field 1999). But even though many contemporary government employees spend countless hours in karaoke clubs, they must also be discreet about their whereabouts because they are the moral models for the state. Modern karaoke clubs are separated into private and public spaces in order to serve varying levels of governmental and civilian clientele. Private spaces for karaoke (called reserved rooms or *baojian*), designed to protect identities, are usually built on the upper floors of a disco. One enters the club through a public disco space and can enter the upper floors only with a reservation. Food and drink are ordered through a hostess, who discreetly services the rooms. As one government employee told me, "We can only hang out in these little rooms and can never go down to the disco because our jobs can be threatened if people know we are here."

Entertainment available in contemporary establishments is reminiscent of China's late-imperial and Republican eras, but there have been many changes to the structure of this social realm. Sex is still referred to euphemistically and usually not the main service on offer, so men can still provide a "tip" (*xiaofei*) for "special service" (*teshu fuwu*) at a massage parlor or hair washing salon as they did at courtesan houses during Republican times (Henriot [1997] 2001). Most of the women who serve men in contemporary China, though, are not the educated, erudite women imperial literati demanded, although it is not uncommon to hear of a college student providing sexual services. This is perhaps a reflection of the contemporary clientele, who are defined by wealth rather than scholarship—a cultural shift validated by the many masseuses, hair washing girls, *sanpei xiaojie,* and brothel-based sex workers who serve these men (Armajo-Hussein and Beesey 1998, Parish and Pan 2004).[10] There is a saying that men and women often recounted to me: *fugui siyin ren bu fengliu zhi wei pin* (the man who does not chase women is surely poor, for wealth and success always leads one to think about sex). Wealthy entrepreneurs and other men with access to wealth (including government officials) use sex as a means of distinguishing themselves and protecting their status, much like elite imperial men. But the men who consume sexual services in contemporary China often view their pursuit more as work than the leisurely activities that helped to distinguish and protect the status of imperial era men.

The integration of entertainment services into China's patron-client system has generated an "economy of desire" (Zhang 2001), which has created an environment where government officials now have the option of exchanging their power over useful resources and allowances for something that cannot be legally acquired through their rank. Du Jun, a businessman in Beijing who entertains government officials, said to me, "Government officials are people too, and many may not be satisfied with their own wives, but have no other way of finding anything because in their work unit they have to be a model, they have to be a leader, they have to speak, and guide the work. So, if you're a government official, you have to grab the means of the people who are using you for your power to satisfy your own private desires . . . to make an exchange. It's a type of communication." People often recount *you quan, cai you qian* (you can only have wealth once you have power). Indeed, the power imbued in positions of authority in China allows men to procure signs of wealth and male status through the system of *guanxi,* which in turn converts symbolic capital into social, economic, and now sexual capital.

These types of scenes, used to build relationships between elite men in karaoke bars, are certainly not unique to China. The hostess club is part of the elite male business culture found in many parts of Asia (Allison 1994, Cheng 2000, Hwang 1996, Micollier 2004). However, only Chinese society seems to have created a "sexual-political subject" (Jeffreys 2004) within the context of the karaoke club. In *Nightwork: Sexuality, Pleasure, and Corporate Masculinity in a Tokyo Hostess Club,* Anne Allison (1994) discusses the culture of corporate masculinity inside Tokyo hostess clubs; the book became a foundation for me as I prepared to study Chinese men's habits in a similar environment. Allison describes how Japanese *sarariiman* (white collar workers) are expected or even required to go out to hostess clubs with their boss and colleagues after work in order to solidify their relationships. She describes this as a nexus of work and play. But even if the environments and activities are similar, the karaoke bar plays a different role for government officials and businessmen in China. Japanese *sarariiman* work very hard during the day and play hard with their colleagues at night as a way of rekindling the "humaneness" of their work relations. This, argues Allison, "is the principal aim of corporate entertainment" for the Japanese *sarariiman* (14). Participating in karaoke is necessary for demonstrating the human relations that help a Japanese *sarariiman* maintain his position, but success is determined through his performance inside the office. Work in this context is defined by activities that take place inside the office. Activities that occur inside the karaoke bar afford leisure, although they do serve a homosocial role in Japanese culture that strengthens relations between male colleagues. Success for Chinese businessmen or even government officials, however, is more dependent on the skills they demonstrate inside a karaoke bar than on their professionally related skills (Dickson 2008). Men often told me a good leader is considered someone who occupies his time with hosting and entertaining guests rather than office work. A leader who is frequently found in the office is perceived as a failure and will likely lose his position to someone who can manage the unit or bureau more effectively by delegating the responsibilities of the office. Consequently, in this virtuocratic bureaucracy a government official's ascent up the ladder of success is based more on the relationships he builds over food, drink, and entertainment than on the technical skills he can demonstrate in the office. This has turned such behaviors into an unofficial requirement of work-related duties, making them, as one man told me, an occupational hazard rather than simply a group of individual behaviors.

Work in the Chinese Context

Work or "*gongzuo*" is a dynamic term in socialist China that carries specific meaning associated with position rather than labor. To "have work" (*you gongzuo*) in China implies you are employed by a state-owned enterprise or work unit (*danwei*), a position that entitles employees to provision of social and welfare resources including housing, schooling, health care, food, pension, and even marriage documents (Entwistle and Henderson 2000, Lai 1995). All other types of work are categorized according to function. For instance, someone who does business is said to "*zuo shengyi*," a peasant is said to "*laodong*" (do labor), and a migrant worker is said to "*dagong*" (do manual or menial work). All are forms of work, but generally, only work inside a state-owned enterprise is officially called "*gongzuo*," a privilege that carries an expectation of party loyalty demonstrated through adherence to strict moral and political standards. To say someone has a job (*ta you gongzuo*) also implies that he or she must protect his or her reputation in order to maintain that position.

This institutional framework has led to an ambiguous definition of the activities associated with "work," which often transcend the expected purview of a given position into a realm dictated by cultural and political expectation. The Communist Party views work as a tool used to demonstrate party loyalty. This characteristic is increasingly manifesting itself in a very particular manner, though, as government officials and wealthy entrepreneurs look for ways to forge the gap required for successful operation of China's market economy.

A typical workday that I observed for a government official or businessman in Ruili starts at 8:00 in the morning and often does not end until 2:00 the next morning. Their days often begin by hosting guests at a popular breakfast spot in Ruili that serves typical local Dai dishes of rice noodles topped with meatballs, stewed spiced beef, or a hot paste made from the flour of yellow peas, called *xi doufen*. On most mornings, this restaurant is quite a meeting place for Ruili's high-level local officials, before setting out for the day to accompany guests on tours to survey (*kaocha*) local situations in Ruili's countryside. At 11:30 the officials invite their guests for lunch in the rural township they have gone to visit. The requisite alcohol used to show respect to business or government partners always accompanies lunch, which consists of more local delicacies. Lunch is often followed by a siesta period (*xiuxi*), which lasts until 2:30, and the work-related duties resume in the afternoon until 5:30. The hosting official and his work unit invite their visitor to dinner in the city at 6:00, which consists of more local delicacies and more toasting between the host and their guests to express their mutual respect and appreciation. After dinner the host invites his guests out for entertainment (*yule*), which can include hair washing (*xitou*), massage (*anmo*), foot reflexology (*xijiao*), or a trip to one of Ruili's disco and karaoke clubs for singing, dancing, and more drinking. Karaoke is often followed by a midnight meal (*xiaoyan*) at one of Ruili's night markets or sidewalk restaurants. Any one of these forms of entertainment can be accompanied by a female service worker who may also provide some type of sexual services, sometimes involving a massage girl (*anmo xiaojie*) or a "three accompaniment miss" (*sanpei xiaojie*). Alternatively, guests are offered a brothel-based sex worker, who is discreetly solicited by the government official's driver to the guest's hotel room. This typical day of hosting and entertainment, officially referred to as *jiedai keren,* often ends at 2:00 a.m. and can define six or even seven days of an official's week.

Men constantly stressed to me that the activities structuring this typical day were an essential part of their work. Wang Yantao, the midlevel official who was diagnosed with AIDS in 2002, was previously designated by his work unit as one of the primary people responsible for hosting and entertaining. Consequently, he spent five out of seven nights every week entertaining guests (*jiedai keren*). He always regretted his actions but said to me, "Our work made us do these things. When a superior (*lingdao*) came down to visit we would go eat with them. Then when we finished eating and finished drinking we would all go out to sing and dance together. And after singing we would go do reckless things including all the soliciting of prostitutes that comes along with it (*luanqi bazao shenme piaochang de shi ye laile*)."

The activities Wang Yantao described have become unavoidable in a virtuocratic bureaucracy, where they impart evidence of party loyalty. As one man told me,

> Nanren bu piaochang
> > duibuqi dang zhongyang
> Nüren bu zuoji
> > duibuqi Zhu Rongji

> (A man who does not solicit prostitutes has betrayed the Party Central,
> A woman who does not work as a prostitute has betrayed Zhu Rongji)[11]

This couplet is a parody of the hard-line anti-corruption campaign that Zhu Rongji waged in the 1990s, but it is also indicative of the important role commercial sex plays in political bargaining in China. Men constantly reminded me how important these types of activities were for protecting their political careers and promoting their economic success. Lower-level officials who successfully entertain higher-level guests (*jiedai keren*) may receive more opportunities for advancement and favorable reports about the status of their work. Their bosses may also reward them with extra pay for performing these duties. As one retired government employee told me:

If you want to be an official and advance up the ladder, you must have personal relations (*renji guanxi*). You cannot advance without these personal relations. And where do personal relations come from? You have to invite them out to eat, for a massage, shoot the shit with them, solicit prostitutes for them and then they'll see that you're useful. Our country's policies do not permit these things, but our local officials desire them. So slowly, if you give them the impression that you can do these things, you will gradually advance in rank.

Many of the men I met complied. Zhou Lin, who worked for the local Party Committee in Ruili, told me he hosted and entertained six or seven days a week. When his boss called him to a banquet, he said he had no choice but to drop everything and go for the evening. And then he reluctantly said to me, "You have to betray your own wife (*yao duibuqi ni ziji de laopo*)." A government worker at a gender training workshop in Kunming who was asked to comment about the health risks of being a man in China spoke about provision of sex work during his work unit's hosting and entertaining activities. He said that although he does not like participating in these activities, he feels compelled to accept the services of a sex worker when hosting and entertaining with his boss in order to strengthen and maintain relations with his superiors and limit any potential threat to his own career. A tall, confident, and successful man who owned a restaurant, hotel, and casino that catered to men who depended on easy unofficial access to the border told me, "You especially have to *yingchou* with the government officials because that can make or break whatever you do as a businessman." Like most men, he dreaded the nights spent drinking with government officials and other colleagues, but believed such a fate is often unavoidable for maintaining and growing a business. The many nights spent drinking, eating, smoking, and singing in karaoke bars translated into strong trusting relations with the local government officials, border control, and members of the Public Security Bureau, who often turned a blind eye to the materials and people that crossed the border to his casino and restaurant. Men could of course refuse the sexual services offered to them, but they feared ruining their reputation and instead acquiesced as a face-saving mechanism (*mianzi*) to protect the individual social prestige gained from successfully performing accepted social roles (Hu 1944).

It is also important to realize that *guanxi* cannot be ignored once it is built. One needs to work hard at maintaining the relationship in order to sustain the strong sentiments (*renji guanxi*) that bond two people together. A relationship is established only after three meetings. A first meeting acquaints people, they become familiar with each other on a second meeting, and then they can be considered friends after a third meeting (*yihui ren, erhui shou, sanhui you*). This requires men to repeatedly engage in *yingchou* with the same partners to maintain their business or climb their way up the political ladder. One man who worked for a state-owned utility company that was facing competition from privately held companies spent most nights in karaoke clubs and massage parlors entertaining local customers in order to maintain their business. This is necessary, he told me, because people in Ruili are comfortable doing business only with people they feel are trusted friends. As someone responsible for relationship development and maintenance in the company, his job kept him away from his home and family most nights so he could engage in *yingchou*.

The men participating in these constant sessions of drinking, smoking, eating, and entertainment realize the impact on their health, as do their families, but many feel as if they lack the agency to change their behaviors because doing so could sacrifice their success. The daughter of a high-level official in Ruili once commented to me, "My father's not very healthy because he always has to go out and drink a lot." Another high-level government worker who married his wife after helping her through emergency surgery for cancer in the late 1980s said to me, "She's healthier than I am now because she doesn't have to *yingchou* like I do." And several of the successful businessmen I met in Ruili were trying to restore their health after years of excessive drinking and smoking. One man in particular, who had worked hard toward success, eventually stepped back from the regular banqueting and smoking to restore his health. He did this by attending regular sessions of a procedure at an outpatient clinic within the prefectural hospital, which slowly stripped his blood of all the fatty deposits that had collected over the years of banqueting.[12]

Party efforts in post-Mao China to maintain an ideological hold over flourishing entrepreneurialism are leading to development of new ways of demonstrating party loyalty that are redefining politicization of the Chinese body (Anagnost 1997, Tsai 2007). Work-related requirements used as a means for demonstrating party loyalty have increased state control over individual, family, and collective lives by moving the social focus out of the home and into the work place. Many businessmen, government officials, and government workers are kept away from home at night because of work-related responsibilities to entertain, which often include soliciting services from a commercial sex worker. Many families are not comfortable with these requirements, but men often sacrifice the masculinity imbued in loyalty to their family for professional success, which also contributes to their masculinity. A man who was being considered for a minor official position told me he was seriously thinking of refusing the opportunity. He said to me, "Becoming a government official means sacrificing my family. Many families are broken after the husband becomes an official because of all the responsibilities to *yingchou* and *jiedai keren*. You have to stay out all the time and do a lot of drinking, and then there are the "unmentionable things" (*buhao shuo de shiqing*).[13] So many people aren't responsible to their families these days because they want to advance their careers, and I don't want to have to choose between my family and my work." But Wang Yantao's wife once said to me, "There are a lot of pressures on these men when they *jiedai keren*. They eat and drink and sing karaoke and then finally they have to go to solicit prostitutes (*piaochang*). A man's masculinity is questioned if he doesn't *piaochang* when the other men say to you, 'Let's see if you're a real man.' And of course every man wants to be seen as a real man." Still, many women are frustrated by the time their husbands spend outside the home and blame the party (as well as their husbands) for the time they spend alone at home taking care of a child. The wife of an employee for a state-owned company who comes home only one or two nights a month said to me, "When work calls they have to go, they can't avoid it. But when your wife calls you home, you can avoid it, you don't have to go home, because we don't have that kind of power over men. Only the Communist Party has that kind of power over men. So this is all their fault."

This trend is facilitating development of a network of sexual relations in urban China that is continuously growing ever more complex. Not only do women believe that power begets money (*you quan cai you qian*), but it is only through money that men become evil (*you qian cai neng bian huai*). The entertainment industry in Ruili and other areas of China is primarily supported by either wealthy businessmen or people with access to money (Osburg 2013, Otis 2012). An economy controlled by patron-client relations that is in the hands of men who desire the comfort and corporeal services offered by entertainment establishments, but who cannot financially or politically afford to access these services on their own, contributes a major source of support for the industry. According to these men and their wives, quasi-compulsory participation in these types of clientelist relations can influence their lives. Both Wang Yantao and his wife lamented about his character when he first started working for the government. He was a quiet, conservative (*baoshou*) man, they said, until he started answering the call of his duty to host and entertain the many guests who came to visit his work unit in Ruili. In an era of competing loyalties between family, state, and market, it is the state that seems to be winning because of the power it wields over individual success. Such competing and discordant loyalties may benefit the state in the short run but also result in some unexpected social outcomes that are emerging partially in the form of influences on health. Addressing these issues will not simply be a matter of teaching people the dangers of engaging in such behaviors. It will also require creative use of the social, cultural, and political structures that motivate people to engage in certain practices.

2 Constructing the "*Nanzihan*"

Hegemonic Masculinity in Urban China

AS I WALKED DOWN A SMALL STREET IN KUNMING ONE afternoon in search of lunch, I perused the menus of a cluster of restaurants that specialize in fried rice (*chaofan*). Big placard menus hung on the walls outside each restaurant, about a dozen or so in the row, but only one stood out to me. This was the menu that listed *nanzihan chaofan* (manly fried rice). How could my research on Chinese masculinity be complete without ordering a plate? So there it was—the decision on lunch was made. "What makes this *nanzihan* fried rice?" I asked. The proprietor told me it was distinguished by its spiciness (*hen la de*). When I asked about the connection between a manly man and a spicy plate of rice, she explained all the pressures contemporary Chinese men endure in their daily lives: "They have family pressures (*jiating yali*) and social pressures (*shehui yali*) that they deal with on a daily basis, which makes their lives very stressful. Family pressures are particularly burdensome because the man is expected to support his family. A real *nanzihan* is a man who can eat such hot and spicy food without saying it's hot." I inferred this meant that he can handle the various pressures placed on him without cracking under duress.

As ridiculous as it may sound to compare a man to a plate of rice, the proprietor's brief explanation encapsulated everything I was learning about men and how they and the women in their lives describe a man worthy of Chinese categorization of a *nanzihan*, a manly man. Descriptions of masculine cultures are typically rooted in the sexual practices and behaviors often associated with hegemonic forms of masculinity, which define the boundaries of normative and alternative male performance. The strong culture of masculinity in Latin America, for example, is defined by the hegemonic archetype of the macho man, who falls on his sword in defense of his family's honor and spreads his seed among multitudes of women (Lewis 1951). As Matthew Gutmann (1996) so adeptly demonstrated in his classic ethnography on men living outside Mexico City, however, many men do not identify as *macho* and in fact consider fatherhood as an important aspect of their masculine identity.

In China, hegemonic masculinity deviates from the global paradigm that associates maleness with sexual behavior and practices, to occur more at the nexus of social relations that have become integral to shaping the economic and political structures that govern post-Mao society. Sex may be a medium for men to achieve certain rewards. But masculinity in China, as I discovered, is more closely tied to a man's social and professional status. The descriptions I heard from both men and women placed masculinity, or identity as a *nanzihan*, at the center of differing sets of relationships that occurred both inside the home (*zai jia*) and outside (*zai waibian*) in the broader social sphere. Inside the home men are expected to maintain relationships with parents, wives, and children. Outside, they are expected to establish and maintain a strong set of relationships with friends and professional networks that can ensure success in business and government. This organization of masculinity around institutional structures of state, workplace, and family is classic in both China and the contemporary Western world (Connell 1993). The social and political milieu in post-Mao China, however, also requires men to compartmentalize the varying aspects of their lives, resulting in a social life filled with "homologous opposition" (Bourdieu 2001) for those striving to achieve this hegemonic status of *nanzihan*. The need to not only fulfill but to isolate their social and political roles from one another creates a unique dynamic among men striving for success in contemporary China, which distinguishes their particular brand of masculinity. These tensions, which characterize this brand of masculinity, also create vulnerability to STIs and HIV despite the fact that men occupy the more powerful side of the gendered dichotomy.

Gender in China

Studies of gender in China, as they are in many contexts, are shaped by descriptions of women and femininity. The volumes of "gendered" literature on women in China have offered an opportunity to peer into the domains of the inner sphere and learn about women's lives in a world where history was made and told by the men who controlled the public sphere. But we still know little about masculinity, or what men say and do to define themselves as men, despite the fact that we know a lot about what men say and do in contemporary and historical Chinese society. This void in knowledge of one half of China's gendered structure has impeded our ability to gain a true understanding of cultural meaning in China (Butler 1990, Sedgwick 1985). Historically we do know that sexual association with women (or even men) imbued men with the symbolic capital (Bourdieu 1991) necessary to enter the ranks of the elite (Brownell and Wasserstrom 2002, Furth 1988, Henriot [1997] 2001, Hershatter 1997, Sommer 2000). But the consumption of women was and is just one aspect of male performance that helps to define men of a certain class. The construction of Chinese male identity is much broader than a man's sexual practices. Masculinity in this context, as Rhacel Parreñas (2011) has described among men in Tokyo, is "buttressing." Historically, masculinity in China was primarily associated with husbands and fathers, and education that gave men entrée into an elite class of literati who were responsible for governing China (Louie 2002). This is true of the men I met in contemporary China as well. Although relationships with women are clearly important to men, they are not prioritized in the construction of male identity. Work, family, and health are more often identified as the most important elements necessary for raising men to a level where they can pursue success. Men who meet the expectations of a *nanzihan,* though, have the social flexibility to establish sexual relationships with women outside their marriage. These relationships do play a role in underscoring the symbolic capital that identifies them as a *nanzihan.* But it is the relationship and not necessarily the sex that occurs between a man and a woman that solidifies his masculine identity (Farrer 2002, Osburg 2013, Xiao 2011).

The performance of masculine practices has also become intertwined with political power and bureaucratic legitimacy in post-Mao China despite Mao's own attempts to degender society. Mao expected men and women to identify with revolution and the nation instead of trivial individual and bourgeois matters like gender differentiation. This robbed men (and women) of much of their identities, rendering men powerless and at times even feeling as if they had been castrated (Li 1999, Zhang 2001, Zhong 2000). Gendered, and in particular masculine, performance has regained importance in the post-Mao era as a medium for fueling economic growth. But these practices are little understood and misinterpreted because Chinese masculinity remains under-examined and undertheorized. The *nanzihan* adheres to a specific model of masculinity that expects men to fulfill a prescribed set of professional and personal roles and relationships. Some of these roles and relationships exist in tension with one another, forcing men to develop a contemporary discourse that has also become integral to defining masculinity in post-Mao China. This type of masculinity, which applies only to the elite in business and government, is arguably only one "class-specific form of masculinity" (Connell 1995). But it represents a hegemonic ideal of masculinity in China, which it is important to establish before tackling any masculine problems within this context. It is also the type of masculinity mediating risk for STIs and HIV among this class of men that fuels China's commercial sex industry.

The hegemonic "masculinity of success" these men aspire to is the type of masculinity required to build the social and symbolic capital necessary for attaining economic and political status in contemporary China. Hegemonic masculinity is often a problematic category because it describes a dominant idealized form of masculinity that may be practiced only by a minority of men who claim hierarchical superiority in relation to other marginalized and subordinate forms of masculinity because they engage in certain normative practices (Connell 1995, Connell and Messerschmidt 2005, Cornwall 1997). Nevertheless, an examination of hegemonic masculinity within a certain context is useful in understanding the construction of power within that society through description of the normative expectations against which all other forms of male practice and behavior are evaluated. Performing the norms related to hegemonic masculinity is important for men aspiring to economic and political success. This chapter begins with a brief examination of three men who claim or wish to claim status as a *nanzihan,* as an initial lens into how hegemonic masculinity is directing men's practices, behaviors, and risk in post-Mao China.

Constructing Stories of Manly Men in Urban China

Wang Jun

Wang Jun was thirty-eight years old when I first met him. Although his identity card (*shenfenzheng*) and appearance readily revealed his identity as an ethnic minority, he lived the model life of a Han Chinese civil servant. Wang Jun moved to Dehong Prefecture from his natal hometown after graduating from university. At the time, he held a midlevel position of responsibility in the party apparatus and lived with his wife, who also worked for a local state-owned work unit, and their son. He had held this position for many years but was regularly promoted in his rank. Wang Jun knew his status could be raised by working his way into a better position, but he said he was happy at this level where he could command respect without working very hard. Wang Jun and his family originally lived in the one-room dormitory allotted by his work unit but used their savings to buy a newly built apartment with multiple bedrooms and bathrooms. Of course one may question how a family living on two government incomes could save up enough money to buy a brand new apartment. But Wang Jun was very close with a group of local male entrepreneurs who depended on his government connections for facilitating many of their business ventures.

Wang Jun, who earned his reputation as a real Chinese man through demonstrating his role as a dedicated father, responsible husband, and loyal son, could often be found at home after work, cooking dinner for his wife and son, relaxing in front of the television, or doing chores around the house. He constantly strove to fulfill a promise he made to be eternally responsible to his wife after she survived a serious illness before their marriage. He was also a proud parent to his son and an extremely filial son to his parents and grandparents. Wang Jun often returned to his natal town to visit his parents and also drove two days to visit his grandparents' graves during the Chinese grave sweeping festival (*qinming jie*). He constantly reminded me of the importance of being filial to one's parents. He was also careful to fulfill responsibilities to his affairs outside the house by maintaining his reputation as a loyal party member and employee. When he had the chance, Wang Jun always invited his superiors (*lingdao*) out for dinner and took the opportunity to demonstrate his respect through toasting them with cups of China's famous white spirit (*bai jiu*). Wang Jun was known around the prefecture as a fierce drinker who was skilled in the popular numerical drinking game *hua quan*. When he was not at home or out to dinner with his superiors, Wang Jun could be found spending time with his close network of friends, either listening to their latest business plans or playing cards late into the night. Wang Jun was loyal to his friends and told me he would go to any length to help the men in this close-knit group, which consisted of several of Dehong's successful businessmen and one of the prefecture's top doctors. He and his friends often played cards in one of their homes, or in a local hotel room, until the sun came up the next morning. I asked Wang Jun if his wife ever became suspicious of him after spending an entire night outside their home, and he always assured me that she trusted him implicitly and never questioned his whereabouts.

Confident that he had fulfilled his responsibilities at home, Wang Jun also exercised his right as a man in Han Chinese society to be a good lover (*qin-ren*) to several women. When I knew him, Wang Jun was engaged in several long-term sexual relationships with mature and educated women outside his marriage. He enjoyed exploring sexual possibilities with these women and did not feel it detracted from his role as a good husband to his wife or father to his son because he did not love these women and therefore was devoid of any responsibility to them. Consequently, they posed no threat to his marriage. And although he had sex with these women, he was attracted to them because of the opportunity for stimulating conversation. Aside from these long-term sexual relationships, he and his friends also told me that Wang Jun, who is a tall, thin, and handsome man with a respectable government position, was often sought by young women who find this type of man attractive. He admitted to toying with these young girls in the karaoke clubs. But Wang Jun said he never pursued sexual relationships with such women, who did not interest him and whom he believed might carry sexually transmitted infections.

A Rong

At thirty-five, A Rong was close to hitting the pinnacle of his success in business. This allowed him to start thinking about finding the second wife (*xioa laopo*) who could help him increase his demonstration of filiality to his parents, through producing more descendants. He identified as Han Chinese on his identity card but was one-quarter Dai and grew up surrounded by many Dai cultural influences. Still, he considered himself a traditional Chinese man who was influenced by the ways of Confucianism. He regularly reminded me that many of the customs he followed as a Chinese man were motivated by China's Confucian history and told me he is a Confucian (*rujia*) at heart.

A Rong and his wife met in high school and started dating while attending university in Kunming. After graduation, they were both assigned to government positions in Ruili, where they settled and gave birth to a daughter. They originally lived in the three-room apartment assigned by her work unit. A Rong left his position after a few years to pursue a life in business (*zuo shen-gyi*), where he could become wealthy. Over the years, he dabbled in many business ventures, searching for success. He started a successful cross-border business conglomerate with several friends and colleagues (including Wang Jun), just about the time I arrived in Ruili.

This life of peripatetic business pursuits brought A Rong a reasonable amount of financial success. When I first met him, his family lived in a large gated mansion in Ruili's district of wealthy people (*furen qu*), a neighborhood in the southeastern quadrant of Ruili filled with similarly opulent homes. But they sold their house and moved back to the small apartment allotted to them through his wife's work unit by the time I left Ruili. His new business venture was located five hours away from Ruili and was where he spent most of his time. He returned home an average of only one or two days every month, which left his wife feeling very lonely in their big house. She preferred to be surrounded by friends and colleagues rather than the silence of their large, isolated house.

When I met A Rong, he demonstrated the model of responsibility expected of a Chinese man. He was a good husband, concerned about protecting his wife and providing her with everything she needed, and a good father devoted to securing his daughter's future. And like his good friend Wang Jun, A Rong was committed to being a good filial son. As the eldest and most capable (according to his accounts) child in his family, A Rong was responsible for supporting his retired parents, as well as his brother, who was unlucky in business. Part of this filial commitment included producing more grandchildren to extend their lineage. Many people in Ruili were able to skirt the one-child policy, but this was prohibited for civil servants like A Rong's wife. An extra child would be at the cost of her job as well as the state benefits that accompany civil service employment. As a result, part of A Rong's quest for financial success was motivated by his need to find and marry a minor wife (*xiao laopo*) who could help fulfill his filial duty.

It seems A Rong was quite a playboy before I met him. He was a confident and good-looking man who enjoyed chasing after women (*pao niu*) when he was younger. He believed his good looks and success attracted all these women. He also spent a lot of time drinking and singing in karaoke bars as a way of building up his relationships with the people who held the key to his success. At the tender age of thirty-five, though, he had had enough. He was tired and basically done playing around. "*Wo wan(r) goule*" (I have partied enough), he said to me. He still felt compelled to smoke in order to maintain and solidify relationships with business acquaintances and government officials, but he no longer participated in the type of lifestyle that required him to

drink heavily and stay out in clubs late at night. At this point most of his networking was conducted over banquet-style dinners, where he could show his
respect through eating, simple toasting, and exchanging cigarettes. He also
spent a lot of time maintaining the solid network of friendships he shared
with Wang Jun and others during their long nights playing cards.

Xiao Mei

Born to a rural Jingpo family, Xiao Mei strongly identified with his ethnic
identity but also aspired to the success he witnessed among the many Han
and even Jingpo men in Ruili's urban environment, where he lived when we
initially met. He constantly negotiated the expectations to fulfill the requirements of Han masculinity while grappling with his own identity as a masculine Jingpo man (*jingpo hanzi*), which limited his ability to conform to the
restrictions of order and responsibility that go against the grain of someone
raised in a nomadic culture.[1]

When I first met Xiao Mei he was just a boy (*xiao huozi*) of twenty-seven,
so considered because of his relatively low social standing. He was, however,
married and had a young son. But he rarely saw his wife or son. Although they
technically shared a home, he returned there only once or twice a month. He
and his wife were not happy together, but the marital customs associated with
their Jingpo ethnic origins proscribed them from divorcing. In addition, as a
traditionally minded person, Xiao Mei had a disdain for divorce. As a result,
like many other men I met, he was more an inhabitant of the city than his
home, darting around from hotel to hotel in search of a room where he could
catch a few hours of sleep.

Xiao Mei was the eldest of three children born to a rural Jingpo family in
Dehong Prefecture. He considered himself a *jingpo hanzi,* but knew conform-
ing to the ideals of Han Chinese masculinity was necessary for success as a
man in his new urban environment. When I met Xiao Mei he was employed
as a low-level staff member for an official in the party apparatus. He strove to
become merely a low-level official in order to gain some of the status needed
to rise to the ranks of masculinity in his adopted Han-dominated world, but
lack of education meant that even a low-level position eluded him. As a middle
school graduate, he was considered fairly well educated by Jingpo standards
but virtually uneducated and thus lacking culture (*meiyou wenhua*) by Han
Chinese standards. A wealthy relative gave him an opportunity to move to
Ruili when he was younger, and another relative eventually gave him the

opportunity to work for the party. For several years he looked for ways to raise his status as an urban man, either by trying to increase his chances of becoming a low-level official or through looking for ways to do business. He failed on both accounts but eventually found an opportunity to move into a similar low-level government staff job in Kunming, which he felt would improve his opportunities at finding the symbolic capital he longed for. This move was made independently of his wife and son, who remained in Ruili.

As the eldest son in a traditional Jingpo family, Xiao Mei was born with relatively little status. Though Jingpo culture prefers boy babies, and men are dominant in the family, the eldest son receives no inheritance. Family property is passed onto the youngest son, who is eventually responsible for supporting his parents in their old age (Leach 1959, Wang 1997). In addition, although sons are necessary in the family for their strength, they are considered a burden to the family's resources because the bridegroom's family in Jingpo culture is responsible for providing a bride price to the bride's family. Thus, for the Jingpo, "A daughter no matter how unprepossessing, is just like a tree-ear-producing tree trunk: a source of wealth. A son, no matter how dull-witted, is still a shoulder-bag hook on the wall: parents can get meals in the house" (Wang 1997: 158). Jingpo folklore also believes that "to have a son can protect a village, but to have a daughter can help acquire nine villages" (*sheng nan shou yige zhai, sheng nü kede jiuge zhai;* Jin 2003: 274). Xiao Mei did benefit from the hierarchical Jingpo marriage system, which promotes marriage of commoner men into the aristocracy (Leach 1959, Wang 1997). His wife was a descendant of a Jingpo chiefly clan. Marriage into the family resulted in a marginal increase in his social and political status but not quite enough to lift him to the position he coveted.

Xiao Mei attempted to account for the voids in his political and social status through economic demonstration, which is often emblematic of a successful businessman in China. His job in Ruili gave him access to an expensive car, which seemed to form part of his identity when he lived there. He also found ways to access expensive clothes, watches, and mobile phones, all status symbols in urban China. He further took advantage of the responsibilities associated with his job to access a network that could affect his social status as well as opportunities to satisfy his sexual desires and curiosities. Responsibilities for his government job often took him away from Ruili for several days at a time, or kept him out in Ruili until one or two o'clock in the morning. On the few nights he did not have work-related responsibilities, he could still be found in one of the town's disco and karaoke clubs, or out at one of his favorite massage parlors solidifying relationships that were important for building the human sentiment (*renqing*) he knew was necessary for succeeding in China's Han-dominated society. Regardless, each situation usually ended with a late-night meal (*xiaoyan*) at one of Ruili's night markets. Most nights Xiao Mei returned to sleep either alone in the dormitory room assigned to his wife by her government work unit or at a hotel with one of the women with whom he maintained long-term sexual relationships. On rare occasions, he returned home to the house his in-laws built for him, his wife, their son, and themselves.

Constructing the Hegemonic Chinese Man

These three men occupy different positions and roles in Chinese society, both ethnically and professionally, but all aspire to be successful as men—to achieve the position that earns them the respect and title of a *nanzihan,* a man who has succeeded in the realm of family and at business or government, within China's Han-dominated society. Earning this title can open up the privileges accorded to China's most elite men.

Men who earn the status of *nanzihan* have reached an ideal gendered state, representative of "the most honored way of being a man" (Connell and Messerschmidt 2005: 832) in elite Chinese society. These men, who hold the most powerful positions in male Chinese society, are the symbol of hegemonic masculinity in China and maintain their status through institutionalizing this elite form of gendered performance (Connell 1995).[2] This was historically performed through the civil service exam system, which socialized elite literati through study of the Confucian classics. Unique access to a form of female-centered entertainment reified their class-based masculine status outside the study hall (Peterson 1979). This type of "corporate masculinity," a masculine performance used to reify organizational and institutional power, is common among the upper echelons of business, military, and government, where positions of power are often maintained through displays of racial or ethnic superiority and visible evidence of heterosexual identity. But these displays of masculine performance are only part of the hegemonic form of masculinity that characterizes elite men in the Chinese context. Understanding the true structure of the corporate masculinity associated with Chinese men of status is also dependent on examining the remaining practices they use to define themselves as men.

The model I present is not just an ideal, but the lived experiences of men I have observed striving for the title of *nanzihan*. It is a model of masculinity that Chinese men use to obtain and remain in power. Constructing this model will be useful for understanding the contemporary Chinese institutions and practices that distinguish China's modern-day elite men. Outlining a hegemonic model of masculinity will also be useful for examining and understanding other groups of men who embody alternative masculinities outside of this dominant pattern, including rural men or those who have sex with other men, two separate classes whose vulnerability to HIV infection is also influenced by their gendered performance.

The Importance of Relationships

Discourse around gender is often feminized, and even when it is masculinized it is rarely viewed as a relational structure (Connell 1995, Gutmann 1997a). Beyond this relational dimension, though, there are many other relationships that may affect individual performance of gender. For example, men and women maintain homosocial relationships with each other that affect how femininity or masculinity is performed. I learned the importance of looking at these relationships through my own research process. Men easily accepted me into their homosocial circles but also felt it was important to introduce me to their wives because homosocial bonds are so important to Chinese society. The women I spoke with also fulfilled various roles in men's lives, and they realized the importance of their opinions and voices in constructing a model of Chinese masculinity because of the objective stance they offered as outsiders looking in at the other side of a relationship they helped create.

Women are an important part of constructing and understanding male identity within a relational model of gender, but in China we must also consider the other relationships important for constructing male identity. Chinese society is centered around five core relationships of which only one—that between a husband and his wife—consists of a relationship between a man and a woman.[3] Men, who are at the center of all the five relationships that structure Confucian culture, value all of these relationships in constructing their identity. This remains true among contemporary Chinese men.

The first part of constructing an identity as a real Chinese man entails fulfilling an expected responsibility as a husband, father, and son. As one man told me, "Family is very important to 90 percent of Chinese men and those are the 90 percent who are responsible men. The others are not responsible." In only one instance a wife and husband, both of whom were uneducated, told me "a real Chinese man is a man with money, which goes hand in hand with power." For them, the richest man in town was the best example of a *nanzihan.*

The nuclear family is now the norm in urban Western societies, where life centers on the dyadic relationship between a husband and wife. Despite the fact that an increasing number of people are living within nuclear families in China, life is still organized vertically, centered on the male lineage. It is the relationship between a father and his son, or even a mother and her daughter-in-law (Fei [1947] 1992), that continues to structure Chinese family life. Fulfilling the social roles that support family and society has thus become integral to defining men. A man without children may be accused of being infertile or unable to produce descendants, amounting to one of the greatest potential insults to his masculinity. This is true all over China, even for men who engage in homosexual relationships or identify as gay. Many gay men still marry women, without revealing their sexual identity, in order to bear the children that will help fulfill their filial duties and affirm their masculine status. This has created a class of *tongqi,* the wives of gay men, who are often stigmatized and neglected once their husbands achieve their traditional goals and effectively abandon their wives to live out their own ideals of sexuality.[4] A wife thus can act as an important source and symbol of status for Chinese men. A man's relationship with his wife, however, is not nearly as important to him as the vertical relationships he has with his parents and children, who extend his lineage within China's patriarchal tradition.

"Wei wo de houdai": Constructing a Man's Lineage

Children (most importantly a son) are not merely a sign of male potency in Chinese society; they are a sign of security for a man's lineage. Men go to great lengths to protect and promote their descendants (*houdai*) to guarantee the maintenance of not only their lineage but also their parents' lineage. This is a form of filial piety and a marker of true masculinity. This was particularly true for Xiao Mei, who had not yet achieved the qualities necessary for true masculinity in the Han world. He had produced a son, however, which he knew did grant him a modicum of masculine status. As for Wang Jun, he told me the most important person in his life was not his wife; nor was she the love of his life. His parents were the most important relationship in his life because they represented a part of his lineage that could not be replaced. He claimed he could easily find another wife if something happened to this one. After all, he had all those young girls chasing after him in search of a man who could raise their status. If he somehow lost his son, he could also have another one. But he only had one mother and one father, and they could not be replaced.

Responsibility to parenting for a man is another issue that is separate and distinct from fatherhood. Chinese men do not work as hard to spread their seed as the stereotypical macho man. But masculine expectations in China also do not extend into the daily duties of parenting as they do for the truly masculine men Matthew Gutmann met in Mexico (1996). Chinese fathers are responsible for ensuring the family's economic stability and for facilitating their child's entry into the outside world. The domestic side of parenting, which includes a secure, comfortable, and supportive environment, falls within the realm of a child's mother. Consequently, Chinese men have traditionally assumed a distant role in their children's lives.

Women's increasing role in the public sphere, as well as pressures from global influences, are placing more expectations on men to become involved in daily parenting needs in contemporary Chinese society. At the same time, many of the men aspiring to successful positions as *nanzihan* are trying to hold on to their Confucian roots. More involvement in parenting would require more time at home, which could detract from their opportunities for success. Still, these men are constantly concerned with fulfilling responsibilities to furnish the best opportunities for their children's education and future. Many of the successful men I met in China asked me to spend time with their children tutoring them in English. They knew this type of skill was important for their children's success in a modern, globalizing nation. Despite their concern, they also prioritized responsibilities that frequently took them away from home. I asked them to explain why they spent so much time away from home, if they had so much concern for their children. They always explained that they sacrificed this time with their family for their children and their descendants (*wei wo de houdai*). That one exclamation stymied any and all criticism against a father who was absent too often because he was doing the important work of preserving China's future by securing his lineage, one of the primary responsibilities of a *nanzihan*.

Despite this type of masculine discourse prioritizing a man's role outside the home, I often wondered what type of tensions were created within these men who seemed to enjoy spending time with their children. Many of the men I knew rarely smiled or joked, but their attitudes changed when they were with their children. Suddenly their faces lit up and they became demonstrative, affectionate, and playful people. Wang Jun was always happy to receive a phone call or text message from his son reporting some good news like top placement in a swim meet. The first time I met his son, Wang Jun introduced the tall and thin teenager as "my proudest creation" (*wo zui deyi de zuopin*). Even Xiao Mei, who rarely returned home and practically divorced himself from his domestic life, was happiest and most at ease when with his son.

One may wonder if these men are truly devoted to their families, but broaching such a subject was difficult because questioning a man's devotion to his family is even more threatening to his masculine status than public demonstration of affection to a child. Such questions were always met with hostile responses from men who assured me that they absolutely prioritize care for their children. The threat was so great that men even defended their friends against such accusation. Any perceived neglect of one's domestic responsibilities is tantamount to disreputable behavior, which can result in loss of face (*mianzi*), another component crucial to the construction of masculine status in urban China.

A Rong was perhaps most deserving of these suspicions. He maintained a strict division between family and business when I first met him but felt a need to compromise this comportment as he tried to maintain commitment to both family and entrepreneurial success after establishing his cross-border business far away from home. His business operations were located five hours away across the border in the Kachin State, but the social and political relationships necessary for his success were centered in Dehong Prefecture. This forced him to connect with both professional ties and family during his brief periodic trips back to Dehong. He contacted me during one such trip. I had not heard from him in several weeks, but one day he called to invite me to join him, his wife, and his daughter to celebrate his mother's sixtieth birthday at his natal home. He said to me, "We Chinese people are very filial (*xiao*), and celebrating our elders' birthdays is very important to us." That night he hosted a big banquet in a restaurant, with enough people to occupy two circular tables that seated twelve people each in a private room. But only some of the people in attendance were family who had come to honor his mother's birthday. His wife, daughter, mother, sister, in-laws, and niece and nephew sat at one table. He sat at the "head" table with the government officials and business contacts he had also invited, which is where I sat as well. His mother's birthday became a pretext to return to his home town, but his attention seemed to be dominated by the officials and business partners present who could influence the success of his business venture. I became the added piece of symbolic capital, as the educated American from an Ivy League university, who could increase his status with the local officials.[5]

A Rong and his family returned to his parents' home after dinner for the decorated birthday cake that has become a requisite for modern Chinese birthday celebrations. It was obvious from his distracted look and constantly ringing phone that business continued to call. Despite silent protest from his wife, A Rong left the house around eleven o'clock that night to tend to some business (*shiqing*) that had suddenly come up, without paying much attention to his mother, whom he had supposedly come to honor. He said, "I have some affairs to attend to" (*wo you shiqing*), a mantra that often excuses men from obligations, and quickly exited the house. Having important affairs to attend to (*shiqing*) outside the home has become symbolic of a *nanzihan,* who is busy becoming successful. *Shiqing* are also proprietary. A man need not divulge the *shiqing* calling him to duty. The specifics are also never questioned but rather protected by a social code of privacy. It is important merely to have *shiqing,* announcement of which is automatic evidence of his masculinity and excuses him from responsibilities to family, friends, or lovers. Consequently, hindering a man from attending to his *shiqing* is a threat to the masculine success he is entitled to in "a society characterized by sexual inequality and an ideology of masculine superiority" (Chodorow 1978: 181). As a result, I often heard businessmen and government officials in Ruili say they had to attend to *shiqing* whenever they needed an excuse to exit one situation for another they prioritized in their individual lives. Xiao Mei, who was constantly searching for the opportunity that would give him access to the truly masculine world in urban China, relied on this discourse of *shiqing* more than other men I knew in Ruili. This was the one scenario that created a perception of masculine performance around him that no one could question, despite his marginalized status as a low-level, uneducated, ethnic-minority government employee.

This cultural justification, which favored men's success over all other responsibility, freed them from the onus of negotiating some of the conflicting tensions in their lives but caused further anguish for others, primarily the women in their lives, who had to assume these responsibilities. A Rong's wife and other wives I met told me of their frustration with husbands whom they believe failed to truly fulfill their domestic responsibilities. One woman I met said to me, "Men say they respect their wives and are responsible to their families, when in fact they're not. They don't really fulfill these responsibilities." In an interview with A Rong's wife, who constantly lived with these frustrations, she also told me, "Chinese men always say their family is the most important thing to them, but that's not demonstrated at all." She did not fully believe that men work so hard just for their family or their *houdai,* and in her case she did not think her husband was being very good to his own family. She said, "There's no real gender equality in China because the man can do what he wants and they are never with their family." Men, however, always defended themselves and their friends against these types of accusations. Liu Dun, another member of Wang Jun and A Rong's close network of friends, said to me one day, "Even though I spend a lot of time outside the home (*zai waibian*), I still do a lot of things for my family." For Liu Dun and the other successful businessmen I met in China, the money and opportunities they supplied for their families fulfilled their ordained social responsibility as a husband and father.[6] This satisfied one dimension that helped to establish their status as a *nanzihan.* These are the types of tensions I constantly saw arising in the gaps between evolving expectations for men, to assume an increasing amount of responsibility at home and the pressure to achieve political and economic success that is emblematic of the Confucian men who are also still revered in Chinese society. They are also the types of tensions that are resulting in varying social problems that are not yet being addressed in a society prioritizing its economic development over its social development.

A Chinese Man's Best Friend Is His Best Friend: Homosocial Networks in Urban Chinese Society

The centrality of family to Chinese men detracts from the other relationships that complete Chinese social lives, including those between friends. Relationships between friends represent the one nonhierarchical bond prioritized in the Confucian social structure. Unlike the other bonds, the one between friends was not valued for ordering society. The special homosocial bonds formed through these friendships, however, created an elite process of socialization reserved only for the men who were responsible for establishing and guarding that order. When they were not with their family, where men and women occupied separate spheres, elite men bonded with one another inside the exclusive institution that trained them for the civil service exam (Goodman 1995, Kutcher 2000, Mann 2000). They became like brothers, *xiongdi,* a term very close male friends still use to refer to one another. The benefits of homosocial bonds eventually spread to the merchant class, who could turn to networks of men organized by local guilds and native place associations, for support and even aid on their frequent trips away from home (Mann 2000). Such networks among both elite and merchant class men helped to maintain control over the resources important for protecting masculine status in imperial China. This tradition continues in contemporary China, where a strong homosocial culture helps men maintain control over the economic, occupational, social, and political resources that govern society. A strong culture of hegemonic masculinity, which prioritizes homosocial relations, gives men the social space to socialize with one another inside informal institutions that are aligned with men, such as tea houses, restaurants, massage parlors and karaoke clubs, and exclusive men's clubs (Osburg 2013). Inside these spaces, men build up relationships with one another and gain exclusive domain over the structures that support the form of masculinity that placed them in positions of power.

Analyzing the roles homosocial relationships play in men's lives requires paying close attention to their lived experiences. We hear a lot in both scholarly and popular discourse about men's responsibilities to relationships with wives, children, and parents but not to their friends. It makes sense, however, for a society structured vertically around lineage and not marriage to prioritize homosocial bonds. In the rural Chinese society that Fei Xiaotong described, men and women generally did not mingle outside situations of reproduction and work and saved their emotions and affections for homosocial environments (Fei [1947] 1992). This type of homosocial divide is still evident in today's families, where husbands and wives live with a palpable void (*fuqi kongjian*) between them, which allows the flexibility and space for men and women to lead their own social lives and explore their individual social needs. I often found myself alone, as the only woman, out with a group of men who were eating and drinking together, singing together, or playing cards together. When I asked about their wives' whereabouts, they usually responded by saying, "She does her thing and I do my thing" (*ta you ta de, wo you wo de*). The husbands and the wives had their own set of friends and they did not socialize together. Instead, they met at home and left it together only for family-related events. Their activities were also gendered. Male friends often sat around a beer or tea, shooting the breeze (*chui niu*), while women preferred strolling through the streets (*guang jie*), shopping, and chatting (*liao tian*). And while men networked over alcohol, cards, karaoke, and cigarettes, women networked and built relationships over facials (*xilian*). After months of drinking and singing karaoke with men, I was almost relieved when relationships with male informants had been stretched to their limit, and fieldwork shifted toward women. I am not fond of browsing around clothing shops, but I was happy to get to the point where I was invited to more facials than to long evenings in karaoke bars.

I first became cognizant of the important role homosocial bonds play in constructing Chinese male identity during a conversation with Liu Dun. He advised me to pay attention to a man's close network of friends if I truly wanted to gain insight into masculine identity in China. Chinese men, he said, have several circles of friends, each assuming a different role in the man's life, and you can understand each man by observing the differences between these various networks. I had always seen young men walking arm in arm or draped over each other passing the time, but I hadn't realized that these physical bonds, which do not imply any type of sexual relationship, may represent more masculine bonds as well.[7]

Most of my lessons about the importance of homosocial bonds among men came from Wang Jun and his close network of friends, which included Liu Dun. Liu Dun was the first man I met from the group. We were introduced through a mutual friend in Kunming who is also one of his business partners. An introduction through a trustworthy contact provided me with immediate rapport through a relationship automatically imbued with *guanxi*. It also meant that he could introduce me to his close network of friends. I immediately became an honorary woman in this small "band of brothers," and they became a living classroom for me to learn about the structure of men's lives in Ruili. This group of friends consisted of Wang Jun and four successful businessmen (A Rong, Yang Xing, Liu Dun, and one other local man). Yang Xing, in particular, took it upon himself to actively teach me about being a man in China. One of his lessons offered a detailed explanation of the distinctions men make between their friends. He described them as a series of concentric circles that fit inside one another:

First of all there are your "acquaintances" (*shu ren*). Then there are the people with whom you eat and drink. They may be the people you network with over food and drink (*yingchou*). There is a lot of *yingchou* a man needs to do and it's so important for doing anything. You especially have to *yingchou* with the government because they control your success as a businessman. You have to have good "relations" (*guanxi*) with them and that's obtained through *yingchou*. Then there are friends (*pengyou*) and they come and go like migrating birds. Next there are good friends (*hao pengyou*) with whom you may be friends for a while but are still not people you can totally trust. Finally there are your "bosom buddies" (*zhiji*). These are the friends you will have for life. When I was young I thought I had so many friends and I used to boast to my parents about the number of friends I had. Then they would tell me, "You'll see none of those people are really your friends and you can only count on your *zhiji*."[8]

Trust and confidentiality are the most important aspects of a friendship between men. Unlike Western society, where the most private things are shared between a husband and a wife, Chinese society reserves these privileges for friends who often share the strongest bonds of trust and personal sentiment. There are many things a Chinese man will share with his close friends that he will not share with his wife, either because it could harm their relationship or because it does not fall within a woman's domain. Some men introduced me to their close friends by saying "we are the best" (*women shi zui hao de*), meaning they share implicit trust with each other. And A Rong once said to me, "If I didn't have my [male] friends, I wouldn't have a life." These men, who were like family, were crucial to his success and livelihood because, as he said, "You can only do business with men who you trust as brothers" (here he said *gemen,* a northern Chinese term used by men to refer to their most trusted friends). This close relationship was solidified and maintained over countless hours of cards and mahjong, which they often played when they met at A Rong's house to talk business until daybreak. Wang Jun served the role of Yang Xing's most trusted friend and repository of his most precious secrets. One day Yang Xing said to me, "I am friendly with both A Rong and Wang Jun but I cannot implicitly trust A Rong. I can share about one-third of everything with A Rong but I can share about 95 percent of things with Wang Jun."

The strong homosocial structure in Ruili affected my relationships there as well. In some respects, I was considered one of the boys, which enabled me to socialize with men. Many men were willing to accept me as part of their circle of friends because my personality as an American woman is perhaps more characteristic of local men than of women. People were often willing to confide in me because they didn't see me as a foreigner. I spoke relatively fluent Chinese and had settled into the community. Some men commented to me that they felt as if they were talking to a man when speaking with me. I also developed relationships with men's wives (among other women), but this too took a homosocial direction as relationships with husbands and wives developed in parallel to one another. For example, my relationship with A Rong started long before I had a friendship with his wife. His wife was always at their house when I first met him, but at that point I was fostering relationships within his homosocial network, until he identified a need for me to do so for a separate but parallel friendship with his wife. One day he said to me, "I am happy to be your friend, but I would also like you to be friends with my wife." Suddenly his perspective of me had shifted toward the way he would view a typical woman. For several days he deliberately placed me in situations with his wife and told us to go browse the shops (*guangjie*) together. They had developed problems in their sex life that involved her chosen contraceptive method. Knowing I was a medical anthropologist, A Rong mistakenly thought I had medical training and believed his wife would be willing to confide her problems with me and seek advice from me, if she could trust me as a friend. I also developed friendships with several women who never introduced me to their husbands. These were useful after the novelty of hanging out with an American woman wore off and my relationships with many men began to dissipate. Unique business connections, from which I was excluded as a foreigner and an outsider, helped to sustain men's relationships with each other. This consequently precluded me from relationships beyond the "classroom" into the level of a *zhiji* where the most sensitive and intimate conversations between men occurred. As a result, I found myself engaging with more and more women by the time I left Ruili, increasing my opportunities to learn more about women's opinions on masculinity during frequent invitations for facials.

Making the Chinese Man: The Innate Characteristics of a *Nanzihan*

Aside from the social capital a man attains through relationships, a Chinese man is also judged according to various types of symbolic capital gained from position, *suzhi* (a term that defines a person's perceived quality and potential contribution to society), face (*mianzi*) or perceived social reputation, and to a lesser degree material wealth.

The Importance of Position

Position has always been an important status marker in Chinese society. During imperial times, scholars (*shi*) occupied the pinnacle of society, followed by peasant farmers (*nong*), artisans (*gong*), and finally merchants (*shang*), this last group enjoying little status during that era. Today men of high political or economic status are considered most successful. Government officials are valued for the authority and respect imbued in them through the Communist party, which also typically shuns businessmen, who symbolize the antithesis of socialism.[9] In post-Mao China, however, where "to get rich is glorious,"[10] success in business is a new source of symbolic capital that yields both status and power for a new class of men.

Men in these positions fuel a large commercial sex industry and support many mistresses and lovers. But their masculine identity is embedded within their political and economic status, and not in the sexual opportunities that status makes available to them. As one woman argued, "Yes, men have a lot of sex these days, but I often think their behavior is merely a result of curiosity for new experiences and the fact that everyone has basic needs. They are really defined by their abilities." This was certainly true for A Rong. He was particularly proud of the fact that he was not only the most talented person in his family but also the most capable person from his cohort of high-school classmates. His talent and capacity at succeeding in business gave him a strong sense of being a man. Wang Jun also knew that success in government was necessary for solidifying his masculine identity and often felt insufficiently masculine because he had not achieved a high enough position in government for his age. The discrepancy between Western and Chinese measures of success became clearest, however, after speaking to the family of a man who was an accomplished infectious disease doctor integral to the local HIV/AIDS response. A man whom Western HIV/AIDS experts respected for his knowledge, skill, and determination was shunned as a failure within his own family. After once praising his medical abilities to his sister, she disappointingly said to me, "He can't even become a high-level official, so what good is he?" Clearly, the education, knowledge, skill, and respect he achieved among national and international HIV specialists, for his success and dedication in treating and responding to one of the country's most serious HIV epidemics, was not nearly as valued as the *guanxi* and prestige the family could gain through a high-level position in government.

The Status Inherent in Quality

As post-Mao China embarks on an effort to strengthen itself as a nation and raise its own status on the world stage, it has defined the type of citizen necessary for helping to accomplish this goal. The type of person who the government believes will help raise China from the ranks of the "Sick Man of Asia" is thought to be someone imbued with *suzhi,* a discourse popularized by the post-Mao state that broadly refers to a person's ability to contribute positively to society. There are countless articles and books that debate the meaning of *suzhi* without definitive conclusion. In general it is associated with the physical, intellectual, and ideological characteristics of a person. Urban people are generally viewed as having more *suzhi* than rural people. Likewise, ethnicity and education (*wenhua*) are also important determinants of *suzhi* (Anagnost 1995, Murphy 2004, Hairong Yan 2003). *Ta meiyou wenhua* (he has no education, which can also be understood as "he is very unacculturated") is often analogous to saying someone is lacking in *suzhi* (*suzhi di*).

People like Wang Jun and A Rong are considered among those with high *suzhi* (*suzhi gao*). They have a university education, which affords them access to privileged positions of status in society. Yang Xing was a successful thirty-five-year-old hotel and restaurant owner in Dehong, with only a high-school education. His refined style and dilettante manner, however, helped compensate for his lack of education and granted him access to the necessary *suzhi* expected of the *nanzihan* he felt he embodied. Yang Xing held great interest in preserving local ethnic culture through collecting, restoring, and displaying local looms at his restaurant. This itself represented a civilized man. He also had a great ability to orate in a very literate style. He often said to me, "Watch me if you really want to understand Chinese men." One evening during Spring Festival (*chun jie*), he stood up at a banquet he organized for some close friends and colleagues (we had all invited and been invited to quite a few cups of awful Thai whiskey at this point) and began orating on what it means to be a true *nanzihan*, most of which was delivered in a style of literate prose beyond my capabilities of relatively fluent but yet foreigner-level Chinese. Many of us around the table were initially reluctant to empty our glasses (*ganbei*) yet another time after a long meal. But his eloquent performance moved us all to empty just one more glass in honor of what we all believed was an invitation to drink coming from a true Chinese man imbued with a level of *suzhi* demanding of our respect.

Many masculine behaviors in China develop out of a need to protect face (*mianzi*), a concept related to the amount of social prestige and honor ascribed to a person and his or her reputation. *Mianzi* is crucial to the "symbolic capital" (Bourdieu [1980] 1990) necessary for men to maintain their status in Chinese society. Naturally then, men are always concerned about how a certain action may affect their face or *mianzi*. Men who perform their expected social roles are ascribed with *mianzi* (Hwang 1987: 960). Those who do not will sully their reputation through loss of an equal amount of *mianzi*. A man deserving of *mianzi* is thus "the man who will fulfill his obligations regardless of the hardships involved, who under all circumstances shows himself a decent human being. It represents the confidence of society in the integrity of ego's moral character, the loss of which makes it impossible for him to function properly within the community" (Hu 1944: 45). Simply put, *mianzi* has a lot to do with following through on promises and expectations. A man cannot respectfully bow out of a promise, no matter how lofty or trivial it may be, and expect to maintain his *mianzi*. He is basically as good as his word and is also judged on his ability to fulfill responsibilities such as supporting his family.

The strength of one's social network and the perceived worth of the people in that network further establishes *mianzi* in society. This leads men like Xiao Mei, who are trying to access the "symbolic capital" inherent in good *mianzi*, to demonstrate symbols of power that signal the wealth and social status of the people in their network (Hwang 1987, Oi 1985). For him this often came in the form of showing a picture of himself with a high-level official, who he may have met with his boss. He carried these photos in his wallet as a badge of success. His perspective as an outsider to Han society may have given him the perception that this could award him *mianzi* and social status, but in all honesty feigning the breadth of his network of symbolic capital reduced his credibility and consequently depleted his *mianzi*, further detracting from his status as a *nanzihan*.

The Status of Symbols

Entry into the world of hegemonic urban masculinity can be difficult for men who truly lack the status afforded by *suzhi*, education, or economic or political status. Like Xiao Mei, these men look for alternative routes or symbols that may help represent such status. Xiao Mei, who lacked education as well as command of literate Han language, was sequestered to marginalized status in society. However, his marriage to a more educated woman holding a higher-level position helps him account for part of the stigma against uneducated people in China. A Jingpo woman from Ruili told me many uneducated Jingpo men marry Han women or more educated women in order to achieve some status in the city. Xiao Mei took advantage of his indirect access to high-level government officials at all bureaucratic levels as a way of demonstrating connection with the political system. His job also gave him access to gifts such as watches and expensive cell phones, which he used to demonstrate a connection to wealth. He used all of these status symbols to overcome his low *suzhi,* a common strategy among men who lack access to education and other elements of personal quality. Tiantian Zheng encountered similar uses of symbols that help men create status during her research on hostesses in a karaoke club in Dalian (northeastern China). One customer at the karaoke bar said to her, "Men like me who do not have any education cannot impress others with degrees. So we have to resort to money and potency to prove our ability and talent. Otherwise, I am really nothing in the society" (Zheng 2003). Such symbols may serve as a proxy in the short run but are not a substitute for the relationships and qualities that truly make a *nanzihan.*

Positioning Alternative Masculinities

The model of masculinity I present here is certainly not the only path to being a man in China. It represents a dominant hegemonic form of masculinity, founded on principles of responsibility, relationships, and status, that offer a man entrée into the realms of respect and success in mainstream Chinese society. Men who do not adhere to these principles are marginalized and not considered worthy of the type of man representative of Chinese society. Gay men, for example, do not fulfill the filial responsibilities expected of a *nanzihan* or a man eligible to be a leader because they are not attached to a woman and do not have children. This has led to many men simultaneously living a gay life and a life with a wife and child. Older gay men, who grew up before an era of globalization ushered gay pride and LGBT rights into China, do not identify as gay or bisexual. They simply carry on two parallel lives that allow them to claim dual identities of masculinity. Failure to fulfill the filial duty of extending one's lineage is not the only quality that denies men association with the privileged identity of *nanzihan.* One must also be responsible, have *mianzi,* and hold status. These requirements precluded Xiao Mei, who was a recognized masculine man (*jingpo hanzi*) in his own culture, from attaining status as a *nanzihan* in his adopted Han society. Jingpo men are cut from a cloth of strong free-spiritedness characteristic of their nomadic society. This type of masculinity, which is more characteristic of the archetypal *macho* man, is not valued in Han Chinese society, where men are expected to be responsible to their families and society.

A large part of Jingpo culture is structured around gender. The totem, known as the *munau*, that sits at the center of every community depicts a series of gendered symbols highlighting the important roles women and men play in the culture. Men are typically portrayed as brave hunters and warriors who are capable of meeting the challenges presented to them by the mountains and jungles that dominate their homeland.[11] One Jingpo man told me "Real Jingpo men have tattoos." The tattoos I saw carved into Jingpo men's bodies were all depictions of dragons and text imparted from martial arts masters who served as their mentors. These tattoos, representative of the closely networked communities that hold much of male Asian society together both at home and abroad,[12] were a symbol of a man who had been indoctrinated into a certain type of learning and method. These men all told me their tattoos indicated a real Jingpo warrior.[13] Jingpo men also described representations of guns and knives used to support a life of hunting and fishing. Indeed, many of the rural Jingpo men and boys I saw still carried the traditional Jingpo sheath draped over their bodies. Other Jingpo men I met in the city still identified with their rural roots and recounted stories that seemed phantasmagoric, probably stemming from their animistic origins. Whether truth or fiction, I felt these stories were an expression of true Jingpo masculine identity. I also learned about the impulsive and violent nature Jingpo men felt they were forced to control in urban society. Even A Peng, an elegant and refined Jingpo man trained in the Western traditions of ballet and modern dance, told me he constantly battles with the need to control his innately fierce Jingpo nature. He once said to me, "I am so Jingpo," meaning that underneath his refined manner lay a man ready to explode. This character, they said, comes from their highland origins. Consequently, they told me, "As Jingpo men we don't want to be controlled or to listen to anyone telling us what to do." Such characteristics contrast with Han society, which requires adherence to rules of hierarchy and order as a means of advancing through the social order.

Jingpo men who migrate to an urban environment are suddenly met with a different masculine culture that challenges and confuses their identity as a man (*hanzi*). In the city, Jin Liyan, a Jingpo scholar at the Yunnan Academy for Social Science, said that many Jingpo men search to regain their status as a *nanzihan,* since they are so accustomed to being a masculine Jingpo man (*jingpo hanzi*). But they are unsure how to achieve this status in a society where the definition of masculinity is so different. As a result, they try to attain that important masculine status by mimicking the patterns of masculinity they encounter in the city. This was certainly true of Xiao Mei. Like him, many of these men, who are of rural origin and uneducated, have difficulty adapting to the requirements of their new cultural surroundings.

The Pressure of Being a *Nanzihan*

From what I have described, a *nanzihan* lives a fairly privileged life in China. He is among the elite and enjoys success in marriage, fatherhood, and friendships as well as professional pursuits in business or government. He is also among the more educated and considered as someone worthy of bringing China into its new era of global success. Yet these men lament about the pressures of being a successful *nanzihan*. Men often perceive the social frameworks required to achieve hegemonic masculinity as a restrictive imposition on their lives (Carrigan, Connell, and Lee 1985). Many of the Chinese men I spoke with lamented the pressures of these social frameworks almost as a form of gendered oppression. Xiao Mei once exclaimed to me, "It's so hard to be a Chinese man because we always have so many things to do" (*women de shiqing tai duo*). Yang Xing's lessons to me emphasized how tiring (*lei*) it is to be a Chinese man. He would say, "There are so many things Chinese men have to worry about, like politics, finances, business, family, society, and of course saving face (*mianzi*). It's the men who go out and do everything. They are the government officials, they go out to do business, and they have to take responsibility to support the family." Some men even claimed that their need to seek relaxation in the services of a commercial sex worker stemmed from the pressures and demands they felt from their wives. Masculine pride does not permit them to reveal any weakness in front of their wives, but this does not preclude them from unloading their psychological stress on a woman outside the family who can also provide some sexual relief.

The gendered agenda is most often framed by a feminist agenda that tries to increase women's agency and correct their vulnerability to men's actions. Increasingly, however, the gendered agenda is turning toward men and inciting a modification in men's behaviors and practices in response to recognition that men are also vulnerable to normative forms of masculinity, which can impose rigid expectations that restrict their agency as well (Dworkin et al. 2013, Lynch, Brouard, and Visser 2010). I saw more attention turn toward masculinity in China as well, but often to the end of justifying the behaviors and practices that impose vulnerability on both women and men. In the fall of 2004, for example, China Central Television (CCTV) aired a serial program called *Zhongguo nan tongzhi de xinli yali* (The Psychological Pressures of Chinese Male Comrades,)[14] to help rationalize the behaviors of China's successful men. As is evident from the title, the program took a very male-centered approach and empathized with the pressures on men in contemporary China. One episode in particular addressed men's needs for commercial sex work because of the various pressures that weigh on them at work and at home. It urged Chinese women to be tolerant of this type of behavior, which was portrayed as a logical consequence of the pressures they face. Experts who spoke at Male Health Day in Beijing that same year also spoke about how the pressures of modern life have encouraged unhealthy lifestyles among Chinese men ("Experts Urge Men . . . " 2004). This was a surprising turn in official discourse that was not even supported by some of the successful men who taught me about masculinity and masculine practices. I do believe, however, that a feminist approach to the study of men in China (Gardiner 2002) can be valuable in understanding the origins of their vulnerabilities and those of their sexual partners.

The pressures successful Chinese men face are not necessarily those related to their roles in government, in business, or at home but rather the need to isolate the various parts of their lives into compartments as they aspire to the status of *nanzihan*. Businessmen, civil servants, and government officials all work hard to manage the competing demands of family, work, friends, and sometimes lovers, which are all part of achieving this social status. Many successful men in China also balance responsibility to one or more minor wives. They must also work hard to maintain relationships with the various actors who serve a number of roles in their lives. All of these varying roles and responsibilities are socially accepted, and many of them are expected of the man who wants to become a *nanzihan*. For the man operating within the social and political environment of contemporary China, though, many of these roles must be kept distinct from one another. This alone places psychological demands on men. One civil servant I met, who is very responsible to his family but also must answer to the demands at work (which sometimes include soliciting the services of a commercial sex worker), is either socially or politically precluded from sharing many of his concerns with his wife. He said to me, "Chinese people have a lot of psychological problems because there are so many things they can't tell other people." Xiao Mei was often frustrated by the competing loyalties that caused him to feel hardships and miseries (*beishang*) in his life because he couldn't share his experiences with anyone else. "Everyone's stomach hurts (*duzi teng*)," he told me, "but you can't tell anybody else what makes your stomach hurt." The hardships that make some men's stomachs hurt may be related to work or family. Work can be very demanding, keeping a man out of the house both day and night. Many do not willingly engage in all the activities related to their jobs but feel they have no other choice. Many officials in contemporary China are expected to keep mistresses as a symbol of status. Even secretly gay officials hire symbolic mistresses (Palmer 2013). The tensions are twofold: first at home, where men try to isolate their wives from knowledge of their mistresses, but also in the official world, where explicit knowledge of an affair can threaten not only an official's reputation but also his position.

A Rong, like many men, had the flexibility to discuss plans for seeking a minor wife with his wife because he was a businessman whose status could grow only through acquisition of a *xiao laopo*.[15] As a woman living under the guise of marriage laws that elevated a woman's position in society, his wife was opposed to his plan, but A Rong did not acquiesce, hoping to fulfill his ideals as a Confucian man. He felt he had a responsibility, though, to his family to apprise his wife of his plans and not hide anything from her. Many men, however, and particularly those in government, conceal minor wives and the children from those relationships from their wives. The many government officials who are rumored to have minor wives risk their position and status, while other men simply choose not to share this information with their wives. I did meet men and women who told me about families with multiple wives that live together under one roof.[16] Many men aspiring to be a *nanzihan*, however, must daily juggle a set of expectations and responsibilities, at home and outside, with various actors who cannot meet one another. They live at once in two social worlds, which on the one hand opens up the social space and sets expectations for men to engage in relationships with women outside their home. On the other hand, they also operate under a legal and political system that proscribes such behavior. This creates a set of multiple competing discourses that these men must negotiate as they establish their masculine status. So while they earn the entitlement of masculine success in the various social circles around them, these men also suffer from the pressures of their achievements. This becomes difficult in a small city. Both Xiao Mei and Wang Jun described relationships with their lovers to me, relationships that they felt entitled to as Chinese men but that were relegated to closed spaces because of other social and political restrictions requiring they keep these women separate from their wives, colleagues, and friends. In order to satisfy all these demands, men construct a dichotomous life that distinguishes between what goes on at home (*zai jia*) and what goes on when they are outside the home (*zai waibian*).

Homologous Oppositions in Chinese Men's Lives

A gendered division in imperial China assigned women responsibility for the "inner quarters" (Ebrey 1993) while men were in charge of the public sphere. A wealthy family was even able to separate men and women at home, with women literally occupying the inner quarters and men occupying the outer quarters (Fei [1947] 1992). This sexual asymmetrical (Rosaldo 1974) organization of society denied women access to public careers. Public society, in this instance, was instead defined by men and their masculine practices. This type of public-private dichotomy is a common global trope that associates men with business, government, organized religion, and the literacy needed to write books, while women are assigned the duties of running the household and all its related domestic affairs (Ortner 1972). These gendered roles and distinctions are often structured by a "system of homologous oppositions" in which opposing activities are divided among men and women almost as they would be by a system structured according to the forces of *yin* and *yang* aimed at finding balance and harmony in the social order (Bourdieu 2001). "Imbued in the things of the world," Bourdieu argues, "the masculine order also inscribes itself in bodies through the tacit injunctions that are implied in the routines of the division of labor or of collective private rituals" (24).

Contemporary China no longer makes such a neat distinction between the spaces that men and women occupy. Men still hold most high-level government positions and dominate China's entrepreneurial sector, but women are supposed to hold up half the sky, and have emerged from the inner quarters in business, government, education, and all manner of menial occupations. The social milieu governing contemporary China, on the other hand, expects men to dedicate more of their time to the home front. So, although women are still primarily associated with protecting and managing the domestic sphere, men are expected to demonstrate responsibility to the inner sphere while maintaining their public roles outside the home. For many of the men I met, this presented a dilemma of sustaining their own dichotomous lifestyles, dependent at once on maintaining a domestic persona at home (*zai jia*) while simultaneously maintaining a more public persona on the outside (*zai waibian*). As I've demonstrated, relations with wives, children, and parents that are dependent on traditional Chinese structures of filial piety, marriage, and fatherhood characterize their inner domestic lives. Reliance on traditional social norms, however, is still pulling men toward the roles that structured men's lives before 1949. After he fulfills his duties at home, a manly Chinese man (*nanzihan*) leaves the responsibility of maintaining domestic order to his wife (Bray 1997, Ebrey 1993, Ko 1994), while he pursues status accessible only through a rich life outside the home. This outer life consists of a man's role in business and government. A successful man's life outside the home is also dependent on a broad network of homosocial relationships with friends and other acquaintances.

Much of this division is prompted by men's concern with maintaining the integrity of their family, which I have discussed, as one of the most important aspects of establishing and protecting their masculine identity. A man's time at home (*zai jia*) with his family is thus strictly separated from the time he spends outside the home (*zai waibian*) with the networks of homosocial relations that are equally important for determining his success as a man. But even though the two are equally important for structuring a man's masculine status, they are mutually exclusive as they carry equal weight for either determining or disrupting the verification of a *nanzihan*.

Distinction in the sanctity between inner and outer for a man is perhaps most evident through his phone conversations. A bureaucratic phone system that made it difficult for individuals to access phone service years ago served as a catalyst for rapid development of mobile phone technology in China. Mobile phones, which are useful for keeping people connected in a society built on networks, have thus grown to permeate and control life in contemporary China. No matter the time or place, people are expected to be always available and ready to answer their mobile phone. The first question a caller asks when someone answers a phone call is "Where are you?" (*ni zai nali*)? The answer, for the men I met, was always framed by the dichotomous life between their domestic and outer lives. They would answer by saying either "I'm at home" (*wo zai jia*) or "I'm out " (*wo zai waibian*) rather than revealing a specific location. The answer to this question would determine the tone of the rest of the conversation depending on its appropriateness for the context of the call recipient's location.

I was considered part of a man's outside life, which was evident in the tone they used with me over the phone. Men always cut phone calls with me short when they were at home. I could often detect if a man was at home when he spoke to me using the local Ruili dialect, which concealed the fact that he was speaking to an "outsider." This was a cue that I had interrupted a time reserved for maintaining family relationships and responsibilities, a sphere that outsiders were not permitted to enter or permeate. As a man once said when I called him on the phone, "I've been home for the past few days" (*zhe jitian wo dou zai jia*), a statement that served to stymie any further conversation. This was an indication that those few days were dedicated to spending time with his family, a world I was not privy to as part of his outside life. Weekends were also a time when men were often not available because of the competing need to demonstrate concern for their family. Weekend nights were the only opportunity many men had to demonstrate expected responsibility in their role as father and husband through the family meal. Many would religiously reserve at least one night on the weekend for a "family meal opportunity" (*jiating jihui can*). Business at the local disco and karaoke clubs was surprisingly slow on Friday nights because many men went home to "accompany their wives" (*pei laopo*). It is more than just the walls of their house that distinguish men's lives in urban China, though. They also assume different personas inside and outside the home. One woman told me the home is a place where only serious things are discussed, but once a man leaves home he turns back into a boy (*xiao huozi*) and is free to play. Home is also a place where many men told me they find peace and solace within the comfort of a stable domestic environment. For many men, there is palpable tension between upholding responsibility toward their family and domestic lives and the expectation of pursuing important and potentially lucrative *shiqing*, affecting their lives as they strive to achieve the important status of *nanzihan*. Coming home to that solace gives them a needed respite from the stress.

As I mentioned in the beginning of the chapter, the man who has achieved the elite title of *nanzihan* often reifies this status through the consumption of women, which signifies him as elite. This is not part of his masculine identity but certainly an entitlement that comes along with masculinity in Confucian society. For these men, who also identify as modern Chinese men, relations with various women outside the boundaries of marriage do not represent a cultural or psychological contradiction, for they marry out of obligation and social, political, or economic need. Their emotions (*ganqing*) are distinct from the physicality of the body (*routi*). This theoretically gives men (and increasingly women as well) free reign to explore their sexual desires outside of marriage. But as we will see in the following chapter, this can be difficult under the watchful gaze of a Leninist system that still feels the need to control private lives.

3 New China, New Life . . . Sex Included

Negotiating Private Lives and Public Discourse in Post-Mao Urban China

THERE IS NO DOUBT CHINA IS MORE OPEN SEXUALLY, both in public and in private, than it was before Deng Xiaoping came to power. The streets are filled with reminders of sex, from the shops that sell sexual products[1] to the many magazines on newsstands that sell sex on their covers, not to mention the karaoke clubs and brothels (which bill themselves as tea shops or hair salons) that often make themselves visible to passers-by with their telltale pink lights. The period of sexual silence that gripped China during the country's Maoist era has been replaced by a new era where sex can now be put on public display. Sex is available everywhere, and people are not ashamed to consume it. This has prompted many questions around a sexually open culture that seems to have suddenly emerged from within a society popularly perceived as sexually conservative. Many claim this rapid social transition is a sexual revolution, prompted by China's opening up to the West and the effects of neoliberalism as the state recedes from its role in providing the social safety net that allowed it to intrude into personal lives. Whether the influence originates from the outside or inside, it presents challenges to a state that demands loyalty and self-sacrifice but must now navigate the sense of individual identity accompanying this new period of sexual openness. China navigates this new field through its own model of governmentality, which preserves a state of authority even in the wake of the government's retreat from providing social services. Examining this model of governmentality is very useful for understanding how sexuality is developing in post-Mao China. First, however, we must distinguish between the model Foucault used to develop the concept of governmentality (Foucault 1991) and the model that has developed in post-Mao China.

The modern European state Foucault highlighted in his discussion of governmentality engendered a new citizen capable of self-cultivation and self-discipline, which in turn helped the government maintain control over its population (Barry, Osborne, and Rose 1996, Burchell, Gordon, and Miller 1991, Rose and Miller 1992). Government in this model still works to promote health, welfare, security, and happiness for every individual as well as the population as a whole, but it does so through a reduced role in the governing of individual lives because the people are trusted and capable of governing their own conduct (Dean 1999, Greenhalgh 2008, Lemke 2001, Sigley 2004). Although the Chinese government has also reduced its role in providing public goods, it still cannot be considered neoliberal (Kipnis 2007). This raises questions on the applicability of the very concept of governmentality to the Chinese context. Foucault's discussion of governmentality, however, is very useful for understanding the changing role of government, and I would argue its application is not only to cases that entail a neoliberal shift in state management of bureaucratic processes but also in a case like China, where the state is still very much in control of society but through a mode that removes it from direct contact with the daily management of individual lives.

Social management in post-Mao China is governed by *"community"* (*shequ*)[2] structures that replaced many of the daily roles served by state-owned work units (*danwei*) previously responsible for protecting the public welfare of their employees.[3] These quasi-governmental units, which may resemble neoliberal organizations in structure, are actually a crucial agent in facilitating state surveillance over society in an era of government recession. Their role in facilitating provision and management of social services and social welfare primarily serves a state needing to monitor the actions of individuals. This helps the government, which has receded from some of its previous roles in providing a social safety net, to still achieve its goal of prioritizing protection of the state over individuals, which is clearly distinct from the shift modern European governments experienced when they transitioned to a neoliberal state. In China, the same community agents who are expected to facilitate distribution of public goods are also expected to ensure that residents comply with state-mandated campaigns such as the one-child policy, and monitor any deviant behavior that may compromise state integrity. This helps the state maintain its role in guiding and even controlling individual action, notwithstanding its official withdrawal from supporting the welfare of those individual lives.

The tensions that result as China navigates this new territory produce a sexual culture existing within a contradictory space between the country's social and political goals and the individual desires growing with development of the market economy. This creates a particularly challenging dilemma for preventing sexually transmitted infections, including HIV, among the many men who depend on the state and profess their loyalty in search of economic and political success. These men are informally encouraged to engage in commercial sex as a means of governing distribution of the resources responsible for expanding China's economy. At the same time, the party that supports them and needs their loyalty to survive prohibits such actions, which can threaten their very legitimacy. Periodic campaigns in the past, cracking down on government officials who transgress party values, reminded officials of the party they are committed to serve. The reminders are even stronger under Xi Jinping. These campaigns underscore the party's authority but do little to change behaviors. Instead, they usually just force men to veil their actions in deference to party authority. Stories abound, after Xi Jinping initiated his austerity campaign, of men who simply moved their banqueting from public view into the private spaces of their own homes or to other more-out-of-the-way locations beyond the scope of the state panopticon.[4]

These types of competing discourses have created a unique sexual culture in which people are seemingly free to explore their individual sexual desires but at the same time must restrict public perception of their sexuality in order to adhere to the expectations of a Leninist state that prioritizes its needs over those of individual citizens. The Chinese state has historically been an enduring feature in defining and shaping sexuality. State discourse has influenced varying degrees of sexual freedom, ranging from the sexual entitlements granted to the scholar gentry of imperial China to the extreme sexual austerity that characterized Maoist China. This has created a culture where the state and not the individual ultimately governs the realm of sexuality, and where behaviors must be veiled in order to avoid any unwanted state retribution. This is the type of dynamic that sets the Chinese sexual experience apart from those in other modern industrial nations and that subsequently presents challenges to the organizations promoting international health agendas targeting individual behaviors.

Post-Mao China's Sexual Revolution?

China's explosive rate of economic growth has captured global attention over the past three decades. Within its borders, though, many social scientists are discussing a "sexual revolution" associated with the growing access to wealth and to Western culture that has accompanied market reforms (Altman 2001, Farquhar 2002, Zhang 2011). The Chinese government often downplays this relatively recent opening up of its sexual environment as being like the flies Deng Xiaoping recognized would come in once he opened the window.[5] Certainly some flies have flown in, as Deng predicted, but it would take an infestation to effect so drastic a change of a sexual culture in such a short period of time. To do so, argues Zygmant Bauman, is "like accepting the alchemist's authorship of the gold found in the test tube. . . . It takes more than greed for profit, free competition, and the refinement of the advertising media to accomplish a cultural revolution of a scale and depth equal to that of the emancipation of eroticism from sexual reproduction and love. To be redeployed as an economic factor, eroticism must have been first culturally processed and given a form fit for a would be [sic] commodity" (Bauman 1998: 122). Nevertheless, a Leninist party faced with the need to protect its legitimacy in the face of a rising sense of individualism sees a growing market and exposure to foreign ideas as a perfect scapegoat for the growth of such an open sexual culture.

Many of the government officials and workers I met while conducting fieldwork for this project were model representatives for the propaganda that aimed to protect state legitimacy in the face of China's emerging sexual culture. People often told me that the open (*kaifang*) sexual attitudes taking hold in contemporary Chinese society came from the sexually liberal attitudes they see on American television. Deng Xiaoping's China promoted a new vision of openness through market reforms, which are referred to as *gaige kaifang* (reform and opening) in Chinese. Aside from opening its economy, China has now also become open to the West. And it has opened socially to a point where people are also considered *kaifang*. To be *kaifang* implies one is open to new ideas (*sixiang kaifang*) and also open sexually.

Kaifang is a familiar discourse to a modernizing and developing China that looks outward as opposed to isolating itself (*fengbi*). During China's Republican era (1911–1949), government practiced an open form of governance characterized by participatory politics and political diversity. Open borders also fostered a trend of global outlook and open minds, nurtured through a progressive education system and religious tolerance. Republican-era China also benefited from open markets (Dikötter 2008). Maoist politics reigned in much of this openness, but recent opening up to the West has allowed China to observe from afar what it now perceives as a modern vision of *kaifang* after a long period of isolation. As one man said to me, "We see America as so *kaifang*, so we think if it's good for America it should be good for us, too." This notion of *kaifang* that he and so many people speak about in conjunction with the United States usually refers to sexual openness. But if China adopted its contemporary sense of sexual openness from the United States, then surely something went wrong in the translation. There is much more open consumption of sex in China than in the United States. Urban streets are dotted with sexual product shops (referred to as *baojian pin dian* [health protection product shops], *chengren yongpin dian* [adult use product shops], or just plain *xing yongpin dian* [sexual use product shops]),[6] and brothels that are frequently openly visible to the street. Karaoke clubs also furnish opportunities to have sex with a sex worker in the back of many private rooms. One can hardly avoid sexual offers in China, especially in hotels. Many hotels subcontract out to a madam who operates from somewhere inside the hotel or its environs and has access to the hotel's phone lines. Sex workers call each room every day, beginning sometimes at nine o'clock in the morning and continuing until midnight or one o'clock in the morning, offering a hair wash or a massage (*xi tou, anmo*), a euphemistic way for offering sex. I once stayed at a hotel where women called about twenty times every day, from morning till night. Of course, they hang up when they hear a woman's voice. High-class hotels are not excluded either. Two gay friends, who came to visit from the United States while I was conducting fieldwork, stayed in one of the four-star international hotels in downtown Beijing. Their idea of a relaxing first night included dinner and then an early morning jog through the city. I politely asked how they had slept, when I went to meet them the next morning. They said, "We slept fine but got two odd phone calls around midnight asking if we wanted a hair wash or a massage." I had to explain to them why that happened and then politely asked the manager to block those calls from going to my friends' room. The women, I said, had obviously called the wrong room. The most upscale hotels do not give such access to madams, but this does not stop the women from following unsuspecting men into the elevator. Many of the men I met assured me these "harassing phone calls" (*saorao dianhua*), as they are known, were common in such a *kaifang* country like the United States and insisted I was wrong when I told them that phones in hotel rooms do not randomly ring in the United States.

State and popular discourse prompt us to believe that the *kaifang* attitudes so dominant in contemporary Chinese society are part of a newly emerging trend, but many are actually emblematic of China's rich sexual culture. Unlike Western society, where sex is primarily associated with reproduction (Bauman 1998, Herdt 1994), the Chinese cosmological order celebrates sexuality outside the reproductive realm. Historically, Chinese tradition has viewed sex as a normal part of life that was important for health and vitality. Taoist manuals instructing people in sexual conduct were traditionally an important component for ensuring that sex contributed to overall health. This included restricting ejaculation of semen (*jing*), which like blood is considered a vital resource in China for preserving health and longevity. The words *jingshen* and *jingli,* meaning vitality and energy, use the same character, *jing,* which means semen. Excess loss of semen is believed to rob a man of his longevity and virility. Men are also instructed to have sex with multiple wives and concubines as a way of maximizing their longevity (Kleinman 1981, Zheng 2009). Access to sex and assignment of certain sexual roles also played an important role in defining status in imperial Chinese society. Men who filled the ranks of China's elite class of literati were socialized through their interactions with courtesan women. Unlike Western society, where a man's attraction to a woman is always associated with reproductive outcomes, reproduction in Chinese cosmology is considered as separate and distinct from the functions of the body erotic. Reproduction, as Charlotte Furth has illustrated, is accomplished through the gestational body in Chinese society. But Chinese bodies also consist of a generative body, reserved for the body erotic (Furth 1999). Individuals who fulfill their paternal duty to society are allowed to exercise their sexual subjectivities through this androgynous body not bound by any corporeal restrictions or biologic expectations (Furth 1988, Sommer 1997, Sommer 2000).

The rich sexual culture characteristic of imperial China was primarily reserved for elite men. As the merchant class grew by the end of the Qing dynasty, though, the class of men who could access these entitlements also expanded. Merchants, who craved more sexual services than erudite courtesan entertainment, nurtured growth of a lower-class prostitution industry. China's expanding foreign and economic relations also ushered in new modes for delivering sexual services. For example, Russian prostitutes were introduced into the massage parlors in Shanghai in the early twentieth century (Field 1999). The importation of novel forms for delivering female-centered entertainment continues to proliferate in post-Mao China. The karaoke bars, which have almost become emblematic of urban China, were imported from Japan, and the hair washing[7] that so many people enjoy is a typical Thai tradition. China's contemporary sexual environment is often framed as a global phenomenon resulting from the country's opening up to the West. But when we look at the trajectory of China's sexual culture, including the various modes used for delivering sex in post-Mao China, we see many more regional influences from countries that share similar Confucian and Buddhist backgrounds than global influences.

Despite state propaganda, the sexual subjectivities developing in China today are a result of discourses of the nation, as well as a linkage to some familiar others, rather than an imposition from a new foreign intruder (Boellstorff 2003). Within this structure, sexual culture, where I observed it most intensely in Ruili, is dependent on the interaction between Han attitudes toward sex and the attitudes of varying ethnic minority cultures as well as of China's neighbors along its borders. The open sexual culture I witnessed in Ruili, for example, occurs at the nexus of two contending indigenous minority cultures, the Dai and the Jingpo, as well as influence from their Han intruders and their Burmese neighbors. Dai culture allows a certain period of open sexual pursuit during the year, and Jingpo culture allows men to have multiple wives. As with other ethnic minority cultures around China, the Han interpret such allowances as sexual looseness, without considering the foundation of such cultural structures. Misinterpretation of the Mosuo tradition of *zouhun*,[8] as a sign of a sexually open culture, for example, has led to a lot of sexual exploitation within the community. Lugu Lake, where the Mosuo live, has been turned into a remote haven for commercial sex. The Dai and Jingpo similarly believe that Han misinterpretation of their culture resulted in the transformation of their homeland into a sexually open haven for customs and traditions (like sex work), which local ethnic minority cultures do not support. Burmese sexual culture also permeates the border. Pictures of Burmese Lady Boys (known as *renyao* in Chinese or *kathoey* in Thai) are a staple in Ruili tourist shops, a local sexual symbol not associated with Chinese sexual culture but certainly considered part of the local sexual culture. Somehow we are led to believe, though, that China is experiencing a sexual revolution imposed through Western ideas.

Uncovering the roots of contemporary Chinese sexual culture is not easy in an environment where the state needs to promote a different image. My own conversations around sex with the men in my network were heavily influenced by a propaganda game, used to protect state legitimacy, until I built a sufficient amount of rapport within the community. As men began to trust me, they proudly started proclaiming themselves as Confucianists (*rujia*), telling me they were following Confucian tradition in seeking out multiple wives, lovers, and sex workers, a cultural trend that is once again defining "real men" of a specific class status in China (Xiao 2011).[9] Toward the end of my fieldwork, a government official who had become a close friend admitted to me, "You know, we always tell you our sexual openness results from Western influence, but that's not true. We know the sexual openness happening in China is really a revival of Chinese tradition." The breakdown of these barriers allowed me to move away from thinking about contemporary Chinese sexual culture as part of a globalizing phenomenon and more as a result of a particular set of cultural influences. This realization also let me explore the very strong political influences on contemporary Chinese sexual culture, which result from a demand for selfless devotion to the state at the expense of the individual.

The Balance Between State and Individual Through Chinese History

Sexuality is one of the deepest forms of expression we experience as individuals. It is an articulation of who we are and how we perceive our bodies in relation to others. In China, where the individual is subordinate to the state, sexual culture must also adhere to collective goals that promote state supremacy. The individual in China has historically been subordinate to the family, kinship groups, and the emperor as a way of ensuring state order (Pye 1991, Yan 2011). This state-ordered system has left little room for development of the self in Chinese society (Elvin 1985, Mauss 1985), despite periodic emergence of certain figures with a strong sense of self. Mencius, one of Confucius' earliest disciples, expressed frustration with the rigid institutional structure he saw as a constricting force on the individual. The Ming neo-Confucian philosopher Wang Yangming advanced ideas of individualism akin to what we find in Western thought. And late Qing reformers such as Tan Sitong and Kang Youwei went so far as promoting an end to institutions that formed the basis of Confucian collectivism, including the family, which they saw as a mechanism for usurping the equality and personal freedom needed to develop the individual self (Elvin 1985). The Chinese state does not tolerate such sentiments of individual thought, however, and it often reacts by marginalizing or even exiling dissenters who represent a heterodox position. The state works hard to further underscore its loyal base through expressions of benevolence (*ren*) and service rewarded in return for individual self-sacrifice[10] (Pye 1991, Saich 2008). The party stands behind a motto of *wei renmin fuwu* (in the service of the people), which is often veiled and insincere, but nevertheless effective in building public loyalty.

Cultivating self-sacrifice was crucial to Mao's project of establishing a strong new China (*xin zhongguo*). This created expectations to shift the loyalty typically expressed toward family, kinship groups, and the emperor during China's imperial era to socialist collectives, the Communist Party, and Chairman Mao after 1949. Mao expected complete selflessness, proclaiming awareness of oneself as unhealthy. Anyone favoring individualism and liberalism risked expulsion from the party (Madsen 1984, Saich and Apter 1994). Daily messages promoted through the state propaganda machine reminded people of the duty they owed to the state in exchange for all the sacrifices the party made in its commitment to lift the Chinese people out of poverty and liberate them from feudalism. One revolutionary song, in particular, that has become a mantra for political self-sacrifice reminded people:

> If there were no Communist Party
> there would be no new China
> (meiyou gongchang dang, jiu meiyou xin zhongguo)
> The Communist Party has taken delight
> In working for all ethnicities
> The Communist Party has used all its heart
> To save China
> She gave the people the road
> To liberation
> She led China in the direction
> Of brightness
> She persevered through over
> Eight years of war
> She improved the people's lives
> She built the basis for a long-term struggle

Following the anti-Japanese conflict
She implemented many benefits of democratic rights
If there were no Communist Party
There would be no new China[11]

The post-Mao state has refocused its efforts toward building the powerful economic and political infrastructure needed to climb onto the world stage. This
has forced it to look outward, leaving more room for individuals to express
themselves and pursue their personal desires. Officially, however, Chinese citizens still live within a moral code that prioritizes collectivism and service to
the people (*wei renmin fuwu*). The tension that emerges from this "disrupted
space" (Wong 1997) between two opposing systems forces individuals to
negotiate between the new space they have for developing personal lives and
the restrictions the collective imposes on that space. Individuals who quickly
learn that their personal lives are potentially under constant state scrutiny
and surveillance redefine privacy in this realm. This creates a very precarious
situation for the men governing the distribution of economic and political
resources in post-Mao China, for they are not only pursuing the individual
benefit that is now accessible through the market economy; they also have
the opportunity to explore new forms of individual self-expression as part
of the process of governing distribution of these resources. The process they
use to distribute resources encourages these men to engage in casual sex, but
they must also be very discreet in order to project a perception of loyalty and
devotion to a state that prohibits such activity. This places a new set of restrictions on men who are simultaneously taking advantage of a renewed space for
exploring sexuality in post-Mao China and demonstrating state loyalty. This
type of competing discourse weighs heavily on the men aiming for success
in post-Mao China because of the double standard they are trying to meet in
carrying out their formal and informal duties.[12]

Monitoring Individuals in China

Growth of a market-oriented system in post-Mao China has incited a greater
sense of individualism than the party was previously able to suppress. This
has heightened the party's need to ensure individual loyalty to the state and its
goals. This is not a new aim for the Chinese state, but they do need to develop
new approaches for maintaining state loyalty in the advent of a bifurcated

system challenged by competing ideologies. Confucian government was structured in a way that ensured state loyalty through promotion of loyalty in the household. A confluent system viewing the state as an extension of the family ensured that duty to one's parents through expressions of filial piety would also result in expressions of state loyalty. But whereas imperial China stressed the importance of both loyalty to the state and filiality to one's parents, the Communist Party discourages people from expressing personal loyalties. Functionally, Mao subsumed the role of the family into the work units (*danwei*) he created to coordinate all the needs of an individual. Doing so helped to direct an individual's loyalty entirely toward the state. The *danwei* is centered around a work function, but all people employed by a single *danwei* are part of a discrete community created to serve a specific state need. Employees of a state-owned department store, for example, all belong to one community that strongly identifies with the department store and with the state, which supports and owns their work unit. The *danwei* provides their employment, basic communal housing on or near their place of work, education for their children, health care for their family, and a communal dining hall. It also manages family planning, granting permission for timing of pregnancy and the number of children allotted to each household.[13] This structure dispelled the function of the family as the primary provider of social services. Even eating, a function that furnishes a focal point for Chinese families, was delegated to the community. This shift, framing identity around the state vis-à-vis the *danwei* instead of the more traditional association with family (Lu and Perry 1997, Saich 2008), has become a new frame of reference that continues to guide urban Chinese life even as the system is being dismantled.

Those not employed by a *danwei* lived in areas monitored by residential neighborhood committees (*jumin weiyuanhui*). This system, loosely derived from the late imperial household registration system (*baojia*), organized residential neighborhoods into distinct units for monitoring individuals and social service assistance (Ch'ü 1965, Yang 1988). Neighborhood committees have now expanded in both size and importance as the state dismantles the *danwei* system to concentrate more of its effort on implementing market reforms, strengthening its economy, and raising itself onto the world stage. They now encompass communities (*shequ jumin weiyuanhui*—also known as the *juwehui* for short) that span an area much wider than a single neighborhood and have responsibility for facilitating many of the services previously associated with *danweis*.

Dismantling of the *danwei* system has resulted in dissolution of a state institution that commanded the type of loyalty demonstrated to family. The state has aimed to rebuild this sense of commitment through the *juweihui*, but it cannot achieve the same results through an organization that technically lies outside the formal state apparatus and has no state funding. Both the *danwei* and residential community committees foster a condensed living environment that is easily monitored. But the *juweihui* is technically a self-governing nonparty apparatus. This makes it a more independent environment that does not readily command collective loyalty and identity. The *juweihui*'s administration under a very low-level party unit, however, allows it to act as a quasi-state organization capable of representing state power and authority over individual lives. But they merely facilitate provision of public goods and do not lend the support that created loyalty within members of a *danwei*. The lack of state support also limits the *juweihui*'s ability to monitor the behavior of local community members (Bray 2006). Most are staffed by retired grannies who have both the time and the necessary moral integrity in the eyes of the party to serve as a model for the community. They are primarily responsible for facilitating provision of public goods, mediating local disputes, and mobilizing support for unemployed members of the community who are entitled to subsistence allowance (*dibao*). They also facilitate moral and political education, supervise periodic mass mobilization campaigns, and identify deviant behaviors within the community, which can include anything from hairstyle and dress to listening to questionable music, gambling (card playing and mahjong), household decorations, and sexual liaisons (Saich 2008, Yang 1988). Their service is important for maintaining the legitimacy of a state that is no longer structured to fully monitor and support individual livelihoods (Hoffman 2006), but they carry no real authority. This limits their ability to monitor individuals and deprives the *juweihui* of the type of state loyalty built up through the *danwei* system.

Many see this as a neoliberal shift in Chinese bureaucracy (Rofel 2007). I argue, though, that bureaucratic institutions in post-Mao China are not analogous to the neoliberal institutions that grew out of the process of state recession in the West. Such organizations fill a role previously served by the state with a primary goal toward protecting population health and welfare. Transition of the Chinese state as it recedes from its role in supporting and monitoring individual lives seeks, however, to maintain its presence in the popular conscience in order to sustain the level of loyalty necessary to support the state. Placing facilitation of many of the social services previously provided by a *danwei* into the hands of the *juweihui* allows the state to step back from its role as caretaker while still ensuring that the organization responsible for promoting community health and welfare will prioritize the state's goals over those of the individuals within the community.

As an example, we can look at how governmentality is now affecting injection drug users (IDUs) in urban China. The Communist Party has traditionally treated narcotics as a matter of public security. This changed in 2008, when the government required residential communities to add responsibility for monitoring IDUs to their long list of duties. A new anti-narcotic policy required neighborhood residence committees to establish detoxification and rehabilitation programs (*shequ jiedu/shequ kangfu*),[14] which charged the staff of the *juweihui* with the additional task of supplying current and former drug users in the community with psychosocial support, job training, and the skills necessary for reentry into society (Narcotic Control Law . . . 2008). They are also responsible for conducting periodic urine screenings to detect current drug use among registered drug users in the community. Those with positive results are sent to compulsory detoxification centers (now operated by the Ministry of Justice).[15] Members of the residence committee, who have no training or inclination to work with current or former drug users, staff the community-based drug detoxification and rehabilitation programs. This makes them incapable of providing the necessary social services to fulfill their stated mission of helping drug users reintegrate themselves into society. The technical aspect of administering a urine test for the presence of drugs, however, is fairly easy and perhaps more efficiently administered through the community than through the Public Security Bureau. In this way, the community-based drug detoxification and rehabilitation programs, like so many other functions of the *juweihui*, serve the needs of the state much more than the needs of the individuals within a given residential community. The state is dependent, however, on institutions that can exert control over individual lives to maintain their legitimacy and authority. This is perhaps nowhere more important than in the control over the sexual lives that threaten state legitimacy through their challenges to official party morals and values.

Monitoring Sexual Lives in the Chinese State

"The state," argue Elizabeth Bernstein and Laurie Shaffner (2005: xiii), "has a sexual agenda." In the West, states rely on a moral vision to regulate sexual conduct. The Chinese state does not regulate sexual conduct. Instead, it has historically relegated sex in a way that allows individuals to express themselves sexually in spaces that protect the state from the threat of personal expression. Confucian order relegated erotic desire to outside the home, as a means of preserving both family and its associated state order. Prohibitions against sex, still for the purpose of state preservation, did not come until the late Qing dynasty, when the Yongzheng emperor declared that gender and not status should be used to structure China's system of sexual values. He made this decision in an effort to avoid the potential disruption in marriage markets and a rise in concubinage that often preceded dynastic decline (Sommer 2000). Consequently, sex, which had been celebrated as a vital force of both health and enjoyment for the individual in premodern China, was suddenly transformed into a burden truly reserved to serve the state (Van Gulik 1974).

Sex continues to be an agent for controlling individuals and preserving state order in post-1949 China, where it is now facilitated through more formal institutional mechanisms. This first occurred through the 1950 marriage law, which formally institutionalized marriage in China as an equal arrangement between a man and a woman and explicitly stated that marriage should honor a system of one husband and one wife (*yifu yiqi zhi*), clearly prohibiting bigamy and concubinage (Tran 2011).[16] Prohibiting feudal marriage practices was seen as a crucial component of moving China into the ranks of modern nations. Marriages arranged between two families were outlawed in favor of a new institutional form of marriage that gave women a voice in who they married. It also provided a legitimate platform for permeating personal intimacy (Warner 1999), aided by a vision of nurturing a healthy population. Under the law, brides and grooms were required to undergo a specific set of medical exams as a way of controlling the "quality" (*suzhi*) of the population of new China.[17] The law also allowed the state to regulate eligible partnerships and made available the material that shaped the public's normative vision of sexuality. Further, the marriage law facilitated the state's ability to reach into the most intimate space of married life through the one-child policy. The same grannies who, under the marriage law, were granted entrée into people's homes to educate them about proper marital relations now use that privilege to penetrate into the most intimate space of an individual's life, where they carry out the duties that help the state meet its population goals. This includes monitoring women's menstrual cycles, distributing contraceptive pills, and scheduling pregnancies. This helped the state establish a new mode of "bio-power" (Foucault 1978), useful for creating a specific body politic that could serve the state's goals (Friedman 2005, Scheper-Hughes and Lock 1987, Sigley 2001).

The new social institutions that the state established after 1949 were crucial to Mao's efforts to mobilize the mass effort needed to raise the country out of poverty. The institutionalization of marriage and centralization of public discourse around sex that happened through the marriage law gave Mao the power to control the libidos of the masses, which he saw as a threat to the Communist Party (Wehrfritz 1996). Rather than issue a series of regulations and prohibitions against sex, though, the state suddenly silenced any public discourse on sex that had developed through the institutionalization of marriage. Gone were the state manuals about feminine hygiene, marital relations, and sexual health. Mao simply desexed China through an absence of discourse. The silence was deafening to a populace that didn't quite know what they were permitted to do. Local cadres had unspoken rules about sexual conduct. Officially, however, there was no prohibition against sex, just an implicit expectation of selflessness for the benefit of the state. This left the door open for people to surreptitiously serve their self-interest. Emily Honig (2003) discovered many accounts of self-expression of sexuality during the Cultural Revolution, including female sent-down youth[18] who supplied sexual favors to cadres in exchange for permission to return home. She also details other accounts of out-of-wedlock births and abortions, which she argues were not uncommon. This era epitomized the popular Chinese adage that people can only do it; they can't talk about it (*zhineng zuo buneng shuo*). No one could talk about sex during the Cultural Revolution for fear of political retribution, but from Honig's accounts it seems few things changed under the radar screen. Sex was erased in public, though, where sexual discourse lacked any legitimacy in front of a state that depended on selflessness.

Emergence of the Sexual Self in Post-Mao China

The din of state silence on sexuality spawned an impression of a sexually repressed culture that still dominates popular global perceptions. People looking in for the first time see the current emergence of sexuality as a sexual revolution stemming from Western influences. Unlike many Western states that oppose sex, however, China's sexual culture was able to survive because the state's opposition was aimed at the feudal bourgeois tendencies suggested by free expression of sexuality rather than at sex itself (Honig 2003). So what appears to be a sexual revolution is a sexual culture that has been able to rapidly reemerge after being hidden under the weight of state silence. People in post-Mao China can once again enjoy sex, albeit under continued state relegation. To do it is OK, and to speak of it is also OK. For the first time in Chinese history, people are also becoming agents of their own sexuality through a new ability to choose their sexual partners. Recession of the state is giving people more personal space to develop their sense of self, which is increasingly informed by the hedonistic ideals that accompany development of a market economy (Wang 2002). This places the state in an uncomfortable position, where it must balance the desire to build a strong economy with the need to maintain loyalty of the selfless subject. It negotiates this gap through the boundaries placed on individual sexual freedom. Anyone considering marriage or birth is constantly reminded of the state's ability to intervene in private lives. Increasingly, however, people are pushing the limits of the boundaries to explore the sexual choices and possibilities available in the post-Mao era.

A Meng, an educated Jingpo man who had spent most of his life living outside Ruili in some of China's biggest metropolises studying an art that relied on development of his own bodily sense, articulated to me the changes he had so closely observed in post-Mao China:

A lot of people are changing, including me. I'm changing. You start to choose yourself. People are starting to think about themselves. Me, how about me? What do I like, what should I have? A lot of people are starting to think like this. I need money, what kind of money do I need? How am I going to earn money? They're starting to think. Including thinking about sex, that's the same. In the least, a lot of people are starting to choose the person or the sex they like. They're starting to discover themselves because this world is different. Before they would say, "It's good enough if I can get married and have children when I grow up." They couldn't think about their attitude toward sex. But sex is also a way of life and a necessity of life. Perhaps before it was a creation of the body. But now it may have an association with mindset (*sixiang*) or lots of other things that can even include economic concerns. So why are there people who can even marry a prostitute (*xiaojie*)? There are, I know some. This was impossible in the past. In the past, how could you have married someone who sold sex? But now there are people who see the girl, her inner personality, as well as sex. They say, "I've had sex with her, our sexual relations are really good, we get along well and she's a very good woman. But either because she wants to earn money or is very poor and needs money, she worked as a prostitute. But she can still make a good wife."

Availability of this space to prioritize oneself and make choices, he argued, is also causing a reawakening of sexual awareness in people after a long period of time when they had to repress any feelings or attitudes toward sex. "The people who I know and understand, including myself," he told me, "represent a typical trend of an awakening (*juexing*) attitude toward sex among Chinese people. I think a lot of people are a lot more conscious nowadays, whereas they weren't very conscious beforehand. In the past it was eat, get married, and raise kids. . . . Go to work, go to meetings (*kai hui*). They didn't have any sense of how it should be, what type of life I should have, what type of wife I should choose, what type of work I should have, what type of days I should live."

This new ability to make choices is changing people's attitudes and perceptions toward sex. Wang Xiaolin was a businessman in Beijing who had once worked in government but also sold sex to men in the late 1980s, observed changes in China's sexual culture over the past several decades. As he explained to me:

Before the period of economic reform (*gaige kaifang*), extramarital relations were very rare. Or, you could say they were common but didn't come to the surface. But they slowly became more public after economic reform. People were blind to them during the initial period of economic reform. "Wow! All you have to do is give that girl a little bit of money and you can have sex with her. That's great and it's better than having sex with my wife. My wife has to have a child and other things. This is much better." Then sex was very much a matter of perception (*ganxing*). It was enough to smell something new. Now it's very common, everyone knows a lot of people who are doing this. It's really a matter of rationale (*lixing*) now. Men have choices. The biggest indicator of this rationale (*lixing*) is that men have choices. There weren't any choices in the past. To meet a woman other than your wife who you could sleep with wasn't easy. Now there are lots of choices everywhere. There are high-priced, middle-priced, and low-priced. There are even those that don't require money like lovers. The space for choice is big.

These expressions do not associate global influences with the transformation in China's contemporary sexual culture but with the effect of the relaxation in political control as China reopens itself to the world. Yet people still have difficulty articulating this renewed sexual consciousness because Chinese lacks a term for the concept of sexuality. The space itself has been liberating though, particularly for men who felt castrated by Mao's silencing of sex. As one man told me, "Men no longer have to eat meat everyday; they can also eat vegetables if they choose." They are loyal to their families but also want to explore a sexual realm not available at home. Sex workers provide them with that opportunity to explore the sexual possibilities they can now discover in post-Mao China. Foreign sex workers, from Russia in the north or Burma and Viet Nam in the south, are also very popular because of the perception that they offer even more varied sexual experiences. Many men (especially young men) also want to experience sex with other men, not as a statement of their identity or sexual orientation but because this presents yet another option in the realm of possibilities now included in the panoply of sexual choices available to Chinese people in post-Mao society.

Other men take advantage of China's more open sexual culture for purely practical reasons, or to mitigate their own sense of loneliness. Many of the men I met spend long periods of time away from home, during which they can choose to have sex with a sex worker, or a steady lover, or even set up a separate family in the city where they work. Government officials can also be posted away from home for a two-year span. Low-level government officials from the central bureaucracy are often fast-tracked by performing two years of hardship duty in some remote area that nevertheless holds strategic importance for the central government. Many feel entitled, as a Confucian man, to either casual or more long-term relationships with other women, decisions that are supported in an emerging society that accepts and supports such relationships. I often met men who had no reservations telling me about their multiple wives, and even women who told me of other women in their family who are part of a polygamous relationship. Many even live together as wives and minor wives, as they would have during China's imperial era. Visiting a sex worker has also been normalized. One evening while drinking coffee with a madam in an open air café in Ruili, a man who happened to be one of her steady customers walked by our table at one point to say hi and to let her know to expect him later on that evening. I was surprised a man would speak to her so candidly and in the open, but she assured me his actions were not risky at all because coming to a brothel had become so commonplace.

Men—and even women—are happy to have these choices. This, however, forces their wives to develop new attitudes and approaches toward sex as well, in order to maintain their husbands' interest. A new discourse of sexiness (*xinggan*) is emerging in urban China, which forces women to learn what it means to be sexy, after being relegated to a Mao suit for several decades. They must pay more attention to how they look through dress and makeup, to maintain their sense of sex appeal after having a baby. As one woman told me:

> A woman is very much judged by how she looks and how she dresses. She has to be thin, young, and beautiful as well as dress sexy in order to attract men. And she has to remain that way in order to maintain her husband's interest. Otherwise he will stray away to find a woman who is young, pretty, thin, and dresses sexy.

Sexiness is moving beyond aesthetics as well. Much like the late-imperial gentrymen who visited courtesans for their talents and erudite knowledge, men in post-Mao China want to find women who they can engage in conversation. Their wives are often uninteresting, chosen only for their family status. Men want to talk to women but often go outside for such stimulation. The multitude of sexual choices opening up in post-Mao China is creating a revolutionary feeling as they explode into the streets. Meanwhile, the joys and freedom are restrained by a state that does not tolerate transgression of its own ideas and values.

"Contradictory Consciousness" on the Minds of Chinese Individuals

As A Meng pointed out to me, the proliferation of choices for people in China today is acting as an agent of social change. People think more about themselves and less about protecting the state and its values. This of course places the state in a compromising and uncomfortable position, where it must constantly negotiate the individual freedoms that are necessary for strengthening its economy and becoming a member of the global community. Ascending onto the world stage requires development of fields that have flourished in other modern nations, such as the arts. China now produces some of the most accomplished modern dancers in the world as well as abstract artists and novelists, fields that rely on individual introspection and expression. There is also an expectation for the development of civil society, which would require the state to relinquish some of its authority to independent members of society. Developing a modern twenty-first-century society incurs a certain amount of autonomy, which the state must carefully navigate to succeed as a rising global power. All of this is difficult because it recognizes a space for individual agency and allows development of a society where individuals think more about themselves than about the values and principles that serve the collective state. These competing state discourses, emerging where two divergent ideologies exist alongside one another, have considerable consequences for the many people who want to enjoy the new sexual freedoms allowed in post-Mao China while avoiding any accusation of violating the party's ideals. The amount of power the state is able to wield over personal intimacy (Friedman 2005) limits the development of sexuality in China even in the wake of the seeming revolution occurring on its urban streets. The Communist Party not only created a new China, but as a song at the top of the Chinese charts in the early 2000s reminded us, it also controls and enables the spaces where people conduct their lives, including their sexual lives. The song, which parodied the famous revolutionary ballad that reminded people of all the Communist Party had done for China, extended the message to include the party's control over individual sexual lives. It began with the traditional line "*If there were no Communist Party, there would be no new China (meiyou gongchang dang jiu meiyou xin zhongguo).*" But the lyrics continued: "If there were no new China, there would be no new life (*meiyou xin zhongguo jiu meiyou xin shenghuo); if there were no new life there would be no sex life (meiyou xin shenghuo jiu meiyou xing shenhuo);* How would you expect me to live without a sex life? (*meiyou xing shenghuo ni jiao wo zenme huo).*" Such reminders of the constant presence of the state in people's individual and sexual lives create a lot of hesitation and concern to tread carefully in order to avoid overstepping any boundaries.

Much of the state's control over sexuality is imposed through censorship of sexual discourse. The state is no longer silent about sex. In fact, it became vocal about sex again after the Cultural Revolution ended, by renewing distribution of the state marriage manuals that instruct married couples in sexual conduct. The state initially used these manuals as a mechanism to control development of the sexual culture opening up in post-Mao China. Sexual publications have since broadened into the realm of print and electronic media. The newspaper stands that line China's urban thoroughfares are replete with commercially published magazines that promote and teach about sex, from Chinese versions of *Cosmopolitan* and *Men's Health* to more local publications. In 2001, I picked up several issues of *Healthy Girl* (*jiankang nühai*), which discussed a different sexual topic every month of that year. Likewise, I've picked up issues of *Men's Health* that promote sex. One issue proclaimed "more power, more sex" (*gengduo quanli gengduo xing*). Bookstores are also replete with books on sex, but they are often hard to find because they fly off the shelves so quickly. Even academic books by scholars such as the sociologist Li Yinhe are difficult to find because people are curious to read anything about sex.

The media we see on the newsstands and in bookstores are those that are sanitary enough to get past the state censors' definition of a "healthy" vision of sex. These types of outlets promote a sexual culture that meets state expectations. Sexuality in China has a need, however, to develop beyond state boundaries and definitions of "healthy sex." This happens in the spaces that elude attention from state censors. It can also occur in spaces that operate just under the radar screen, on a plane where their influence is not quite hidden from the government but extends just wide enough to influence only a limited number of people without threatening state legitimacy. While a play like the Chinese adaptation of *The Vagina Monologues* has the potential to become very successful in China, it is kept at bay so as not to offend government censors. The play's producers chose to limit production to periodic performances in packed small venues rather than apply to stage the play in an official theater (Tatlow 2013). That would require approval from state censors, who would surely require modification of the script. The state can tolerate production of such a play, so long as the audience does not reach a critical mass where it may pose as an additional element of social change.

The type of discourse that cannot get past state censors remains hidden and limited in its ability to influence sexual attitudes. But the demand for such discourse is exploding as people take advantage of the new space available to explore their sexuality. These demands are satisfied in all the small cracks that manage to elude state censors. Many of the men I met, for example, told me they relied on underground movies, in people's homes or over the internet, to learn about sex. This is the only way they can learn about sex. Others turn to internet chat rooms or their phone screens for information distributed via electronic messaging. Far beyond the state discourse that aims to control sexual conduct in China, the flourishing of this type of informal media, which eludes state censors, is playing a crucial role in shaping sexual culture in contemporary China.

The advent of text messaging supplied a perfect outlet for sharing sexual discourse that could bypass state censors. The small accessible screens of the millions of Chinese cell phones have helped to distribute off-color, or "yellow," jokes (*huangsi xiaohua*), as they are called in China, to millions of people. Jokes are a popular way of sharing sexual discourse. Their reliance on popular idioms and colloquialisms constitutes a perfect subtle medium to exchange and promote ideas related to many social issues and problems that cross boundaries of class and education (Diamant 2000, Link and Zhou 2002, Yunxiang Yan 2003, Zhang 2006). Jokes that cross the party's ideal of what is morally healthy, though, can be censored and difficult to distribute publicly. I learned this lesson from a taxi driver who regularly took me from Ruili to the airport in Mangshi. The taxi driver, who knew all about my research, gave me a copy of a DVD with pop songs, including the song that turned the revolutionary ballad "If there were no Communist Party, there would be no new China" into a parody about sex in the "New China" (*xin zhongguo*). That song got past the censors, so he happily gave me the DVD. He also let me listen to a CD a friend had given to him with lots of yellow jokes but wouldn't give me his copy because it had been censored and would be very difficult to procure again. Text messaging has furnished the easily accessible medium that can openly transmit the type of popular sexual discourse people crave in post-Mao China, without the concern for self-censorship necessary to avoid retribution from the state. This has increased access to popular jokes, erotic stories, and colloquialisms that help people in post-Mao society develop a rich sense of sexuality not thought possible in China. The content of these jokes, which often ended up on my phone, are not dissimilar in intent to the off-color jokes we hear in the West, but instead they help to articulate the sexual feelings and understanding that come from within a Chinese perspective on life. Like Western jokes, which are often difficult to explain because of their reliance on puns and metaphors, Chinese jokes also take advantage of the unique lexical elements made available through the Chinese language.

The topics I saw in the yellow jokes delivered to my phone ranged from peasant ignorance over birth control to sexual colloquialisms. Many jokes also take full advantage of the protected space of the text message to exploit rumors about the sexual improprieties of China's high-level officials.[19] In one joke about peasants, a maid from the countryside discovers a used condom in her employer's bed one day. Embarrassed about what the maid may think, the woman of the house says, "You mean you don't make love in the countryside?" The maid replied, "To do it is to do it, but we don't use as much force (*jinr*) as you city folk, shedding a layer of skin in the process." In another joke I learned about the seven reasons "little brother" (*xiao didi,* used as slang for penis) would quit his job, among them a requirement to work in dark, damp working conditions, and the fact that he has to work until he throws up. I also learned about the nine things a man always has on his mind (*jiuxiang*). Among them he thinks about having free prostitutes, making love effortlessly, inexpensive cigarettes, being able to drink without getting drunk, and being accompanied by a virgin every night. Chinese characters also offer a unique way for making a sexual statement. The character *nai* (乃), for example, is representative of the word *vagina* because it resembles a woman's profile with open legs at the bottom.[20]

Beyond just articulating China's modern sexual culture, anonymous text messaging (and now China's microblogging system Sina Weibo) also serves as a "weapon of the weak" (Scott 1985), an everyday form of resistance that people can use to criticize some corrupt practices, including sexual practices of government officials they can otherwise not chastise in public.[21] James Scott speaks of jokes as one form of resistance people use, taking place in public view but at the same time shielding the identity of its authors and skirting censorship. People took great advantage of text messaging during the SARS (Severe Acute Respiratory Syndrome) debacle to articulate frustration and disappointment that was otherwise stymied by quarantine and government censorship. They did not just make light of SARS, though; they also used the situation as an opportunity to criticize the government practices that were emblematic of the events that led up to the epidemic. One joke, titled "What the Party Has Failed to Do, SARS Has Succeeded in Doing," was critical of corrupt practices that rely on interaction between people, something curtailed by the quarantine measures imposed during SARS. The joke lists five failures, including the fact that the party failed to control prostitution and whoring, but SARS, it says, was able to swiftly deal with those problems (Zhang 2006).

These types of messages that covertly criticize China's public officials amount to a constant outlet for people wanting to express silent protest even beyond a major state cover-up that cost several thousand lives. One joke I received on my phone played on the adage *yushi jujin* (keep up with the times), which was a key concept in Jiang Zemin's theory of economic development.

The joke takes full advantage of the richness of the Chinese language and its many homophones by replacing the *shi* (时), meaning time in Jiang Zemin's adage, with the character 食, which is a homophone that refers to food. In the joke, Jiang Zemin goes to the home of the famous actress Song Zhuying, who is rumored to be his lover. When he arrives, she asks if he would like to have dinner first or sex first. Jiang Zemin responds by saying, "I have the constitution of a dragon and a horse, so why don't we have sex and eat at the same time (*zhen longma jingshen, hebu yushi jujin*)?" This play on words, accomplished by replacing time with food, allows the joke to comment on Jiang Zemin's own sexual exploits by adding a sexual innuendo to his economic-development philosophy, to imply he is suggesting that the Chinese people need to keep up with the times both economically and sexually.

Another joke that admonished government officials from the local level to the central level for their corrupt practices demonstrated the hierarchy of gifts (from liquor to cigarettes and women) required to bribe officials at every bureaucratic level. Higher officials logically demand higher prices.[22] The joke color codes the price of bribery to inform its readers that:

Xiangcun gan bu he huangjiu, shuo huanghua, kan huangdie
Village cadres drink yellow liquor,[23] speak about yellow things,[24] and look at yellow butterflies.[25]
Xianji ganbu he baijiu, dabaitiao, mo baitui
County-level cadres drink white liquor,[26] give empty (white) promises, and caress white legs.[27]
Shiji ganbu he hongjiu, shou hongbao, qin hongchun
City-level cadres drink red wine,[28] receive red envelopes,[29] and kiss red lips.[30]
Shengji ganbu he yangjiu, da yangqiang wan yangjie
Provincial-level cadres drink foreign liquor, play foreign tunes, and play with foreign women.[31]
Zhongyang ganbu he mingjiu, chou mingyan, wan mingxing
Central-level cadres drink famous brand liquors, smoke famous brand cigarettes, and play with famous movie stars.[32]

Face-to-face communication is usually much more cautious. Chinese people are generally very careful to censor themselves in order to avoid any problems with the state. Many have noted more open sexual discourse in rural areas, though, where there is less government surveillance (Diamant 2000, Honig 2003, Yunxiang Yan 2003). Even Mao himself noted how much more sexually open and forward rural people are in comparison to their urban compatriots (Hu 1974). I had a similar experience in Ruili, where conditions high up in the mountains and far away from the emperor put government officials at relative ease to articulate their attitudes toward sex. They were not shy about speaking in sexual overtones and subsequently became my own evidence that remote areas in China seem more sexually open than urban China. I don't think this necessarily means they are culturally more sexually open, but just less restricted in their ability to express themselves sexually. After all, the karaoke clubs and brothels in urban China are just as busy as those in more remote areas, but they are more sequestered. Daily conversation in remote Ruili by comparison was replete with words such as *meinü* (beauty) when referring to or introducing women, or *shuaige* (handsome man, or perhaps more appropriately "hottie") when referring to or introducing a man. One evening at a dinner with several male and female government officials, one of the men turned to me and, referring to the women sitting on the other side of the table, said, "You know these women, they all wear skirts, but none of them ever dare to open up their legs!" In another instance with several Jingpo officials, I found out the meaning attached to a woman who takes off her shoes in Jingpo culture. I took off one of my shoes at a dinner to lower my height in deference to a shorter man who had invited me to a toast. The man, who was a high-level local official, insisted I not take my shoe off, after which one of the women present yelled out, "You can't put your shoes back on once you take them off,"[33] a sexual innuendo from Jingpo culture that perhaps embarrassed this government official in the presence of his foreign guest. This type of discourse, which livened up almost every banquet I attended in Ruili, demonstrated to me the rich and open sexual culture that is truly characteristic of contemporary China, even though it is often kept behind closed doors.

Taming the Lion

The explosion of new forms of electronic communication and media presents new challenges for the relationship between state power and personal intimacy. Maintaining control over discourse that influences sexual culture is much more complex in the digital age. State censors work constantly to rid China's airwaves and networks of any "polluting material." But they also rely on the periodic campaigns, that have been a stalwart of Chinese governmentality, to dissuade people from accessing potentially "polluting" material and reminding individuals of the state's authority and limits over personal free-doms. The Anti-Spiritual-Pollution Campaign in 1983 represented the govern-ment's first attempt to reign in any vulgar ideas that might accompany China's opening to the West. Such campaigns are waged every few years to reign in personal freedoms that encourage the vices and social evils Deng Xiaoping vowed to keep at bay in the wake of opening China up to the outside, and they support the moral austerity that is so important to state preservation (Chen 1992). In 2004 the government announced another new campaign to regulate text messages and websites with sexual content. The campaign issued a law targeting the many websites with pornographic or obscene content that the state saw as agents of the rapid social change occurring in China. They conse-quently issued orders to stop these outlets from polluting Chinese society and threatening the health of China's youth. The new law also vowed to punish anyone coercing others to view information with sexual content transmitted via text message. Another antipornography campaign in July 2013 shut down thousands of websites and a Shandong-based newspaper accused of publish-ing vulgar content.

These types of edicts, issued to scare the public into realizing the party is watching over their actions, are unenforceable and often happen in vain, but they are imperative in a state that has allowed a new capitalist system to emerge in parallel with its own socialist ideology. This creates an ideological disjuncture where neither socialist nor capitalist values can prevail over soci-ety. The government negotiates this space with campaigns to remind people that although they are benefiting from one system in the post-Mao era, they still owe loyalty to the system that created the new China (*xin zhongguo*). So just as it does with campaigns against corruption, the government will con-tinue initiating such campaigns as it negotiates between two economic sys-tems that are ideologically incompatible with each other. The campaigns are a necessary measure for voicing state authority and protecting its legitimacy as a party that opposes such strong expression of self-interest even while it pro-motes an economic system that depends on hedonism (Wang 2002).

The Chinese state is rife with competing discourses needed to build a mar-ket economy under the governance of a Leninist state, many of which open up the space for a sex industry that is caught in the cracks between conflicting modes of governance and state governmentality. On the one hand, the state must implicitly support a vibrant sex industry to reach its economic goals, while it also punishes those who sell and buy sex as a way to maintain its legitimacy. The sex industry is indispensable in China, though, because of the crucial role it plays in moving local economies forward. It plays a role in determining distribution of resources to local entrepreneurs but also attracts revenue to local governments that must be financially self-sufficient in the decentralized post-Mao economy. Local economies often depend on cottage sex industries to attract businessmen looking to explore their new sexual freedoms.

Aside from the revenue brothels can supply to some official bureaus and even local governments, they have become integral to the process of economic development. The local Public Security Bureau often owns brothel businesses, which are also usually registered as a legal commercial entity. This increases their value to local officials because they contribute to the revenue base for the local tax collection agency, much as prostitution did during the Republican Era (Remick 2014). This, some have argued, actually amounts to a disincentive to officials from controlling the local sex industry (Farrer 2002, Jeffreys 2004, Pan 2004, Xin 1999). I saw evidence of this in a southwestern town where I conducted a brief period of fieldwork. It was rumored that the party secretary of the city asked the Public Security Bureau to turn a blind eye to brothels and commercial sex activities. Closing them down, he believed, would have serious implications for the economic development in his city, which depended on an active cross-border trade industry. Still, the many men who can legally be penalized for engaging in sexual activities live in a contradictory dilemma, between a world of governance where they are encouraged to engage in commercial sex as a mode of governing the distribution of resources and building their career, and a state attitude toward governmentality that prohibits such practices. So even though many can be found in karaoke bars daily, they are careful to protect their identity from onlookers.

Rather than regulating behavior through constant surveillance, the state provides the space for such conduct but makes periodic reminders of the duty they have to be loyal and uphold the party's moral principles. This is the state's way of saying that although the market is important and we realize such traditions must be used to operate the market, they will threaten our legitimacy if given free reign without any constraints. Annual crackdowns, which usually coincide with Chinese New Year, remind people, particularly government officials who often benefit from informal modes of governance, of the authority and power of a state that is ultimately focused on its most important goal: protecting its own stability and legitimacy. Crackdowns on gambling, officially prohibited in China, target the many government officials who frequently gamble embezzled local funds in regions close to China's borders (2003, IHRD 2005).[34] These campaigns usually "kill a chicken to scare the monkey" (*shaji xiahou*), or in other words target officials with some public recognition as a way of amplifying their statements, a tone that is ringing particularly loudly under Xi Jinping.

High-profile officials are sacked every year for involvement with a prostitute or keeping a mistress while countless lower-profile officials are able to skirt the regulations. The state's power was perhaps most felt in the spring of 2010, when it initiated a campaign of raiding and closing down some of the country's largest entertainment establishments in twenty-six major cities, beginning with the Passion Nightclub (*tianshang renjian*), the exclusive nightclub attached to the Great Wall Sheraton in Beijing.[35] The broad campaign, which resulted in thousands of arrests and disruption to hundreds of high-end, high-profile businesses nationwide, was part of a national effort to control environmental pollution on the streets and ensure order in society. It is almost impossible not to laugh at these crackdowns as "empty talk" (Yunxiang Yan 2003). What meaning do they have if they are waged only as a statement, while other lower-profile officials are able to continue life as usual in order to support the growth of China's economy? This balance between informal governance and rigid governmentality is necessary for developing a market economy under a socialist state (Dean 1999). At the same time, though, it affects the officials responsible for conducting government. These men, who can suffer at the hands of the state if their actions become too public, are constantly forced to hide. Entertainment takes place in private spaces, and crackdowns force these types of activities into even more private spaces for fear of retribution during times of heightened sensitivity. A crackdown on a brothel only drives sex work further underground.

This is especially dangerous for men who engage in sexual activities. They dare not approach medical personnel who work for any government-sponsored, or even quasi-government, work unit for fear of risking their status. Such fears curtail sexual discourse in a far away place like Ruili as well. The men who freely exchanged sexual innuendos with me also periodically said to me, "You know we're just kidding, right?" They were afraid word of their sexual laxness might end up in the wrong hands. This results in men who seek out treatment for sexually transmitted infections in private back alley clinics or who rely on books or the internet for self-diagnosis and treatment.

They shudder at the thought of seeking out testing for STIs or HIV for fear of threatening their position. This leaves them and their partners vulnerable to infection. It is this type of relationship between the public and the private, and the individual, state, and society, that Nancy Scheper-Hughes (1994) argues has the potential for profound effects on a society's HIV epidemic.

The competing discourses that have nurtured a rich environment for reemergence of STIs as well as progression of HIV in China will continue so long as China's Leninist ideals collide with the hedonistic desires promoted through the system of market-based capitalism that is trying to develop. Moral and political values that sit in opposition to one another are vying for competition of social space. Western societies use moral codes grounded in religion to judge their government officials. Chinese social codes, which encourage free exploration of sexual desire, have been encouraged among businessmen and government officials seeking political and economic success. But their practices defy Leninist political code, which demands self-sacrifice for the party, transgression of which can cost an official his job and status. Any attempt to address the problems related to sexuality in post-Mao China will have to address this contradictory space.

4 Negotiating Risk and Power

The Role of Sexual Scripts and Networks
in HIV Transmission

I AM ONE OF THOSE ANTHROPOLOGISTS WHO NEGOTI-
ate married life in the United States with a need to do long-term
fieldwork in a distant and remote location (Jones 1999, Oboler 1986). Luckily,
my husband had a very understanding boss when I was planning this project,
who agreed to allow him to alternate "working" two-month leaves of absence
with two-month periods in his office for the year I was scheduled to be in the
field. This lasted one cycle, because the office he managed at the time had all
but fallen apart when he returned after his first leave of absence. He followed
me around for my initial period in the field, though, and in fact opened up
many doors with the crimson Harvard crest that adorned his business card
at the time. Association with an American from Harvard was a status symbol
that men in Ruili could use to build *guanxi*. In fact, my husband was most
likely the key to my introduction to Wang Jun, who was so instrumental in
my research. But Wang Jun wanted to connect with my husband as well. That
meant being able to speak directly to him, so when we first met, Wang Jun
asked if my husband could also speak Chinese. Sadly, he could not,[1] but still
Wang Jun said to me, "Well, he must at least learn one very important sen-
tence. Little girl you're very pretty, I like you (*xiao guniang, ni hen piaoliang,
wo xihuan ni*)." My husband and I laughed but were admittedly a little surprised to hear a man make such a suggestion (even if it were in jest) to another
man in front of his wife. Once my husband returned to the United States,
Wang Jun and others often asked, "Do you think your husband is soliciting

prostitutes (*zhoa xiaojie*) when he is all alone in America?" I answered by saying, "Knowing my husband, he spends most of his time at work and then spends time with friends on the weekend." They subsequently told me that I did not understand my husband and further did not understand men in general. Any man left alone at home, they said, would most certainly need to find a prostitute to satisfy his sexual needs.

I eventually realized that these types of comments resulted from the local scripts that guide men's decisions and choices about sexual partners. "Scripts," as William Simon and John Gagnon (1984) tell us, "are a metaphor for conceptualizing the production of social life. Most of social life most of the time must operate under the guidance of an operating syntax, much as language is a precondition for speech" (29). The scripts that inform our decisions about sex, including who we have sex with, when we have sex with them, where, and what we do, are motivated by patterns of social conduct that are derived from within our local context (Lauman and Gagnon 1995). The role that sexual scripts play in men's decisions about sexual partners consequently influences the construction of the sexual networks that are so instrumental in determining the spread of HIV. Consideration of sexual scripts and sexual networks is particularly important in China, where social networks are a key component of daily life. Within this context, cultural constructions of masculinity, family relations, and *guanxi* work together to produce a set of sexual networks that satisfy desire by fulfilling the needs that also structure China's power relations.

Knowledge and Risk

Public health approaches to disease prevention typically employ functional models in promoting scientific knowledge as a means for changing behaviors that expose individuals to risk for a particular disease. This assumes risk is a calculable measure that individuals can control and readily avoid, through rational decision making when armed with knowledge about nature's inherent dangers (Ewald 1991, Lupton 1999). This scientific and individualistic approach, which admittedly guides most public health intervention theory, employs a perception of knowledge as a disembodied rational structure that can independently guide intentions, observations, and expectations in isolation from the systems of ideas and social relations that can ultimately determine an individual's exposure to various elements in nature and society (Hirsch et al. 2010, Lupton 1999, Paiva 2000, Young 1981).

Chinese men who enjoy the privileges of wealth and power perceive risk as something that can be negotiated within their social environment. Those tasked with protecting the public's health, though, take a standard knowledge-dissemination approach that does not recognize such nuances of social risk (Hirsch et al. 2010). People in China are constantly bombarded with knowledge and information about HIV, on billboards, on buses, and in subway stations. These media typically inform people about "three modes of HIV infection" (*sange tujing*), which many Chinese people can recount verbatim. When I ask Chinese people about HIV, they say, "Oh yes, HIV can be spread through three pathways (*sange tujing*): blood, sex, and mother-to-child transmission." Sexual transmission, they are told, can occur when a person has too many sexual partners (*xing banlü yue duo ganran de weixian yue da*). This official discourse also informs people that blood-borne transmission can occur through sharing injection equipment and by using tainted blood for transfusion, in addition to the possibility of mother-to-child transmission. Further, official discourse includes information on pathways that do not carry risk for HIV infection, in order to dispel stigma and discrimination. So people are informed that hugging, sneezing, and using the same pool, toilet, phone, or tools with an HIV-positive person will not place them at risk for infection. Condoms are part of more directed education efforts, but not the official discourse communicated to the general public. For example, local policy in several provinces instructs all hotels to place condoms in all their guest rooms, a subtle governmental recognition that hotel rooms often serve as spaces for illicit or potentially risky sexual contact.[2] Armed with this knowledge, men (and the rest of the population) are expected to heed warnings and limit their risk (and the risk of their sexual partners) to sexually transmitted infections and HIV. But most of the men I met believed either that they could limit their exposure to HIV outside of this information or that knowledge about HIV, a disease that affects only marginal people, did not apply to them.

Such reactions are not surprising, given that production of knowledge about HIV risk often stems from statistical data around the disease's effects on socially marginalized populations. When I asked urban men whether they would be willing to engage in information sharing about HIV/AIDS, they responded by saying that type of information is very useful for rural people but there is no need for us people in the city to pay attention to such nonsense. To them, risk that leads to disease or infection is most often related to a burden carried by marginalized people, who act as the political scapegoats for behaviors that are usually associated with sin, taboo, and negative outcomes (Lupton 1999). The organization of social hierarchy in Chinese society easily allows people to assign "badges of difference" (Douglas 1992) to marginalized groups with little political or social status. Thus, in China, and especially in Ruili, the rural ethnic minority drug users and sex workers who dominate HIV statistics have become the logical scapegoats associated with the epidemic.[3] At the same time, the importance of status in China makes it necessary for wealthy and powerful members of society to shun any association with factors that pose a risk to their position. Despite knowledge about HIV, many of the men I met felt threatened by the mere notion that they could come into contact with the taboo elements that could put them at risk for such a disease. Admitting it could endanger their political and social positions.

Consequently, most of the activities that could pose a risk of STI or HIV infection to these men or people in their networks were often glossed over in conversation or referred to as things that could not be mentioned (*buhao shuo de shiqing*). In private, people often discuss the possible vulnerability of wealthy and powerful men to STIs and HIV infection, but in public such discussion is considered taboo because of the threat it poses to the political and social status that is the cornerstone of Chinese society. Even within official Chinese public health discourse, the "risky" activities often associated with these wealthy and powerful men are rarely mentioned. In those instances where I have heard Chinese medical or public health personnel mention the potential role of these men in the HIV epidemic, emphasis is immediately displaced onto another subject in order to avoid associating China's supremacy with a negative attribute of risk that is reserved for only the most marginal members of society.

Risks and Rewards

Public health discourse is designed to assume that activities and behavior associated with disease can result in only negative outcomes. The risk incurred through these behaviors can thus result only in disease. Risk, as a concept, though, can entail either positive or negative outcomes because it refers simply to chance (Douglas 1992). Public health as a field focuses on the negative outcomes associated with behaviors that incur risk for disease. However, many of the behaviors people are implored to change or avoid to avert disease can potentially involve some type of social benefit on an individual level. Avoiding these behaviors can pose the potential for *social risk* (Hirsch et al. 2010). This is certainly true in Ruili, where risk can just as easily result in reward as it can in defeat. For example, many people are inherently tied to the risks of gambling, an integral part of China's cultural script that is part of everyday life. Ruili, like many border towns, serves as a magnet for gamblers from all over China, who cross the border in search of the potential rewards that can be found in the many casinos operating inside Burma. In the modern public-health world, where risk is associated only with negative outcomes, it is difficult to provide persuasive antirisk messages to gamblers who perceive risk as a balance between loss and reward. Likewise, for the men who engage in extramarital sexual relationships, public health messages that warn about risk can be misunderstood because of the ability of these men either to tolerate the negative implications of risk that are balanced against possible rewards or believe they can use their power to mitigate the negative outcomes that possibly await them. Extramarital relations with lovers, mistresses, second wives, and even commercial sex workers are part of everyday practices that help these men achieve certain aspects of social and political status. The risk involved in such relations for them thus toggles between having and not having that status, rather than focusing on disease as an outcome of their behavior. An understanding of the scripts that assist these men in constructing their sexual networks is thus an important component of any program aiming to mitigate the negative consequences of risk that can expose them to disease.

The Role of Scripts in Choosing Sexual Partners

The scant literature on men's pursuit of sex outside of marriage is often framed within behavioral theory. Men's primary motivations for seeking sex outside of marriage, we are told, include desires for sexual variation, access to sexual partners of another age or racial or ethnic identity, or perhaps assuaging marital problems or loneliness (Bernstein 2001). The men I met during this project often echoed the same types of sentiments, arguing their motivation for seeking multiple sexual partners stems from some sort of biological need. I noticed more specific social and political motivation behind their choice of sexual partners, though, when I observed their practices and behaviors, motivations that perhaps they believed were inappropriate to discuss with an outsider. The concept of sexual scripts that Simon and Gagnon (1984) wrote about is a useful framework for understanding the contextual motivations I observed behind men's decisions around both marital and extramarital sex.

Simon and Gagnon describe a multivariate approach to scripting. "For behavior to occur," they argue, "something resembling scripting must occur on three distinct levels: cultural scripting, interpersonal scripts, and intrapsychic scripts" (53). No one level can entirely predict behavior; rather, behavior is determined at the nexus of all three. Cultural scenarios exist at the level of collective life. They determine the specific roles that individuals are expected to fulfill in society. Interpersonal scripts allow the social actor to adapt the cultural scenarios expected of someone in that role to his or her own particular situation. "Interpersonal scripting is the mechanism through which appropriate identities are made congruent with desired expectations," they write (53). These scripts help uncover the nonsexual motives that organize sexual behavior, which may include the gendered scripts that control or oppress men and women in their choice of sexual behavior (Paiva 2000). In my own research, these motives may derive from desires to create the quasi-kin networks that are necessary for success in business and government. Finally, all actors create their own intrapsychic scripting, which allows them to realize the multilayered individual desires that are linked to meanings created within their broader social context (Simon and Gagnon 1984).

The scripts I encountered are multifaceted. Some are based on expectations of fatherhood and responsibility. Others help men articulate their erotic desires. And still others are based on marriage, romance, opportunity, and status. None, however, are mutually exclusive. These scripts operate as part of a complex web where they often intersect. I therefore present them both independently and in sets.

Scripts of Love, Romance, and the Body

Sex in the West often follows the romantic ideal of love popularized in the novels that first developed in eighteenth-century Western Europe (Constable 2003, Giddens 1992). In line with this Western trope is also an expectation that sex and love adhere to religious morality. The scripts that govern sex in China are quite different. Sex in China shares greater association with eroticism than with love (see McMahon 1995). And marriage is often structured on the basis of political or social standing rather than love. Instead, people speak of fate (*yuanfen*) as the element that brought them together in marriage. Indeed, many commoners (*laobaixing*) believe all you need is food and clothing to marry a Chinese man (*jiahan chuanyi chifan*). This was true for Nicole Constable (2003) as well, in her examination of pen pal brides from Asia. As an American woman, she questioned the legitimacy of a marriage not based on a proven track record of conjugal love. But as one of her informants told her:

> Chinese seldom use the word "love," and we never use it as casually as people in the U.S. seem to. To us, love is not demonstrated by a word, but rather by how we treat our spouse, our family and each other. (128)

Marriage in Chinese society is based on a sense of mutual obligation that ensures the stability of the lineage rather than on a malleable quality like love or romanticism (Pan 2006). Many contemporary Chinese couples, as I learned, may start out with feelings of love (*aiqing*) toward each other, but these feelings transform over time into the type of feelings experienced between kin (*qinqing*) as passion (*jiqing*) becomes diluted into the mutual devotion (*enqing*) that sustains commitment between a husband and wife. This transformation, as A Rong explained to me, may come more easily for men than for women because of how they view their bodies (*routi*). "Men," he said, "can separate their emotions from their bodies (*neng fenkai ganqing he routi*), but women cannot separate the emotional from the physical." This distinction, he explained, allows men the freedom to satisfy their erotic desires outside the home because they do not worry that they will disturb their family. I heard similar explanations from women. Yang Huifeng worked in a position at the prefectural level in Dehong that brought her into contact with numerous men, some of whom were attractive to her. She and her husband had a seven-year-old daughter at the time who they were very devoted to, but they no longer had feelings of "love" (*aiqing*) for each other. So she saw no reason she could not have sex with these other men and still maintain her family's integrity. Huang Peili once worked for the Women's Federation, the quasi-government organ established to raise the status of Chinese women. She also believed "it's natural for men to have relations with women outside their marriage (*hunwai shiqing*) and because they can distinguish their feelings from sex, it's not a big deal to have a sexual relationship outside their marriage because it doesn't threaten the marriage." As A Rong and others described to me, this separation of love, the body, and emotions enable the types of relationships we witness in contemporary China, even in the wake of a historical system of marital monogamy between one man and one woman (*yifu yiqi zhi*). *Yifu yiqi* refers only to the bond of marriage, though, and not to sexual monogamy. So this system, which acts as a foundation of kinship in China, is not violated unless the integrity of the kin-based marital unit between a husband and wife is threatened (Tran 2011). Thus married partners can have sexual relations between husband and wife (*fuqi guanxi*) but still leave room to engage in sexual relations (*xing guanxi*) outside of marriage to fulfill their more corporeal desires and needs.

Housekeeping, Fatherhood, and Eroticisim

A man's first responsibility is always to his family, creating one and then maintaining its integrity. This type of familial order, as Confucius dictated, is integral to social and political order. Consequently, a man performs sexual relations with his wife as a way of housekeeping. A man's need for erotic experiences is often fulfilled by women outside his home, in the space Confucius left for this aspect of his sexual life. This bifurcation is partially responsible for structuring a man's sexual networks.

Fulfilling the responsibility toward family is often a challenge for men in post-Mao China living under the one-child policy. The policy curtails their filial duties and also challenges their masculine identity, which is largely dependent on expanding their lineage. Those with money skirt the regulations by marrying a second wife (*xiao laopo*), who can give birth to a second child. This is exactly what A Rong did when he amassed enough money to support two wives. He had to be very careful in choosing a *xiao laopo* in order to honor the responsibility and feelings (*ganqing*) he had toward his wife and their relationship. The woman he chose as a *xiao laopo* had to be young and healthy to produce high-quality offspring. But she also had to be a peasant and not too pretty or intelligent in order to limit any threat to the integrity of A Rong's marriage.

A Rong's *xiao laopo* also fulfilled an erotic need for him because, as he told me, his wife's poor health precluded her from satisfying him sexually. But such justification is usually unnecessary because Chinese men have historically had the space to seek erotic pleasure outside the home. Imperial-era China even assigned this duty to a certain class of debased (*jian*) women, who were permitted to serve elite and commoner men. This was recognized as a method for maintaining these men's vitality and preserving their status. Contemporary Chinese men continue to fulfill their erotic pleasures and passions with a variety of sexual partners, including both committed and noncommitted relationships aside from their wives. Having relationships with one or several lovers (*qingren*) has almost become normalized practice among certain classes in China.[4] As one man argued, "It's really not a big deal in China to have a lover, everyone does it these days. As long as you don't break up your family (*pohuai ni de jiating*)." Many depend on *yiye qing*, or one-night loves found at discos, as a way to fulfill their erotic desires without posing any threat to the integrity of their marriage. Having multiple concurrent lovers is also a common trend in China. A madam at one of the brothels where I conducted fieldwork told me about one customer who she believed maintained concurrent relationships with twenty women considered to be his lovers. Some men establish sexual relationships with women they consider as good friends. The development of a sexual relationship with these women adds an element of fun. Sexual partners outside of marriage also carry an emotional element that many men desire, but without the burden of the responsibilities of sex within marriage, which is tied to the familial bonds with a wife. A relationship with a lover also gives these men opportunities to relax with a woman who can be a confidante, and a more ideal sexual partner who makes various sexual fantasies available to a man. Many men find little cause to go home to their wives, except during an event like SARS.[5] Despite their perpetual absence from home, however, men do recognize the responsibility they owe to their families and their wives, who are at home keeping order in the house. For this, they would make a point of periodically going home to "accompany their wives" (*pei laopo*).

Scripts of Status

For the wealthy businessmen and government officials I interviewed, the script that often motivated them to engage in extramarital sex with a sex worker, entertainment worker, or mistress was associated with politico-economic pressure to please a government official in control of a scarce resource or allowance. Sex workers are part of the everyday practices men use to build relationships that confer the status to access resources, but men of real status are marked by a mistress. Like men of imperial China, mistresses (*ernai*) have become a badge of status that men wear on their sleeves (McMahon 1995, Sommer 2000). Many of the men who support mistresses with cars, condominiums, and expense accounts do not necessarily pursue these women with a sexual intent but instead for their symbol as a status marker. Elite men in contemporary China are often judged on their ability to attract a pretty young woman rather than on the virility they can demonstrate through some sort of commercial sexual activity. Being attached to an *ernai*, and being served by a woman of this status, has become a class privilege. *Ernai* also make good financial and emotional sense for men who operate in multiple areas in China. In exchange for monthly rent and a monthly stipend for his second wife, a man can get home-cooked meals, personal laundry service, and even massages, which would otherwise entail extra costs. He can also get the added benefit of a homelike setting during the many weeks or months he spends away from home in a remote location, as well as an emotional outlet at the end of a long day (Xiao 2011). Pan Suiming (2006) has argued that the women with whom men establish long-standing extramarital relations also serve the romantic need developing in contemporary China rather than simply acting as the badge of status they bestowed during China's imperial era.

Scripts of Trust and Opportunity

In a culture where trust is a valued and often difficult commodity to find, business partners are usually drawn from within one's family or close clique of friends. For men who operate several branches of a business or numerous stores, this familial trust can often be found in multiple wives. When I first met A Rong and his wife, they told me if I had arrived just one year earlier I could have met his wife's uncle, a Chinese merchant who lived in Burma with his nine wives.[6] Each wife was responsible for operating one of his nine stores.[7] The Burmese masseuse who became one of my informants told me similar stories related to herself. She received marriage offers from several Chinese men who traveled to Ruili from other parts of China to engage in cross-border trade. All were married and had children but chose her as a potential mistress for her capacity to offer them opportunities that were otherwise out of their reach. One man wanted to marry her in Burma and have a child with her; this would have helped him skirt China's policies of monogamous marriage and family planning. Marrying her in Burma would have allowed this man to fulfill his filial duties, by having more children, without divorcing his wife. Another man wanted to marry her in order to obtain Burmese residency, which could open up greater business possibilities for him inside Burma. My attractive and intelligent thirty-year-old informant saw opportunities in these arrangements as well that could provide her with a better lifestyle.

Trust, as I learned, was also something men used to negotiate their risk for disease with a sexual partner. Trust and familiarity with both sex workers and other sexual partners is often used as a rationale for avoiding condom use (Farrer 2002, Hart 1995, van Kerkwijk 1995). Knowing a woman translates into confidence about her cleanliness. This attitude is held for sexual relations with commercial sex workers, lovers, and minor wives. Brothel managers told me men who repeatedly visit the same sex worker will use a condom the first few times, but they find condom use unnecessary after becoming familiar with the girl.

Rejection of dirt and the desire to remain clean are universal drivers of a biological necessity to avoid threatening humors. But the hygienic practices used to avoid these agents of disease often differ from one society to another. This variation comes in the form of norms and manners, the culturally pre-scribed rules that promote hygienic practice and limit contact with patho-genic substances (Curtis, de Barra, and Aunger 2011). The condoms promoted by the culture of public health as a normative and accepted means of disease prevention are often discounted because of perceptions of cleanliness or local hygienic practices that dispel a need for such a barrier method. I often met men who believed all sex workers were dirty and who thus had sex only with other women who could not be categorized as sex workers.

To the men I spoke with, cleanliness ranged from regular hygiene to per-ceptions that can be tainted by infection with an STI or HIV. Several men I interviewed told me about hygiene rituals they require their wives to go through before sex, including a belief that a cold shower can cleanse a woman of any potentially infectious agent. Cleanliness among other women is evalu-ated according to varying but different criteria. For example, several brothel managers reported clients who judge a sex worker's cleanliness according to the length of time she has worked at the brothel (a factor that is easily mis-reported by a brothel manager). New arrivals have a greater chance of still being "clean." Some men may find themselves in situations where they cannot avoid contact with a woman perceived as dirty. In this case, as one business-man told me, they often negotiate another way around risk, through anal sex with a sex worker because "sometimes the back door is cleaner than the front door." Women who do not engage in the formal sex industry and cannot be readily identified as prostitutes who are highlighted as "high-risk" may be considered even "cleaner." Doctors at STI clinics told me these women are the most vulnerable to disease because they lie outside the standard paradigms of risk. Men like to have sex with these women, who work in the tourist and restaurant industries, because they are clean. Sex workers have been taught and recognize the value of condoms even if they are not always capable of negotiating condom use. But the newly migrated women who often work in hotels, restaurants, and tourist businesses are not aware of the risks of having sex with male customers. These are also often the women who men prefer to have sex with because their position outside the formal sex industry categorizes them as "clean." The Burmese masseuse with whom I became friendly in Ruili told me of a customer who stripped naked in anticipation of her entering the room.[8] Like many of the customers who visit the massage parlor where she worked, this man was hoping to receive a massage accompanied by "special service" (*teshu fuwu*). She followed standard practice and offered to solicit a commercial sex worker for him from one of the nearby brothels, but he refused, saying, "Those girls are dirty. They have diseases. I want you because you're clean."

The "safest" women are those who men know through committed relationships with mistresses, second wives, and of course wives, because men believe these women are sexually loyal to just one man. Most of the men I interviewed told me attitudes about sex toward lovers and minor wives are different from those held toward sex workers because the potential feeling and sense of commitment involved in these relationships removes the need for concern about cleanliness. Although condom use is often considered necessary during commercial sexual encounters, it is not perceived as necessary with committed sexual partners. Only one man reported the willingness to use a condom with all his sexual partners because, as he said, "I know there are a lot of diseases out there now and I value my life." However, he often spoke about myriad friends who maintain several committed sexual relationships in addition to sexual services they receive from commercial sex workers. None are willing to use condoms, he said. In all other instances, I was told men would never consider using a condom with a committed sexual partner because they are sexually loyal and thus "clean." Using a condom with a supposedly committed and loyal partner implies distrust. One man in Ruili told me he usually does not use a condom with committed sexual partners. He is very friendly with all his lovers and says he knows their sexual history, making condom use unnecessary. Doctors from private STI clinics have noticed that this trend has shifted the burden of vulnerability of STI and HIV infection away from commercial sex workers and onto the other women who enter into committed sexual relationships with wealthy businessmen and government officials.

Exotic Scripts

Finally, many Chinese men follow exotic scripts by seeking out new sexual experiences they believe are embodied within China's ethnic other. Government portrayal of China's fifty-five ethnic minority populations has constructed a sense of what Louisa Schein calls "internal orientalism" (2000) in Chinese society. Official representation of ethnic minority communities has feminized ethnicity in China and eroticized it in cases where feminine practices are also used to characterize the community. Such official discourse is very influential in a society that has had little contact with its ethnic minority communities. One of the taxi drivers Dru Gladney interviewed in the 1990s about his perceptions of ethnic minorities said to him:

> Those minorities sure can sing and dance. . . . I really like to watch those minority girls, they're a lot "looser" (*suibian*) than our Han women. They bathe naked in the rivers and wear less clothing. Our women wouldn't act that way. . . . Some of my friends have even gone down to Yunnan . . . or was it Guizhou? . . . to see if they could meet some minority girls, they are very casual, you know. Han women aren't free like that. It's frustrating. Just like our politics, we can't do anything about it (*mei banfa*). So why try? (1994)

These perceptions persist twenty years later because so many Han Chinese either still idealize China's ethnic minority regions as distant, remote, hard-to-reach places or witness an erotic ethnic façade that local governments put on display for Han tourists.

These façades, ersatz as they are, draw in tourists and their accompanying revenue, but they have distorted Han perceptions of minority culture as eroticized feminine culture. Xishuangbanna built its very successful tourist industry on exotic and erotic perceptions of Dai women. Many of the women who work in the tourist industry in Xishuangbanna are Han but are required to represent themselves as Dai (Hyde 2007). This daily type of performance underscores and caters to the fetishism of ethnic minorities that permeates Han society. It also helps Han men act out some of their erotic fantasies, which they are increasingly able to access in the Mosuo homeland of Lugu Lake. The men who travel to Lugu Lake dream of participating in the local noninstitutionalized form of partnership referred to as "walking marriage" (*zouhun*).[9] Others see sex or marriage with an ethnic minority woman as a requirement for fulfilling national goals. I met many Han-Dai couples in Ruili.[10] One man in particular was especially proud of his ethnic minority catch. When I asked if the woman next to him was his wife, he exclaimed, "No, this is my minor wife (*xiao laopo*). I landed a Dai minor wife" (*wo qile yige daizu de xiao laopo*).

Sexual Networks and Disease Transmission

Much of the research and interventions designed to reduce HIV infection recognize the individual as the agent of change necessary to modify risk-taking behavior. Such approaches neglect the relational elements inherent in HIV transmission though, which stem from interaction between two people with further influence from networks of family, friends, coworkers, and other social relations. Effective response to a disease transmitted through social relations requires knowledge about networks of relations related to risky behavior and why those particular relations occur. Answers to these questions can be found in social network analysis (SNA). Social networks consist of a set of *nodes* (individuals, organizations, or even societies) and *ties* that connect some or all of the nodes. These connections, which can be structured by relationships of kinship, frequent contact, information flows, or emotional and tangible support, organize systems of exchange, dependency, cooperation, and conflict (Klovdahl 1985, Mitchell 1969, Wellman, Chen, and Dong 2002). Because networking approaches look at partnerships as the prime sampling unit and the rules of partnership as the prime analytic task (Morris 2004), they are extremely useful for understanding how relational modes of risk for disease are created (Bond, Valente, and Kendall 1999, Klovdahl 1985, Neagius et al. 1994). The ties that bind the nodes together may serve a specific social role useful for sharing ideas, information, and money, but they can also facilitate the flow of other unintended agents like disease. For instance, a network held together by commercial interests can also enable the flow of infectious agents if communication includes sexual exchange. Highlighting the commercial interests that hold the network together offers insight into the approach necessary for intervening in the risk practices that breed members' vulnerability to disease.

Network analysis is increasingly being recognized as an important component in HIV prevention research, particularly in countries with practices of concurrent partnerships. This type of approach is perhaps nowhere more appropriate, and thus valuable, than in China, where the social culture stresses the importance of a rigid set of social relations founded on devotion, loyalty, and self-sacrifice to close networks of family, superiors, and rulers (Fei [1947] 1992, Kutcher 2000, Lu 1998, Pye 1991). The specific types of ties created with China's *guanxi* networks, including their conditions of establishment, closely mimic the types of relationships tracked within SNA and make them the perfect variable for analyzing the social relationships that can promote disease in China. The scripts I describe in the first part of this chapter are helpful for explaining some of these ties.

Opening Up the Space for the Development of Sexual Networks in China

Ed Lauman and John Gagnon's pioneering work on SNA demonstrated the potential effect that institutional shifts in society can have on the composition of sexual networks. Their work looks in particular at the growth of the nuclear family. Development of this condensed family unit structured around conjugal love and sexual commitment resulted in a limited supply of available sexual partners even for the "sexually adventurous married person" (Lauman and Gagnon 1995). The U.S.-based context that informed Lauman and Gagnon's analysis of sexual networks is structured around a social environment that expects individuals to devote much of their social attention, outside of the work environment, to their committed sexual partners and families. People in a committed marital relationship generally go home for dinner and other forms of "family time" after work. This expectation to socialize together as a single unit or social actor leaves little opportunity to form extended sexual networks among people engaged in committed sexual relationships.

Urban society in China has also transitioned from one structured around extended families to one that lives in a nuclear structure. This transition has not had the same effect on sexual networks, though, because the nuclear family does not serve as the social hub it represents in Western society. China's homosocial culture, in addition to state expectations for individual loyalty, has a strong impact on social structure and sexual networks. Men spend much more time outside their home serving the party in homosocial environments. This in turn creates distinct divisions between work, leisure, and home. This became evident to me when one of my mentors from the West suggested I begin interrogating men's use of saunas. He said to me, "Ask them when they go to the sauna. Do they go on their way home from work?" His question, which seemed so logical and simple from my own cultural perspective, oddly seemed strange to me after living in China long enough to know that "going home after work" was not part of the local social landscape for most of the men I met. A visit to a sauna is essentially a fluid part of a man's day after he leaves home, and not part of leisure or domestic activities. Going home happened only after all the day's activities were complete and they were ready to go to sleep. This daily structure is essential to success in China, where, as I was often told, only men who rarely go home can be considered successful. Men who occasionally go home are considered mildly successful, but a man who regularly goes home after the official workday is surely unsuccessful.

Expectations for party loyalty not only create opportunities for men to explore their sexual desires but also provide a rationale that permits the broadening of sexual networks. The wives who do the "housekeeping" get quite frustrated while their husbands are out building their careers. One woman accused her husband of being out (*zai waibian*) all the time doing nothing but eating, drinking, soliciting prostitutes, and gambling (*chi, he, piao, du*). But she acquiesced to his responsibilities, saying, "You can't expect a man not to stay out because of his work. He may make a little more money by cooperating and entertaining guests and he needs this money to support the family." Such tensions between family and party loyalty and their related responsibilities are leading many men to avoid their wives' frustrations and anger by spending more time outside the home, an acceptable norm in a homosocial society.

China's homosocial culture has created an environment where men and women can easily pursue individual relationships. I rarely met the wives of the men who granted me entrée into their social networks, and when I did it was in a context different from their lives outside the home, where they led individual social lives with their male friends and colleagues. Husbands and wives do not socialize together outside the home, as is common practice in the West. This inherent and accepted space between husbands and wives (*fuqi kongjian*) in Chinese society leaves room for development of complex sexual networks among men and women who are married, single, and engaged in varying levels of committed and noncommitted relationships. In addition, as I have explained, success for businessmen and government officials in contemporary China is dependent on demonstration of commitment and loyalty to the party, which involves social networks that are formed within the work environment and operate on hierarchies of power. The separation of these work-related networks from family and personal networks further facilitates the space necessary to create complex sexual networks within the Chinese context.

This type of culture facilitates an environment where men can easily gain introductions to sexual pleasures outside of marriage through work-related expectations and then rely on the protection provided by work-related loyalties to the party to further explore their newly emerging sexual desires and curiosities. Many of the men I met in Ruili and other parts of China are choosing to avoid their wives' anger altogether and finding both emotional and sexual satisfaction not only in the services provided by commercial sex workers but in relationships pursued with multiple lovers. Some of the men I met in Ruili returned home once or twice a month and spent other nights in hotels with lovers, often telling their wives they cannot come home because of work-related duties. This is easiest for men who occupy high-level government positions or work for high-level government officials.

Mamis (madams) often told me about the ignorance of women in Ruili whose husbands take advantage of their jobs to find spaces for pursuing their sexual desires and needs outside the home. Men, they would say, can easily find excuses to leave the house, claiming they have business to tend to (*you shiqing*) or that they have *yingchou* responsibilities. Their wives ostensibly believe the excuses, perhaps because they feel they have little choice. This gives the men space to solicit a sex worker (*qu zhao xiaojie*) or spend time with their lover (*qingren*). One *Mami* said to me, "The women in Ruili are stupid. Their husbands tell them they have to go out to *yingchou* and the women believe these stories." One female informant told me, however, women just need to learn how to communicate with their husbands. She and her husband both work for the government, and they have a son. She said to me one day, "Women can't get angry and frustrated at their husbands and then expect them to willingly come home. This attitude will just drive them farther away. Rather, women have to learn how to talk to their husbands and say to them 'I understand you have responsibilities to your work, but please don't forget that I come first and not your work.'" At times she asks her husband not to honor a *yingchou* appointment in favor of showing attention to the family, and he always respects her requests. This is a clear demonstration of the effect of structures of power on sexual networks in China and their subsequent potential effect on transmitting sexually transmitted infections, including HIV

(Adegbola and Babatola 1999, Messersmith 2000, Orubuloye, Caldwell, and Caldwell 1991, Parker 1995).

Mapping the Landscape of Sexual Networks in China

A mapping of sexual networks in contemporary China reveals a complex structure of men and women from varying strata of society who meet in both committed and noncommitted relationships (Messersmith 2000) founded on the political and socioeconomic structures that influence gender relations and sexual motivations (Bernstein 2001). Men who occupy varying socioeconomic and political roles as factory workers, taxi drivers, construction workers, dock hands, university academics, business entrepreneurs, and government officials seek sexual experiences with an equally varied host of women who exchange sex on both formal and informal bases through China's underground brothels, at entertainment venues, and in noncommercial relationships.

Ideally, a Chinese man can enjoy the privileges of care, filial responsibility, and sexual accompaniment from a variety of women, including his wife, lovers (*qingren*), a second wife (*xiao laopo*), mistress (*ernai*), entertainment workers, and prostitutes (*xiaojie*) (Pan 2004). These women also vary in origin. Many are uneducated women from the countryside; others may be university students or government workers who are seeking a way to supplement their income. Women from the countryside often come to China's urban areas seeking the opportunity and wealth they know is available in the city. Many work in restaurants, hotels, or other entertainment establishments that do not inherently involve responsibilities of sex work. They are drawn to the city by the lure of a cosmopolitan life, nice clothes, and earnings from a high income that can be brought back home to attract a husband (Hongying Wang 2000). Sex work is officially prohibited in these establishments, but many women do provide "special service" (*teshu fuwu*) as a means of earning extra income.

The women who occupy this range of relationships fit into a social hierarchy mirroring that of their male partners. For many, this equates to a sudden transformation in their status that may otherwise be socially unimaginable. Minor wives (*xiao laopo*) occupy the highest spot in this hierarchical spectrum of women. These women, many of whom gain legal status as a man's wife, may originate from the countryside but then become part of an upper-class urban kinship circle. *Ernai* enjoy benefits of cars, homes, and generous spending accounts (Liao, Schensul, and Wolffers 2003), but often remain distinct and hidden from the man's wife and family. Businessmen who travel but cannot afford an *ernai* hire a "sexual secretary" (*baopo*), a woman who may accompany a man on long business trips without the benefit of expensive perquisites like houses and cars. Short-term itinerant sex workers are also divided into a hierarchical scale that expands their identity beyond the limited category of sex worker that dominates the human-rights and public-health discourse related to women who engage in transactional sex. Most common among this elaborate network of women who engage in transactional sex is the "three accompaniment miss" (*sanpei xiaojie*), so called because she accompanies men in singing, dancing, and drinking in karaoke clubs. Other categories are "calling misses" (*tinghu*), who call hotel rooms to offer massage and hair washing services (as a euphemism for sexual services); and *falangmei*, who work in hair salons (*falang*), massage parlors, and saunas offering both standard (*zhengui*) and "special" services (*teshu fuwu*).[11] Finally, men without much money usually solicit the services of a street walker (*jienü*), a woman who sets her own price without responsibility to a pimp or madam (*laoban*). And according to Pan Suiming (2004), migrant men may also hire a tent girl (*gongpeng nü*), who lives with a group of men in a temporary shelter. Pan argues that many in this poorest class of sex workers provide services to men in exchange for food and shelter.

These are the seven categories that have become standard in the discourse on sex workers in China. But the euphemistic titles used for women who sell or otherwise exchange sex are as varied as China's wide range of cultural and geographic landscapes. For example, young girls who ply the beaches at seaside resorts offer swimming lessons (*jiaolian*). These women may accompany men in the water before inviting them back to a hotel room for "extra service." Migrant women from the other side of China's borders are a separate sector of the sex industry that can be available for either very poor or very rich men. Migrant Burmese or Vietnamese women who often cross borders voluntarily or involuntarily can offer sexual services to a man for as little as 10 RMB, while the Russian women who are coveted for their white skin and blonde hair in Beijing may be the purview of only the wealthiest men in town.

The sexual networks that men weave with women who provide them with sexual needs in both committed and noncommitted relationships are just as complex as China's sexual landscape itself, largely because men often follow several sexual scripts, which may relate to their social, political, or economic situation. These webs become ever more complex when we consider the prevalence of extramarital relations among China's political and economic elite. Many of the men I met in Ruili and Beijing reported that 90–100 percent of the government officials or wealthy entrepreneurs in their networks maintained relationships with lovers and second wives, in addition to the services they solicit from sex workers. These types of statistics are not surprising, considering the many reports of corruption that reveal officials who squander public funds on mistresses (Farrer 2002, Markus 2005, Sun 2004).

These networks are further complicated by the sexual relationships developing among the wives of the many men who are fulfilling the needs of their various sexual scripts in and out of marriage. As I mentioned at the beginning of the chapter, men, but not women, are culturally permitted to satisfy their sexual and erotic desires outside the confines of marriage. However, women are finding ways to transgress the rules that define acceptable sexual practices and structure their own ideas of the "erotic" as they gain more social freedom and flexibility. Many of the wives I spoke with are no longer willing to stay home with their child while their husband entertains business partners and government officials. These women are not following culturally, economically, or politically prescribed scripts that prompt extramarital sex but instead are acting on a desire to explore the sexual possibilities offered in China's newly sexualized era, something available to many women who also benefit from their husbands' success. The men who say they are out pursuing sexual encounters for a reason are now afraid that their wives will stray when left alone because they have access to resources that can open up new possibilities. Many of the men I knew in Ruili called their wives several times a day to make sure they were home and not with other men. If they called and their wives were out, they would ask if they were alone or with someone else. If the answer was that they were with someone else, the response was immediately followed by an inquiry as to whether the person was a man or a woman. A Rong, who eventually requested that I develop a friendship with his wife, asked me to ensure his wife was not fooling around with other men when he was away on business. Many women with access to their husbands' wealth, however, are beginning to embrace a sense of independence by going to disco and karaoke clubs and finding their own lovers. Discos in large urban centers like Beijing have become a site where men can find prostitutes (*jinü*) and women can find "ducks" (*yazi*).[12] It was even rumored that several male prostitutes had started working in one of Ruili's discos shortly before I left the field. For the first time, a new trend among China's most privileged urban women is extending the web of modern Chinese sexual networks outside the barriers of what is culturally acceptable.

Playing It Safe: Governmentality and Risk

For many wealthy and powerful men in an area like Ruili, which has experienced an HIV epidemic since 1989, the risk of infection is perceived as real. Publicity and education campaigns have alerted these men to dangers that lurk among "dirty" and "diseased" prostitutes. For many of these men, however, the threat of these diseases to their political or social status is an even stronger deterrent against soliciting sex work than the risks posed to their health. Impact of the state's attitude toward governmentality has become stronger than the threat of biological risk among China's political elite, who see HIV or STI infection first as a disruption to their political status and then as a risk to their health.[13]

Although the commercial sex industries I witnessed in Ruili and other parts of China still have a strong presence, brothel managers reported to me that their business saw declines in the proportion of local customers (businessmen and government officials) in the wake of the HIV epidemic. But this was not necessarily the result of standard public health campaigns. Men in Ruili who work for the government all told me that even though many of the local officials would like to "taste" the young girls who sell sex in the local brothels and karaoke bars, they refrain from doing so for fear of contracting an STI or HIV. One informant told me he is very happy to go to the karaoke bars where the *xiaojies* sing with him, drink with him, and caress him, but at the end of the night he gives them some money and goes home. Several other informants told me government officials are concerned about protecting not only their health but also their political position. They often told me, "Government officials don't carelessly fool around (*luanzuo*) anymore. There are too many diseases out there and besides, it's too risky for people who work inside work units (*danwei*)." This was confirmed by one of the brothel managers I interviewed, who reported only 40 percent of his clients were willing to use condoms with the sex workers who work for him. According to this manager, men who are most likely to use condoms with sex workers include those who have at least a rudimentary understanding of medicine and those who work inside a government work unit (*danwei*). The former are responsible men who want to avoid transmitting diseases to their wives. The latter fear that exposure to an STI or HIV infection will result in loss of their job and political status, which is consequently a threat to the integrity of their family.

Instead, many government officials and civil servants are fulfilling their sexual curiosities and desires with sexual relationships developed with a female colleague from within their work unit (*danwei*). An informant in Beijing who is close with many midlevel government officials at the national level also told me the officials in his network have become more cognizant about protecting their safety (*zhuyi tamen de anquan*) for fear of the retribution it could bring to their status. For all these men, the political and social status bestowed by their position is more important to their masculine identity than the physical pleasure garnered from a night with a sex worker. This also speaks to the relative value of standard behavioral models for HIV prevention in China. Such messages may be transmitted toward an aim of cultural acceptability, but in the end a culturally compelling message (Panter-Brick et al. 2006) can emerge only from within the context of locally valued practices. In this instance, these are the social practices that prompt the sexual scripts responsible for structuring the sexual networks that transmit sexually transmitted infections, including HIV, around urban China.

11 BUILDING *GUANXI*: THE EFFECT ON CHINA'S HIV EPIDEMIC

5 Tracing the Development of China's HIV Epidemic

CHINA DOES NOT HAVE A LARGE HIV EPIDEMIC. THE prevalence rate hovers around 0.05 percent of the total population, a statistic that pales in comparison to the most affected countries in sub-Saharan Africa, where up to 25 percent of the population is infected with HIV. China's HIV epidemic is notable, however, because it defies the global patterns exhibited in other contexts (Patton 2002). This unique pattern tells the story behind the trajectory of HIV in China, which is grounded more in culture, geopolitics, *guanxi,* and rituals of *yingchou* than in the epidemiologic pathways usually associated with HIV transmission.

Global narratives of HIV typically recount epidemics that begin in urban centers and then spread to more rural regions of a country. China's HIV epidemic took a different path. The first concentrated epidemic of HIV in China was discovered among 146 injection drug users living in remote ethnic minority communities in the county of Ruili, adjacent to the Burmese border in Yunnan Province.[1] The area is so remote that health officials believed the epidemic would never spread into the rest of the country (Wu, Rou, and Cui 2004). But this remote region, which barely makes it onto the map in China, did indeed launch a national epidemic that now affects all of China's thirty-one provinces, municipalities, and autonomous regions.

The epidemiologic paradigms that dominate study and discussion of HIV focus on discrete causal pathways of injection drug use, heterosexual and homosexual contact, and mother-to-child transmission[2] that spread the virus and sustain epidemics. Injection drug use has been the primary causal pathway for HIV in Ruili and its administrative home of Dehong Prefecture. This is not surprising given that Ruili is the gateway for heroin smuggled into China from Burma.[3] Focusing on heroin does little to solve the puzzle of China's HIV epidemic, though, because it is but one of the many products resulting from the complex cultural, economic, and geopolitical network (Taleb and Blyth 2011) that is at once capable of ensuring economic security and triggering an HIV epidemic. Facilitated by rituals of *yingchou* and what I call Ruili's "culture of happiness" (*kaixin*), heroin and other lucrative resources, including jade and rare timbers, can easily flow across the border from Burma to China, unseen in the name of economic security. This chapter goes beyond the role that *yingchou* has played in promoting individual interests and transmitting HIV and sexually transmitted infections from one individual to another, to highlight the role these rituals play in supporting the daily jockeying of the cultural, economic, and geopolitical interests responsible for promoting local economies, national interests, and a nationwide epidemic.

Why Ruili?

To the casual observer, Ruili, and its administering prefecture of Dehong, is a remote area kissed by the bucolic lifestyle often found in subtropical regions. Stepping off the plane in Mangshi[4] can make you feel as if you've left China and suddenly landed in Southeast Asia. The streets are filled with Dai, Jingpo, and De'ang[5] men and women in the long sarongs and longyi that are typical of Burma.[6] The food is also different from that in other areas in China. Complex dishes made with a variety of spices and wild vegetables harvested by ethnic-minority communities dominate local tables. The food is accompanied by a fragrant local variety of rice that is said to be the only one that was fit for the emperor.[7] Dehong also enjoys a year-round variety of tropical fruit crops, including pineapple, pomelo, papaya, and jack fruit.

Visitors to Yunnan are usually greeted with the melodic lulls of the famous song *you yige meili de defang* ("There Is a Beautiful Place"). The song celebrates Ruili's beauty and pastoralism through tales of Dai people[8] who inhabit hidden villages forming a chain among the plains where they raise cows and goats (*mimi de zhaizi jinjin xianglian; pingping de bazi li gan niu yang*). This song was written in 1958 but, for the most part, still describes life in Dehong, where approximately 70 percent of the population live an agrarian lifestyle dependent on simple agriculture of rice, sugar cane, bamboo, rape (canola), tropical fruits, and a small coffee crop.[9]

Life is seemingly simple and carefree in Ruili and Dehong, with the year-round warm weather and abundant harvests. But urban Ruili has a different, more complex face that can make it feel more like the Wild West than a tropical paradise. A lot of trading and deal making goes on everywhere, much of which happens behind closed doors. Several pockets of the city are dedicated to the jade industry, which can be legal, but there is also a large industry of illegal smuggled jade thriving in Ruili. I lived adjacent to a pedestrian mall known as gem alley (*zhubao jie*), where one could buy any manner of jade. The small alleyway where I lived was a residential street at the time, but as China's economy and its appetite for jade expands, the houses have all now been converted into small jade polishing factories. The jade market has also expanded beyond gem alley to occupy that whole section of town.

Moving away from Ruili into the border town of Jiegao brings one into an even more complex side of local life and many more factories dedicated to polishing and selling jade and petrified wood, which is another valued commodity in China. These two aspects of life in Ruili operate side by side, and as I was often told, people can choose to live in either world. One of the men who offered me lessons on Ruili frequently professed to me *ni shuo ruili fuza shi fuza, ni shuo bu fuza jiu bu fuza* (Ruili can be as complex or simple as you choose). It is these complexities, nurtured by a region at the margins of society that is also of economic and strategic importance to China, that laid the foundation for the country's HIV epidemic. Understanding these complexities is important for unraveling the puzzle that undergirds China's HIV epidemic. But this is dependent on piecing together the tale of a complicated web of local, national, and ethnic interests all coming together to support a perverse type of economy that facilitates the local epidemic in Ruili and ultimately affects that state of the epidemic in the rest of the country.

To the sociologist Manuel Castells (1998), the "perverse" informal economies that develop at many of the world's border areas are natural environments for HIV epidemics. Castells describes these areas as "black holes" because of their isolation from formal global economic and financial networks. As a result, people in these regions must turn to informal economies that rely on arms dealing, smuggling, illicit drugs, and selling of sex, children, and even human organs (Castells 1991). A similar situation exists at the Chinese-Burmese border, sustained by a trend of cooperation and interdependence between two governments that depend on this type of perversity for supporting their economies and maintaining local and national security. This has resulted in an economy that is not only perverse but also large enough to sustain the governments and communities on both sides of the border. They have in effect created their own micro economy, which in the aggregate links up with the global economy. Although this resulted in an informal economy supported by lucrative resources, which can prompt an HIV epidemic, it is also an economy that is not quite perverse because it seems more organized and deliberate than the typical border economies Castells describes. This also presents challenges to any plans to disrupt the informal economy because of the important role it serves to official plans for economic growth and security on both the Chinese and Burmese sides of the border.

Maintaining this perversity under the watch of the Chinese government is not easy. It requires a lot of careful negotiation and traditional trust building. The remainder of this chapter will describe the complex cultural and geopolitical environment that structures society in Ruili. Through this discussion I will show that China's HIV epidemic is not simply the product of an epidemiologic pathway but is rooted in a complex social and cultural context shaped by a nexus of historical, cultural, and politico-economic structures between local and national governments and minority and majority populations that shape life in a remote region that nevertheless plays a crucial role in protecting China's national interests.

I do offer one caveat before presenting a description of what is a complex and informal geopolitical structure comprising a web of local, national, bilateral, and ethnic relationships (Raw 2004, Zhou 1999, Lintner 1999). Burma and its border regions live in a shroud of secrecy that is particularly difficult to penetrate. Access to the Chinese-Burmese border is especially difficult because both governments are reluctant to grant permission to foreigners to enter the region. This makes writing on the region difficult at best. I was fortunate to have gained the trust of many local officials in Dehong Prefecture, some of whom belonged to local ethnic minority communities. I also developed relationships with members of one of the ethnic minority governments from the Burmese side of the border.[10] Most cross-border activities, however, are kept under tight cover because they often involve the trade and movement of illicit goods, services, and even people. Foreign researchers were not permitted access to Burma before the political reforms of 2012, and indeed few have been granted permission since Edmund Leach conducted his research on Kachin political structures in the 1940s. Any information related to Burma, even from the Chinese side, is still very sensitive, and even access like that which I gained to local officials and community members did not give me access to restricted or secretive information but just endowed me with a greater understanding of regional dynamics and the players who make the region tick. Writing on this region is thus a little like reading the Rangoon tea leaves, to borrow a term from David Steinberg (2001), something he describes as an art requiring a certain amount of faith more than scientific inquiry. As a result, those who write on this region depend on anecdotal tales from informants, many of which seem implausible at best but are often validated because we hear similar stories and come up with similar conclusions. The information and analysis I present in this chapter is based on the stories I heard from people inside China and the Kachin State, but it is also hauntingly similar to other scholarly accounts on the region in that we often come to the same conclusions on who and what stimulates the seeming perversity that sustains this region at the edges of the world.

Ruili's Importance to China's National Interests

The story of China's HIV epidemic begins with Ruili and Dehong's importance to the country's national interests. Ruili has held strategic importance to China since World War II, when it served as a major staging area for China's defense against Japanese incursion. The American volunteer air corps known as the Flying Tigers, an integral part of the China-Burma-India Theater in the war and run under the direction of General Joseph Stillwell ("Vinegar Joe"), set up a border airbase in Ruili, which is also the entry point for the Burma Road into China.[11] Ruili continues to hold strategic importance for China's national security and economic growth because of the access it offers to Burmese gas and oil reserves.

China's rapid economic development has caused the country to become highly dependent on imported oil. In 2000, China imported a mere 2 percent of its oil, but imports grew to 50 percent by 2008 and are expected to reach 60 percent by 2020 (Li 2010). Eighty percent of that imported oil passes through the Strait of Malacca, making China extremely vulnerable to any interruption in transportation through the Strait. This increasing dependence on imported oil led China to turn to its southwestern neighbor for access to gas reserves and an alternative means for importing oil from the Middle East. This initiated conversations over the construction of oil and gas pipelines to extend from the deep-sea port of Kyaukphyu in the Rakhine State[12] of Burma to Kunming and to cross the border in Ruili.[13] Bypassing the Strait of Malacca not only protects China's energy security but also reduces the cost of transporting oil and gas into the country. Easier access to oil and gas supplies in Yunnan will also aid economic growth in this part of the country (Singh 2013).

Access to Burma offers further benefit to the development of western China's economy because it opens up a second coast for international trade. Ruili is remote but sits at the crossroads of East, Southeast, and South Asia. A trading relationship with Burma is crucial to taking advantage of the opportunity at this crossroads. Although China's many eastern cities have access to a coast, Yunnan and the rest of western China are landlocked. Burma has become the California of China, offering trade opportunities to these landlocked provinces. These national economic interests have resulted in exponential increases in infrastructure investment from China as a way of ensuring access to this coastline and Burma's rich oil and gas reserves, bolstering an already burgeoning trade between the two countries. By September 2010, annual Chinese investment in Burma reached an amount equal to two-thirds the total invested in the previous two decades combined ("China's Relations . . . " 2010). It is estimated that China will invest between 25 and 35 billion dollars in Burma in the coming years. Twenty-three billion dollars alone is currently being put into the high-speed rail line that will connect Rangoon and Kunming. The remainder is being invested in oil and gas pipelines, highways, and large dam projects.[14] The story that ensues is similar to the one we see unfolding in Africa (Brautigam 2009). Western China can finally share in the same economic opportunities as China's eastern coastal provinces. This is being done, however, on the back of a weaker nation in need of China's economic support.[15] China builds large infrastructure projects in Burma, and in exchange they gain access to the country's rich reserves of precious resources.[16] Ironically, most of these infrastructure projects will benefit China's citizens rather than the average Burmese citizen, who continues to live in poverty (Simon 2011).

Few people outside of Yunnan Province or the international organizations that work on HIV/AIDS in China have heard of Ruili, but clearly it serves as strategic a role in China's plans for future economic development as it does in China's HIV epidemic. So, although Ruili is remote, high in the mountains, and far from the emperor, it is also of great interest and importance to

Beijing. This makes regional economic security and stability in Ruili a crucial element to China's national interests. Supporting development of the formal economy, which will be important for achieving China's national goals, consequently requires that the informal economy so integral to local stability remain strong. It also warrants supporting the interests of local populations, which can potentially pose a threat to local stability and security. And finally, it requires maintaining good relations with their Burmese neighbor at the national and local levels. Maintaining and supporting this complex web of interests is accomplished through careful choreography of an intricate dance that happens between China and Burma's national governments, the local governments on either side of the border, and the ethnic minority populations who call this borderland region home.

The Complicated Dance Between China and Burma

Burma is one of the least-developed countries in the world despite sitting on an abundant supply of lucrative natural resources that include jade, gems, rare timbers, and oil and gas (in addition to an abundant supply of poppies, which are processed into heroin).[17] Many of these resources help to sustain informal economies, but not a formal economy that can support a country and its population. Burma's formal economy was stunted during a time when international sanctions isolated the country from the global economy and international aid.[18] This seemed to make little difference for the military junta, the State Law and Order Restoration Council (SLORC),[19] which ruled over Burma until 2012 and supported its needs through a second informal economy fueled by the lucrative resources found in many of Burma's independent ethnic states. This revenue was crucial during Burma's isolation from the global economy (Silverstein 1997), which depleted the government of the resources needed to secure its authority over a country that was riven by civil war with its ethnic states. The government had less than US $9 million in foreign currency reserves when many of these sanctions were put into place in 1988. It turned to China for the arms necessary to maintain military rule. The money used to secure the arms came from sales in timber and other natural resources, including oil, jade, and heroin, that are primarily found in Burma's independent ethnic states. The government secured its access to these resources through cease-fire agreements with the ethnic states, which allowed them to access revenue from the sale of precious resources, heroin being the most lucrative of those resources (International IDEA 2001). Ethnic states cooperate because their security is dependent on peaceful coexistence with the junta. Both thus end up in the careful dance that helps to maintain peace between adversaries depending on each other for access to necessary resources.

Burma was also very dependent on its relationship with China prior to the democratic reforms in 2012, which helped to reinstate relations with the United States. China represented a lifeline to daily resources and arms to support the junta during Burma's period of economic isolation. The value of this relationship to Burma dates back to December 1949, when Burma became the first country to recognize the People's Republic of China after its founding on October 1 of that year. The Burmese government feared that the new government in China would support the Communist Party of Burma (CBP) and needed to open up communication to limit the effects of such a relationship.[20] China did not reciprocate, though, until Zhou Enlai visited Rangoon in 1954 to gain the support of the CPB in their anti-imperialist struggle (Liang 1997). Zhou aimed to establish a relationship of peaceful coexistence[21] and friendly relations (referred to as *Pauk Phaw* in Burmese or *baobo* in Chinese) with China's neighbor to the southwest (Liang 1990). This established the foundation for an extended marriage of convenience motivated by economic and strategic needs, where Burma has been able to access the support it needs to sustain its economy and China has in turn gained access to a second coast and resources it sees as necessary for its continued economic growth.

Relations between the two neighbors can be tense but at other times friendly or even genuinely cooperative. Whatever the mood, they realize the importance of maintaining a delicate balance of cooperation that takes into consideration the small but locally powerful ethnic communities who consider the border between China and Burma as a homeland defining and preserving their culture and livelihoods. On the one hand, the Chinese and Burmese governments would like to marginalize these communities to the extent possible in order to limit their power. On the other hand, they realize that regional stability may be compromised if they do not maintain friendly relationships with these ethnic communities.[22] This results in a complicated dance regulated by a careful negotiation of relationships that help to maintain stability and economic security among local actors at the border and within the capitals of these two nations.

Creating Economic Symbiosis
at the Chinese-Burmese Border

The economic and energy security China seeks through its relationship with Burma is not only dependent on a healthy bilateral relationship, but also depends on maintaining stability at the border that ferries across many of the resources ensuring this security. Ruili is a remote area isolated from national and international economies. Similar to other Chinese municipalities in the post-reform era, this city and the surrounding county of the same name are responsible for supporting their own economic growth and funding local ser-vices.[23] Their success in creating a livable city with modern conveniences is a result of strong cross-border trade in both legal and illicit goods.

China and Burma first opened up their borders for trade with one another in 1988 through an agreement between the Myanmar Import Export Cor-poration and the Yunnan Provincial Import Export Corporation, legalizing cross-border trade for private entrepreneurs, cooperative societies, and gov-ernment organizations (Arnott 2001).[24] At the time, Burma was in need of a friend to help sustain its economy after a decision to isolate itself from foreign investment following a military coup in 1962, and a decision on the part of all multilateral and bilateral agencies to stop aid following the military's brutal crackdown on a nationwide uprising to end military rule during the summer of 1988. Yunnan province was also in need of an outlet to boost its economy. China's turn to development of a market economy had implications for indi-vidual provinces and municipalities, which had to find a way to finance their own local economies. The government's plan for promoting economic growth on the east coast included development of special economic zones that pro-duce goods for export. Access to this coastal route was not possible for inland provinces like Yunnan and Sichuan, so the government looked toward Burma as a possible avenue for export from the western part of the country (Lintner 2002). Trade has been further supported through establishment of another Special Economic and Trade Zone on the Chinese-Burmese border. In 1990, China developed the village of Jiegao, which sits across the river from Ruili, into a tax-free zone to encourage more trade between China and Burma.[25] All resources processed in Jiegao can be imported tax-free into China.[26]

Legal trade supported through a mechanism like the tax-free zone in Jie-gao is only one aspect of the vibrant local economy in Ruili. In 2007 Ruili alone carried out 5 billion RMB (approximately US $650 million) of foreign trade. Two-thirds of the total was represented by exports to Burma (Guo 2010). Actual numbers of trade would increase exponentially if they included illicit trade in jade, which is smuggled over the border, as well as rare timbers, which are officially illegal in China, and the heroin that also easily flows in alongside these other goods. Trade in these goods supports a large informal economy that is equally as important for maintaining and securing the border region around Ruili.

Mention of Ruili often incites negative responses of a city shrouded in perceptions of crime and deceit. But the resources and activities that have gained Ruili its reputation as a capital of *huang, du, du* (referring to prostitution, drugs, and gambling) also play an important role in supporting stability in the region. Revenue from the poppies and other precious resources that can be found in Burma's ethnic states is crucial for supporting the ethnic armies that fight to protect themselves and their communities against the Burmese junta.[27] The Kachin State, for example, has large deposits of jade that they mine and supply to Chinese businessmen who sell the jade in China.[28] The jade passes through Ruili, where a lot of it is processed and sold.[29] Large amounts of rare timbers, mostly teak, cut from forests in the Kachin State are also smuggled over the border. Casinos are an additional crucial source of support to this and other informal economies at border regions across China. Gambling is a national pastime in China, but it is also illegal, and so Chinese businessmen often build casinos just over national borders that cater to Chinese patrons.[30] I have seen Chinese-owned casinos at the Burmese and Vietnamese borders, and even remnants of a closed casino at the North Korean border. They are illegal but lucrative businesses that benefit economies on both sides of the border. Many of the casinos I saw at the Chinese-Burmese border were built on land leased from the Kachin Independence Organization (KIO), the body that governs most of the Kachin State.[31] This is one of the many ways the KIO supports itself and its battle for independence in the wake of government isolation from any resources that are available within the country and government sequestration of much of the revenue produced from the resources found in their territory.

The casinos draw people from all over China to do business in Ruili. They also supply business to many of the sex workers servicing the businessmen and government officials who daily entertain each other while building the relationships that facilitate their success. The casino industry in Burma also helps to fuel small cottage industries in Ruili. At any time of the day, I saw and heard local hawkers offering a ride to the casinos in small microvans commonly known as "bread cars" (*mianbao che*). They usually stood outside the bus station, waiting to catch people who had just arrived in Ruili, shouting "*laoban duchang*" (hey boss, casino?). Ruili's casino industry is primarily supported, however, by a large ethnic-minority-owned business conglomerate that operates the largest hotel in town and the largest casinos on the other side of the border. Every few minutes I spotted a van, with their logo on the side, heading toward the border.[32] All of this is conducted in the light of day, and the proprietors rarely scatter except in the event of a high-level visit from the central government.

Maintaining Stability Through Ethnic Diplomacy

In an environment that is arguably governed more by money than bureaucratic authority, trade of any kind is valued because it brings the needed revenue to the area that facilitates economic growth. Ruili has a goal of becoming the next Shenzhen,[33] a tall order for a remote city at the margins of Chinese society. Doing so will help them look good in the eyes of provincial and national officials, who evaluate local officials partially on the basis of economic growth. Economic security is also important for the border security that supports national economic goals. Local security and stability, however, is also dependent on maintaining friendly relations with the ethnic minority communities who call this region home. This has become an important part of the strategy for protecting stability in the region.

The relationship between Han and ethnic minority communities has always been central to China's goal of socialist construction and social transformation. In 1956 Mao discussed this as one of the ten most important relationships for building a strong socialist state.[34] This socialist need continues to inform state intentions in Dehong today. There is always a palpable amount of tension between ethnic communities in Ruili and Dehong, but local officials actively work to downplay these contradictions in an effort to fulfill the party's socialist intentions.

Dehong is home to five highland and lowland ethnicities, the Dai, Jingpo, De'ang, Lisu, and Achang, that constitute the majority of Dehong's population. Their communities inhabit this area in China but also straddle the border, leading them to consider the borderland area, rather than one nation or the other, as their home. Consequently, they often pursue different goals from the sovereign nations that control their territories and determine their citizenship. This makes it imperative for government at the local and national levels in China to strengthen relations with these ethnic communities as a way of maintaining the regional stability that is so crucial for their economic security. Maintaining this stability is a complicated process that happens on both sides of the border. The process has thus far succeeded through careful coordination of bilateral relations between governments on the Chinese and Burmese sides of the border but also with the independently governed states on the Burmese side of the border whose inhabitants are closely linked to the ethnic minority communities that constitute the majority of Dehong Prefecture's population. A good relationship with the Kachin government on the Burmese side of the border and the Jingpo community in Dehong is particularly pivotal to maintaining stability at this border point because of their independence as a community, their ability to organize, and their secessionist intentions. The Jingpo live under Chinese rule but derive a certain amount of power from access to precious resources as well as from an independent governing body and insurgent army inside the Kachin State of Burma.[35] This contributes to their own project of resistance in response to the state projects that have reshaped both their bodies and their homes (Mueggler 2001).

China's Ethnic Minority Project

Any discussion of an ethnic minority community or autonomous region in China must begin with an overview of the country's ethnic minority project. Ethnic minority communities are often confused with tribal communities. Many of the communities we find in China, however, resulted from a process of systematically identifying officially recognized ethnic minorities as a way of achieving national unity. The new government that came to power in 1949 viewed many of the non-Han communities as rebellious agents at China's peripheral regions, posing a threat to the goal of achieving national unity. This forced the government to ask questions about what it meant to be a part of the Chinese nation and how the customs of non-Han people could contribute to the establishment and unity of that nation. They eventually turned to Lewis Henry Morgan's work on Native Americans and other "tribal" peoples to guide their understanding of some of these concerns (Litzinger 2000). This led to a nationwide ethnographic project, known as the *minzu shibie*, that identified, categorized, and described these "foreign" peoples and ultimately aimed to integrate them into the new nation (Fei 1980, Harrell 1995, Litzinger 2000). By 1962 the *minzu shibie* had identified fifty-four communities as official ethnic minorities (*shaoshu minzu*) in China.[36]

Results of the *minzu shibie* contributed to a state-directed sense of ethnic identity that helped shape a nation of people who first and foremost identify as Chinese people (*zhongguo ren*). Consequently, many ethnic-minority people devote more loyalty to the state than to their own community. The government also realized the importance of expressing public support and respect for local ethnic customs. This demonstrated the value of the socialist message to ethnic minority communities and helped gain their support for the new nation. This nation-building project created a unique frame of ethnic identity that potentially does not exist outside of mainland China but has nonetheless been crucial to strengthening the base of support for the Chinese Communist Party (Blum 2001, Gladney 1994b).

The Jingpo

The ethnic minority referred to as Jingpo is an aggregated group of five related ethnic communities consisting of the Jingpo, Zaiwa, Lashi, Bulu, and Kaku, of which the Zaiwa constitutes the largest part of the population. The largest population of Jingpo live across the border in Burma, where they are known as Kachin and primarily live in the Kachin State, located in northeast Burma.[37] The Kachin are divided into six subgroups, known as Jingpo, Zaiwa, Lashi, Maru, Nung-Rawang, and Lisu[38] (Robinne and Sadan 2007). All of these subgroups also speak varying forms of the Jingpo language. Local folklore traces origin of the Jingpo to a deity known as Ning Gawn Wa, who participated in the creation of the earth. He married a female crocodile with whom he bore an unknown number of children. Their eight grandsons became the progenitors of the Kachin sects as well as some other peoples in the region (Lintner 1997). Every Kachin belongs to one of five original families: Marip, Maran, Lahpai, N'Hkum, and Lattaw. These clans are interwoven into a complex kinship network that also binds the Kachin together into a very cohesive society.

The Kachin originally believed in animism until missionaries arrived during the late nineteenth century. They associate closely with a Swedish-born American missionary named Öla Hansen, who went to the Kachin State in 1890. Most Kachin/Jingpo now believe in Christianity, a strategy highland peoples in this region of southeast Asia have used to maintain their distance from the state (Scott 2009). Christianity provided an institutional grid for social mobilization, and it also helped to create a historical identity through conferral of written language, which was necessary to transmit biblical teachings. This also opened the society up to literacy, education, modern medicine, and material property (Scott 2009) and offered the first opportunity to record written history after a long tradition of oral history.

Within Dehong the Jingpo present one of the largest perceived threats to regional stability because of the independence and unity that define their culture. Edmund Leach's classic study of Kachin social structure (1959) describes a society that values political independence over economic value. Like other highland groups of this region, they are reluctant about projects that may induce oppression through slavery, conscription, taxes, corvee labor, epidemics, and warfare. They have traditionally escaped such threats through the same methods that have driven communities living in expansionist territories to areas of challenging topographies seemingly resistant to the expansionist activities of the Chinese state (Scott 2009). Rural Kachin and Jingpo continue to live in sparsely populated villages dispersed throughout highland areas. This has been one of the challenges in implementing health programs in the Jingpo and Kachin communities on either side of the border. It is very difficult to reach the communities, hindering service and prevention activities. Social and political adaptations developed to help them maintain their distance from the state also make these communities impervious to standard messages delivered from a majority government, or even international actors, from whom they wish to maintain a distance.

Unity is another defining feature of Kachin and Jingpo culture. Jingpo in Ruili constantly reminded me of this with the proclamation *women hen tuanjie* (we are very unified). All Jingpo, no matter where they live, treat each other as brothers and follow a strict code of mutual aid for other members of their society (Wu and Yang 1996). This theme of unity is further represented through rigid rules for marriage, which create an unbreakable kinship circle because people with the same surname cannot marry. The use of glutinous (sticky) rice in all ritual meals is yet another signifier of cohesion among members of the community.

The society has not remained as unified as its culture would dictate, despite the centrality of unity to Kachin and Jingpo society. This is partially due to the impact of socialism on Kachin religion in China. Christianity[39] plays a big role in shaping Kachin culture in Burma, where the church and the pastor are the focal point of the community. Jingpo in China still follow Christianity and are able to attend local government-sanctioned churches. But ideological influence from the communist government prevents the church from assuming a major role in the community. The centrality of religion to Kachin/Jingpo society has created a big divide between the Kachin in Burma, who revere their clergy as their leaders, and the Jingpo in China, who are now forced to revere Chinese government officials as their leaders. A question to a Jingpo government official about whether she believes in Christianity received a quick answer of "No," followed by "I believe in the Communist Party (*wo xin gongchandang*)." This cultural divide limits any influence the Jingpo can have on local government and society given their political culture. This influence is further limited by the tensions that often exist between branches of the ethnicity. Nevertheless, the Chinese government still perceives the threat of organization and unity held within Jingpo culture and society, motivating a cautious attitude toward the Jingpo and Kachin. This has made stable relations with the local Jingpo and Kachin government a priority in local and national strategy, as they try to avoid the threat of a "pan-Kachin" movement that could result from the strongly networked Jingpo society straddling the border.

The result is a government that works hard to maintain friendly relations and a balance of power between ethnic communities and the military government in Burma ("China's Myanmar Dilemma" 2009). Central to this effort is ensuring the economic salience of local ethnic communities on both sides of the border. For example, China provides many of the utility services of water, electricity, and telecommunications (phone and internet; "China's Myanmar Dilemma" 2009) to ethnic communities on the Burmese side of the border to secure basic living standards. They also realize the important role informal economies play in supporting these communities. Ethnic communities on the Burmese side of the border are isolated from any formal economy, but several also live on land rich in such lucrative illicit resources as jade, timber, and poppies, which fuel a large informal economy that also supplies their economic lifeline. This makes the informal economy an element that must be cautiously navigated as part of the government's goal to maintain regional stability. The casino industry is a good example of the relative value of the informal economy that supports regional security at the Chinese-Burmese border. The casinos lining the Burmese side of the border are usually built and managed by Chinese businessmen, who lease land from the Kachin Independence

Organization (KIO). The casinos draw a large influx of tourists and businessmen to the area and also employ a large number of rural residents from Dehong Prefecture. On the other hand, casinos are prone to violent crimes, and sanctioning their activities violates Chinese law. Periodic crackdowns on casino operations caused by increased government enforcement or stories of loan sharks who kidnap and murder people can cause spikes in unemployment,[40] and threats to local business in Ruili as well as the economy in the Kachin State.

Aside from community support, the Chinese government also maintains good relations with the Kachin government, whose high degree of organization is crucial to regional stability and security. The Kachin are believed to be one of the best-organized armed opposition groups in Burma (Smith 1994b), with close ties to their Jingpo kin on the Chinese side of the border. In fact, the KIO is the only nonstate government permitted to operate a representative office in China (one in Ruili and one in Kunming). Stability at the border is further underscored through maintenance of relations with local ethnic borderland elites. Borderlands are often controlled by chiefs, who compete with nation-states for loyalty in these regions. The political project at the state level typically aims to eliminate such cross-border loyalties by making borderland politicians resemble their counterparts in the interior (Baud and Schendel 1997). Until such a goal can be reached, however, stability at the borderland depends on maintaining good relations with the borderland chiefs who ultimately control these networks. As a result, borderland elites often become integrated into networks of central state power and act as allies of the state in its efforts to control borderland society. In this dual role, they claim loyalty to the state but are ultimately most loyal to the ethnic networks they serve and protect. It may seem as if two competing interests are getting into bed with one another, but failing to incorporate these elites into state structure could result in a breakdown of state power and control at the border (Sturgeon 2004, Baud and Schendel 1997).

Traditional Kachin social structure, which was divided into systems of *gumsa* and *gumlao*,[41] was similarly governed by chieftains who rule over a hierarchical society of aristocrats, commoners, and slaves (Leach 1959). The society no longer adheres to the traditional *gumsa* and *gumlao* system, but modern-day Jingpo society in China still operates with a similar structure (Wang 1997). The modern chieftain for Jingpo in Ruili is represented by a man who holds great economic sway within the community and with the local government. I never met him. I was told he was not willing to meet with me, but I certainly heard a lot about him from Jingpo in Ruili, one of whom came from his clan. Thus to me he was almost like a mythical figure, but one who holds great influence over the Jingpo people in Ruili. His integration into central state power, as Baud and Schendel describe, also makes him an influential actor in Ruili society, governance, and economy. This chieftain's influence derives less from political position and more from a high social and economic position that has grown into political influence. Many see him as a savior for the Jingpo people in Ruili. He used his wealth to build roads to his natal village and employs many rural Jingpo in the corporate conglomerate he developed in Ruili, which supports local business development partially through operation of a four-star hotel and casinos across the border. Others view him as a slave driver because of the extreme loyalty he expects of those rural youths he employs. But everyone describes him as a modern day chieftain.

This unofficial leader of the Jingpo community in Dehong Prefecture grew up in a rural village that could not be accessed by road during his childhood. Many of his skills came from service in the army. He then entered the timber trade with kinsmen from the Burmese side of the border when he returned home from the army. He diversified into gems in the 1990s, and his business ventures have now grown into a corporate enterprise that invests in a diverse array of industries. The enterprise gains public recognition from a sixteen-story four-star hotel but also includes businesses in land development, infrastructure and construction, and a newly developed private bank that specializes in microcredit. The hotel opened a five-star resort with a golf course outside of Ruili in 2011 and has plans to build an even more luxurious hotel. He is now also owner of one of China's first private air carriers, Ruili Airlines, which promises to connect Ruili with both China and Southeast Asia. He also owns real estate in Beijing and operates several of the casinos in the Kachin State.[42] Much of this is accomplished through support from his father-in-law who is Han and a high-level official in one of China's major banks. I was often told his father-in-law helped to start his business, but he was also in debt to the government, whose support he depends on as well for success.

This man's position as an actor who assumes the role of a border chief regularly negotiating with the nation-state (Baud and Schendel 1997, Hastings and Wilson 2001, Sturgeon 2004) has helped transform him into an influential agent in Ruili in government circles and within the Jingpo community itself. This relationship, however, is equally important for the state. Like all successful businessmen operating in China, he is co-opted by the state (Dickson 2008) to a certain extent even while maintaining the level of authority required to unofficially reign over the local Jingpo community. As a result, there seems to be a certain amount of quid pro quo between him and the state. For example, through his networks of kinship he continues to have the flexibility to operate casinos in the Kachin State that cater to Chinese patrons, despite repeated attempts by the government to close down casinos over the border. But he is also loyal to the Chinese state, providing for various needs. He operates establishments that allow officials in Ruili to entertain a constant stream of visiting officials. And in 2012 he funded all the major road construction projects in Dehong Prefecture. This relationship of reciprocity allows him to prosper as a businessman and leader in the local Jingpo community while granting the government the necessary entrée to assert control over the local region. The state's support of this man has helped to build his wealth and social capital. In turn the state gains unfettered access to this crucial border region. He is also typical of border chiefs in that he remains detached from the state while benefiting from his proclaimed loyalty. As a local elite, however, he has become a border guardian for the state. This helps maintain his power base and the cross-border connections that, as with many border chiefs in this region, allow him to channel useful information and illicit goods across the border (Baud and Schendel 1997, Sturgeon 2004).

Relations Between the Jingpo and the Han State

Bureaucratically, Dehong is an autonomous prefecture, officially known as the Dehong Dai and Jingpo Autonomous Prefecture (*dehong daizu jingpozu zizhi zhou*), which is entitled to serve the unique needs of its ethnic population.[43] Under the Regional Ethnic Autonomy Law, autonomous governments have the ability to "adapt central government policies that conflict with local ethnic customs, and to use their own languages." Indeed, a government official in Ruili once told me, "There are some national and even international laws that we just cannot follow." At one time there was even a special cross-border license plate issued only to traders in Dehong, to allow them to freely cross the border. It was unlike any other license plate in China in that it was black with red lettering, rather than blue with white lettering, and designated the car as registered to the border rather than to a particular province. The autonomous governments are also permitted to "promote their own customs, to practice their own religions, to manage and protect their natural resources, and to develop economic plans suitable to local conditions" (Brown, Sorrell, and Raffaelli 2005). Regional Ethnic Autonomy Law also stipulates that the assignment of top positions in the government and Standing Committee go to a region's dominant ethnic-minority group (or groups in the case of Dehong, which is inhabited by two primary minority populations), but there is no mention of a requirement to assign ethnic minority leaders to positions of power in the local party apparatus. This then creates only nominal autonomy under a government that consolidates power within a Han ruler who serves to maintain power over local communities. Throughout China, these types of bureaucratic arrangements simply increase tensions between a minority population wishing to govern its own land and the majority nationality that ultimately has the power to govern local "autonomous" regions (Bovingdon 2004, Mackerras 1994). Sensitivity to such tensions is heightened in a border area where the state is particularly concerned with extending its reach in order to consolidate power to protect national security and maintain stability (Saich 2001). The government consequently works hard to maintain authority and stability within the ethnic communities.

Creating Ethnic Diplomacy

The competing interests of ethnic autonomy and state rule are partially negotiated through the performance of local ritual. Dai and Jingpo culture are structured around a major ritual observance that occurs once a year. The Dai celebrate Water Splashing Festival (*poshuijie*) in mid-April[44] and the Jingpo celebrate the holiday of *munaozongge,* which falls on the fifteenth day of the first lunar month. Both are marked with major events bringing the community together to dance, sing, and eat for three days. The state often feels threatened by such large organized gatherings. Rather than cause tension by prohibiting organization for these festivals, the state has chosen to sponsor official celebrations of the major ethnic holidays in the county seats. They do, however, prohibit locally organized events in individual villages.

Munaozongge is a festival steeped in animist traditions celebrating a major transition in Kachin history and society that occurred as a result of their migration from the Tibetan Plateau.[45] The festival is celebrated through organization of a three-day celebration where community elders lead the entire community in the sacred dance of the *munao*. Common folklore dictates that the *munao* was first danced when the God of the Sun invited the birds to dance in heaven.[46] The tradition was eventually passed on to humans. The elders who lead the dance continue to honor this origination story through the traditional dress they wear during the celebration, which includes a headdress adorned with feathers from two of the birds that Kachin mythology holds responsible for the creation of their culture (including peacock feathers) and the beak of a condor, which is also part of their creation story. The festival is initiated with the sacrifice of a bullock or a buffalo, central to Jingpo culture as well. Packets of meat are then distributed to invite the host's relatives and neighbors to the celebration. The dance then officially commences when two elders signify they are ready by waving raspberry branches over their heads and leading the community into the local *munao* square. Kachin/Jingpo communities are traditionally built around a *munao* square, which is identified by the traditional Kachin totem depicting the gendered organization of the culture as well as their creation myth.[47] They dance in a circular pattern around the totem following an S shape reminiscent of the route the Kachin took from the Tibetan Plateau to their current homeland.

Government-organized festivals centralized in each county seat have supplanted the small village-level celebrations of *munaozongge*. These standard three-day county-level festivals are initiated by all the official pomp and circumstance one has come to expect from a communist party event. Speeches by local and prefectural officials stress the importance of the Jingpo community as well as the value of their cooperation with the Han government. This allows the government to maintain control over expression of local culture while demonstrating its official support for local ethnic minority communities. The Ruili and Dehong governments have also extended sponsorship of *munaozongge* celebrations to Kachin communities in Burma as China's relations with Burma become increasingly important.[48]

Local government has extended this type of celebratory diplomacy to its relations with local Burmese leaders as well. In 1999 the government of Dehong decided to mark the *Pauk Phaw* relationship, established through Zhou Enlai's 1954 visit to Rangoon, with an official annual holiday called China-Myanmar Friendship Festival (*zhongmian baobo jie* in Chinese). This three-day festival is celebrated during the first few days of the May Day holiday, referred to as Golden Week.[49] The celebration includes lots of pageantry, with floats and dance troupes representing communities from both sides of

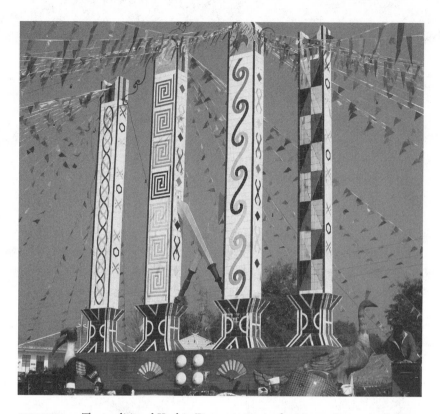

PHOTO 5.1 The traditional Kachin/Jingpo totem in the Munao Square in Ruili. Photo by author.

the border. The constant beat of joint celebrations signifies the importance of this relationship. Cultural representatives from either side of the border get together once again on International Women's Day to celebrate through song, dance, and food, and then again on Dai Water Splashing Festival (*poshui jie*) to maintain the friendliness and good will that supports their strategic relationship.

The complex set of relationships between local and national, minority and majority actors that result in this good will works to maintain stability. But as Janet Sturgeon (2004) noted in her research at the crossroads between China, Burma, and Thailand, it is also the perfect environment for an explosive growth in opium, heroin, and amphetamine trade that is equally important to stabilizing these relationships. In the following section I will discuss the history behind opium cultivation and use in this region. Knowledge of the

PHOTO 5.2 Jingpo elders initiating *munaozongge*. Photo by author.

PHOTO 5.3 Jingpo officials opening *munaozongge*. Photo by author.

PHOTO 5.4 KIO officials at Ruili *munaozongge*. Photo by author.

important cultural and state-building roles that opium has played in Dehong Prefecture and Yunnan Province will shed light on how the various intricate relations previously discussed influence regional stability. It is not an accident that heroin catalyzed an HIV epidemic in this remote region of the world. Consequently, it is important in responding to this epidemic to understand the history behind its cultivation and use.

China's History with Opiates

Opium has played a prominent role in the history of the Chinese state and Chinese society since the sixteenth century. Socially, opium served as a marker for elite men during imperial times. It also constituted a valuable source of revenue that was used for state building at the local and national levels during the nineteenth and twentieth centuries (Baumler 2000). To the public, opium had valuable medicinal uses. It was an effective treatment for symptoms from malaria, dysentery, and cholera. Additionally, it was a useful analgesic and antitussive and was often used to cope with fatigue, hunger, diarrhea, rheumatism, and cold (Dikötter et al. 2004). People in Dehong Prefecture still view opium as an effective treatment for some of the most common ailments that plague the region, including malaria.

The Social Life of Opium

In the West opium has always been viewed as a harmful substance associated with addiction and social deviance. Opium historically held a different status in China, where it played important social, medicinal, and political roles. Men who consumed opium followed a strict ceremonial order that defined its social role and restricted its consumption (Dikötter et al. 2004). The term *addiction*, which we often associate with images of opium dens, developed out of a more Western clinical tradition aiming to capture the quantifiable effects of opium use.

Addiction discourse has become the normative model for discussing opium (and its derivatives), but it is not helpful for understanding China's history with opium. Addiction in the West is a physical property that usually implies reduction in quality of life and does not recognize any positive social effects that can result from using the addictive substance. Addiction to opium in China, however, was not merely about physical dependence (McMahon 2002); it also conveyed messages about individual loyalties.

Opium also had an important social role in imperial China. For elite men, it served as a valuable social lubricant. Much like the cigarettes men offer to one another as a way of opening communication in contemporary Chinese society, opium served as a "welcome smoke" (*yingchou* 迎抽)[50] that demonstrated hospitality and sociability during imperial times. Opium use was popular among high-level government officials and people who occupied various other high-profile roles in society. Of note, Jonathan Spence mentions Chen Duxiu's grandfather, Feng Yuxiang's parents, Hu Shi's stepbrother, and Lu Xun's father[51] in his comprehensive social history of opium smoking in China. But opium use was not limited to the higher echelons of society. Eunuchs and laborers often smoked out of boredom (Spence 1992), which is also a common explanation I heard about why so many ethnic minority men smoke opium in Dehong Prefecture. In Dai and Jingpo cultures, women typically bear the brunt of the work in the fields while men stay at home. Their idle time, combined with the cheap price of heroin so close to the border, has promoted a large epidemic of injection drug use. Opiates also tend to have more influence in places along their trade route. This held true in the Qing and Republican eras, when opium use was often related to opium cultivation. Ann Maxwell

Hill has shown that much of the opium grown in Western Yunnan during the Republican era was consumed locally (Hill 1998). The same holds true in contemporary China, where heroin use is concentrated in places along the major drug trading routes.

China's Long Love-Hate Relationship with Opium

Despite its association with addiction and social deviance, opium has historically been a valuable source for Chinese state building even during times of suppression. Opium provided the revenue necessary for rebuilding local economies following the Taiping rebellion (1850–1864). Political reformers such as Zhang Zhidong (1837–1909) and Li Hongzhang (1823–1901)[52] also realized its value in their self-strengthening efforts as a way of financing special projects and repaying loans (McMahon 2002, Spence 1992). In the twentieth century, opium served as a crucial source of revenue for the Kuomintang (KMT), with the KMT making efforts to control opium during the Republican era; but warlords who saw opium as a lucrative source of taxable income were reluctant to adhere to such measures. There is even evidence that opium supported communist-state building efforts during the Yenan period[53] (Baumler 2000, Chen 1995, Dikötter et al. 2004, Slack 2000, Zheng 2005).

By the time of the mid-Qing, opium was transformed from a source for state building into an imperialist agent that nationalists could blame for many of the catastrophic errors befalling China at the time. Anyone loyal to opium was accused of being loyal to an imperialist product, an addiction that was unacceptable under a nationalist type regime (Dikötter et al. 2004, McMahon 2002). Suddenly the disease theory of addiction made more sense in China, aided by new legislation that ushered in prohibition campaigns against opium. As a result, portraits of the typical opium user transformed from an elite socialite to an addict who looked more like a heartless, slippery person, capable of breaking family ties, disrespecting his elders, and even selling his wife. The campaigns waged to suppress opium were motivated more by a desire to protect the body politic, though, than the individual body. Antidrug campaigns waged during the Republican and Communist eras have also focused on protecting the nation-state rather than the individual (Dikötter et al. 2004, Zhou 1999). Communist efforts to combat drugs, in particular, have been used as a means to build the identity of a "new China" (*xin zhongguo*), which was an integral part of the state-building process during the 1950s. Official estimates show that twenty million drug users lived in China when the CCP came to power in 1949.[54] This was considered a palpable threat to national strength. Consequently, the party prioritized a series of antinarcotic *(jindu)* campaigns that enabled them to declare a "drug-free" nation by 1953. Current drug prevention efforts have revived the *jindu* discourse through antinarcotic campaigns that once again aim to maintain the social order needed for protecting state security, and not necessarily at protecting or preventing disease in the individual user.

Opium in Yunnan

Locally, opium has also played an important role in Yunnan's economy following the decline in imports from British India during the late nineteenth century. Yunnan became a logical replacement for growing the crops that fed China's opium need because of a similar temperate climate and topography that can support multiple annual harvests of both opium and ordinary crops. Soon, however, new legislation was passed to restrict opium cultivation. This met strong resistance from peasants in Yunnan, who had grown to depend on income from the lucrative crop. In Kunming alone, 29,750 *mu*[55] of land was dedicated to opium production by the 1880s. Eradication would have resulted in a huge reduction in peasant income (Spence 1992).

This economic dependence on opium extended as far as China's borderland. Opium cultivation in Burma dates back to the sixteenth century and continues to play a large role in the country's economy (McMahon 2002, Spence 1992, Zhou 1999, Lintner 1999).[56] In Kachin and Jingpo communities, people depended on opium sales to buy daily necessities (Wu and Yang 1996, H'o 2007). In 1956 (the last year opium cultivation was permitted in China), opium sales made up as much as 63 percent of agricultural income for some Jingpo communities in Dehong Prefecture.[57] Opium was primarily used as a means of currency and traded for cattle and other necessities in Jingpo society, but Wang Zhusheng reports that in 1953 a small part was consumed locally (Wang 1997). Writing in 1997, Wang says, "Even today the Jingpo economy remains closely connected with opium use and cultivation" (77). This is partly due to the advantages that opium offers as a crop. Opium poppies are feasible for hill paddy cultivation because they require little work and are easily transported to market. The ease of transportation further reduces the cost of bringing the product to market, thereby increasing any profit that can be made from selling the crop. Additionally, its hardiness limits any damage to the crop during the long journey from the mountains to the valley. Opium does not deplete the soil of nutrients as do rice and vegetables, and it has many varied uses, which again makes the crop more marketable. Aside from its most commonly perceived use for heroin production, opium plants can be converted into oil for use in food or lighting, the lower leaves can be eaten raw as a cold salad,[58] the raw seeds can be used in cooking,[59] the remaining parts can be used as fodder, and the stalk can be burned and transformed into a sought-after dye. This multifaceted nature and high cash yield make the poppy an attractive crop to local farmers and consequently poses difficult challenges to organizations hoping to eradicate opium cultivation in the region (Dikötter et al. 2004, Lintner 1997).

Opium's Continued Hold on Dehong

Opium eradication has long been a priority to both Chinese and international actors concerned with protecting and developing the Chinese-Burmese border (Arnott 2001). Tackling this problem, however, is as complex as the history of Chinese-Burmese relations. Examining the complexity of the problem rather than looking for a solution prompted by Western strategies may help us understand why opium eradiation in this part of the world is so difficult. Much of the modern history of the Burmese opium trade relates to crucial sources of revenue needed to support an isolated economy or protect a country's interests. Sources as early as 1950 trace support for the Burmese opium trade to the KMT and Central Intelligence Agency. It is believed that the CIA used revenue from opium production to support the military operations of KMT soldiers who had escaped to Burma in 1949 in order to "resist the advance of Chinese communism" (Arnott 2001: 74). The Communist Party of Burma also turned to the opium trade as a way of maintaining their armed struggle against Rangoon after Chinese assistance was reduced following the accession of Deng Xiaoping in 1978 (Arnott 2001). In addition, opium supported an economic lifeline for the SLORC and several of Burma's ethnic states that do not have access to a formal economy (Ball 1999, Chang 2004).

Trade in opium, heroin, and other commodities that are illegally transported over the border is sustained through large and intricate networks based on kinship, reciprocity, and patron-client relations. All difficult to penetrate or even describe but important because they form the basis of the local, informal economies that are so integral to regional stability. Unlike formal economies, which depend on global financial networks, informal economies typically develop among culturally and ethnically rooted regional networks like the ones that exist at China's border with Burma. Such organizations benefit from strong alliances of unity and codes of honor helping to maintain their strength and capacity for preservation. Similar to formal economies, these economies too are global in nature. Local regional networks are supported by the global networks of organizations that share similar cultural roots and permit access to a market that demands local goods and resources. In many cases, regional networks can influence politics and law enforcement, much as we have seen in Dehong. The political strength of these networks also promotes an environment that presents significant challenges to efforts to stem drug use (Castells 1998).

Networks that support the drug trade across the Chinese-Burmese border are not new. Much of the trade that originates in Yunnan is facilitated through trafficking networks that descended from the Chinese triads, which began as mutual aid societies in the eighteenth century and only later became involved in opium trading (Dupont 2001, Murray 1994). Alliances among ethnic kin in northeast Burma and Yunnan allowed a more direct trafficking route to open up once China established trade agreements with Burma. Beginning in 1948, some of the ethnic nationalist armies looking to maintain their autonomy established patronage relations with local farmers to support their operations after suspecting they would not be integrated into the new Burmese government. These border polities remain, creating an environment where local ethnic armed groups still exchange protection to local villages for their grain (Sturgeon 2004). They are supported by larger networks of officials who facilitate the elements necessary for moving goods over "borders"[60] in exchange for taxes, levies, and tribute (Yawnghwe 1993). Ethnic links across the border into China have allowed these communities to maintain the staple of their economy through established kinship networks despite the political division between the two nation-states under which they are governed. There also seems to be little government motivation to control drug trafficking. The Burmese junta has traditionally been largely supported by hard currency derived from the drug trade and the gifts officials receive from heroin factories, although the growing gas industry is now beginning to alleviate dependence on drugs. Drug traffickers also have strong ties with high-level officials in Yunnan and other major areas on the international drug trade route such as Fujian and Guangdong ("China's Myanmar Dilemma" 2009, Steinberg 2001).

These dynamics enhance the importance of the dance that local and national officials must conduct at the border area with each other and with the ethnic minority communities that influence stability in the region.

Traditional dependence on a particular crop that has become ever more lucrative in modern times, but also more dangerous, logically fosters the perfect environment for whatever social and biological ills may result from its transformation. The last section of this chapter explains how Ruili's sociopolitical culture has nurtured development of an epidemic like HIV.

The Importance of Being Happy (kaixin): Defining a Local Sociopolitical Culture

Governing in Ruili and Dehong Prefecture is a constant challenge for officials who are under pressure to please their superiors. Performance evaluation for government officials in China's market-reform era is largely dependent on achieving expected goals of economic growth (Saich 2006b). This can be difficult to achieve officially in an area like Dehong, which is isolated from national and global economic networks but close to a host of lucrative resources that support a thriving informal economy. In addition, local officials must ensure provincial and central-level officials that they are maintaining the degree of stability necessary for protecting national security at this crucial border area. Consequently, local officials often find themselves negotiating between the requirements involved in maintaining their vibrant informal economy and in pleasing the people "upstairs." On one hand, Ruili can take full advantage of being in a remote location where the emperor is far away. They can play by their own rules. However, because they are so important to national security, Ruili and Dehong's continued success also relies on satisfying the needs of the many high-level provincial and even central-level officials who often come to survey (kaocha) the local area. They simultaneously maintain the local economy and portray themselves as the model guard of the socialist state through demonstrating what I call a local "discourse of happiness" (kaixin), which aids the common practice of covering things up in China.

People in Dehong are generally happy (kaixin). They enjoy good weather, good food, and abundant crops. In fact, Dehong was one of the few places in China to avoid the devastations of the Great Famine because it harvests two crops of rice annually. This prompted a large wave of Han migrants escaping famine in the late 1950s. People in Dehong also do not worry about many of the political inhibitions that govern life under a watchful central party and the social inhibitions that govern Western lifestyles. The Jingpo, for example, are a highland nomadic (*youmu*) culture, and Dai and Jingpo alike are not limited by many of the sexual restrictions common to Western society. My own Western predilections informed a cautious approach to many of the situations I encountered in Dehong, but all were countered with a standard response of "Don't worry, it's not a problem" (*meishi*). The excessive smoking and drinking that are engendered by local cultures and often unofficially required as part of the local politico-economic process are all brushed off as *meishi*. Even drug use is deemed *meishi*. I was once invited to the home of a local official who came from one of the rural ethnic-minority communities. I was offered opium to smoke during the course of the afternoon, and when I declined the offer I was told, "Don't worry, it's not a problem. This is pure opium and it's not addictive" (*meishi*). The term *meishi* became a mantra for me that defined life in Ruili.

Meishi is acceptable discourse in Dehong where many of the behaviors and actions considered risky in the West or even in the Chinese hinterland (*neidi*) are standard everyday practice. But as the borderland becomes more integrated socially, politically, and economically with the rest of China, locals realize that political and economic survival depends on keeping their accepted everyday practices to themselves. For this they turn to the discourse of covering things up, which is part of standard unofficial practices required for political survival in the rest of China. This realization of the discrepancy between local everyday practices and those that dominate Chinese society and bureaucracy is strong, leading people in Ruili to carefully protect their social and political status. So even though many things may be considered *meishi* (not a problem), they may also raise eyebrows outside of Ruili; hence it is important to keep their cards close. Basically, they live with the attitude that whatever happens in Ruili stays in Ruili.

Maintaining this level of discretion is particularly important to people in the Jingpo community, who work hard to protect their reputation as an honest culture. Members of the community are rarely heard speaking negatively about one another, despite the regional tensions within the community. They commonly say to each other *ni buyao luan shuo* (don't gossip). There are many aspects of Jingpo culture and many things that transpire in their society that may not be understood by outsiders, so they are extremely discreet as a culture in order to protect their reputation. Still, embarrassing or damaging information does spread quickly through a small town, and when information does get out it is quickly covered up through an exclamation of *"chui niu,"* which literally means blowing into the cow (akin to the English saying, you're full of hot air), a term used to dispel the spread of gossip around town.

Covering Up in China

The efforts to cover things up that I witnessed in Ruili may adhere to a specific local discourse, but they are certainly not specific to Ruili. Political cover-up has been a historical necessity in a vertically governed system that blames local error on poor management. This causes officials at higher municipal levels to cover up any action that could lead to local problems, whether they are related to local riots and uprisings that have been historically documented (Kuhn 1990) or major pandemic outbreaks covered up to spare local economies, which was the case with SARS (Saich 2006a).

Ruili and Dehong work hard to cover up the parts of their economy that make the largest contributions to local economic growth yet defy the face of official regulation. Officials in charge of controlling local corruption would tell me they had never seen a speck of heroin in their jurisdiction. Oftentimes, however, officials from higher levels of government seemed to aid local efforts to cover up by announcing the need to prepare the city for the arrival of an important official. During the two and a half years I spent conducting fieldwork in Ruili, the city hosted some of the highest officials from both the provincial and the central levels of government. These included the chairman of the Standing Committee of the National People's Congress (Wu Bangguo), the minister of public security (Zhou Yongkang), the vice-minister for health (Gao Qiang), and vice-premier Madame Wu Yi, who was acting minister of health at the time. The governor and vice-governors of Yunnan also made frequent visits.[61] The local Public Security Bureau always helped to prepare the city for such visits with a two-day notice in advance to all businesses conducting operations that violate national policy. Consequently, brothels closed their doors during high-level official visits. The border was closed to people crossing unofficially to gamble in the casinos located in Burma,[62] and the electronic gambling machines located at the back of the Jing Cheng hotel, where officials usually stayed, were literally covered up with white cloths. As I have described, Ruili's economy and its stability and security depend on supporting the flow of these commodities and industries. Eliminating them would disturb the relations that protect this level of stability. The veils that conceal such activities, however, seem to sufficiently cover up their presence in the face of any of the high-level visitors responsible for both maintaining party legitimacy and supporting regional stability. These illicit activities not only fueled the local economy but also assisted the local officials who depended daily on their operations to promote feelings of happiness (*kaixin*) and contentment among the officials helping to protect Ruili and Dehong from any retribution that could result from sustaining illicit industries.

Having a Good Time in Ruili (*zai ruili wan de kaixin*)

The everyday practices that fill people's time in Ruili and Dehong have created a culture of happiness (*kaixin*) that is also important for political survival. Using the practices of *yingchou*, which have become a customary form of communication in China, local officials are adept in sharing their local way of happiness (*kaixin*) with visitors as a means of ensuring they leave with a good impression. Consequently, a good official in Ruili is one who is skilled at hosting and entertaining his guests (*jiedai keren*) to ensure they have a good time and experience all the best Ruili has to offer (*wan de kaixin wanshi ruyi*). This helps to protect the many illicit industries that support the local economy.

Local government officials aspiring to move up the national bureaucratic ladder are usually careful in their behavior. Officials in many small places often do not have to adhere to such strict inhibitions, though, because opportunities for promotion outside the local area are rare. Inhibitions for officials in Ruili are often weaker still because many prefer to remain in a comfortable political position in Dehong, where they can enjoy happiness every day (*tiantian yao kaixin*). This has fostered an environment where local officials are not afraid to treat their guests to the games and entertainment that help to win over the favor needed to support the local economy that protects stability in this strategically important region. As a result, Ruili became a local and even national playground where such favor was exchanged for the ability to engage in these activities and share in the happiness and good times that are part of the local culture. As many as two hundred officials from around the country could arrive at once while I was living in Ruili, to share in this local cultural attribute. Many were entertained in venues built and operated by the local Jingpo chieftain.[63] As one retired official explained to me, "When the big leaders (*da lingdao*) come down to visit, you have to make sure they are happy (*kaixin*) because the local leaders (*lingdao*) depend on them for promotions and salary raises." If they are not satisfied, they leave Ruili with a bad impression. But simple provision of food, drink, and entertainment, which may include a gift of a pretty girl (*song meinü*), is sufficient to satisfy the whims of an official visiting from a higher position in the vertical system of governance. This helps to promote local and national goals by maintaining the strength of the local economy under a watchful eye, ensuring local officials are keeping national interests in mind.

The visitors to Ruili were often entertained from the moment they woke up in the morning until they went to sleep. Daylight hours were filled with trips to fieldsites to evaluate official work (*kaocha*) but also to popular local restaurants, where the host treated guests to local delicacies of fried bee pupae, or *sa pie* (a dish of cold rice noodles dipped in a bitter mix of cilantro, garlic chives, lime juice, raw chopped beef, and cow bile), and offers of long reverential toasts over *baijiu* that usually included a wish for the guest to be happy and have a good time in Ruili (*zhu ni zai ruili wan de kaixin*). At night they were treated to karaoke, massage (*anmo*), foot reflexology (*xijiao*), hair washing (*xitou*), or a sauna (*sang na*), any of which could be accompanied with the services of a sex worker. In exchange, visiting officials offered career advancement or a blind eye to the industries that support the local economy and the stability of this complex region of ethnic and national relations so crucial to national security and regional economic growth.

Kaixin: A Recipe for Happiness and an HIV Epidemic

Epidemiologic studies have informed us that heroin is at the root of the local epidemic in Ruili and Dehong. But eradicating the epidemic is much more complex than designing harm reduction programs that aim to reduce HIV infection in drug users or promoting alternative crops in place of poppies. Such paradigms, which focus on reducing individual risk, neglect the important role that local cultures, economies, and even bureaucracies play as agents of infection. Responding to HIV in China requires an understanding of the complex cultural, political, and economic context supporting the trade in the opium that ignited this epidemic. This type of response, which may manifest itself as a program rooted in behavior-change communication or harm reduction, must engage the complex networks of kinship, ethnicity, and local and international politico-economic webs that have a stake in protecting China's economic and strategic positions in the region. These networks support a large and perverse economy that helps to maintain stability in this strategically important region though the flow of commodities like heroin, timber, and jade. Their ease of movement does not come freely, though. The businessmen who ferry these goods over the border and who build the casinos that attract a lot of business to the region are trusted government allies. Like many businessmen in China, they have spent countless hours building trust and *guanxi* through practices of *yingchou*. Consequently, unraveling the motivation for China's HIV epidemic goes beyond piecing together the cultural, economic, and geopolitical roots of the perverse economy situated at its border with Burma to understanding the cultural rituals that allow this perverse economy to flourish under the watch of the Chinese government. The men who operate this economy rely on the same masculine rituals as other Chinese government officials and businessmen who have fueled the growth of China's formal economy. In this case, however, the rituals are not just capable of promoting individuals or placing individuals at risk for HIV or sexually transmitted infections. They have become integral to the processes that allow Ruili's perverse economy to flourish, and for a local and national HIV epidemic to develop and sustain itself. In the following and final substantive chapter of the book, I will discuss the importance of *guanxi* making and *yingchou* rituals to the administration of China's HIV epidemic.

6 Engineering a Local Response
to a Global Pandemic in China

F EW PEOPLE WHO PAY ATTENTION TO EITHER CHINA
or to global health will ever forget April 2003, when the world
learned about the first global pandemic of the twenty-first century. An
atypical kind of pneumonia, which the World Health Organization (WHO)
aptly named Severe Acute Respiratory Syndrome (SARS), had been found in
China and was quickly threatening countries and communities throughout
the world. The WHO global surveillance network detected the outbreak of
a strange infectious disease in the region as early as November 2002, but the
Chinese government managed to avoid recognition of the situation for several
months because no international treaty at the time required reporting of the
unknown disease to the WHO.[1] By February 2003, SARS had grown to epidemic proportions that could no longer be hidden. News leaked out through
the internet, e-mail, and text message to the Chinese public and the WHO,
confirming suspicion of a strange contagious disease. China acknowledged
the outbreak of an acute respiratory syndrome on February 11 but maintained
its sovereign right to respond on its own without international involvement,
denying repeated requests from the WHO to conduct further surveillance.
The Chinese government finally granted the WHO permission to tour Beijing
and inspect hospitals on April 18, the day China declared a "war on SARS"
(Fidler 2003, Saich 2006a). This war manifested itself into propaganda and
quarantine campaigns reminiscent of the public health measures used to
eradicate communicable disease in China during the 1950s (Hanson 2008).[2]

They built new hospitals overnight and hailed the health care workers on the front lines as national martyrs. This led to quick resolution of the first global pandemic of the twenty-first century, not because of proven international measures but because of the very local type of response China is so well versed in crafting when faced with epidemic situations. Many have argued that SARS served as the wake-up call China needed to start prioritizing public health, and particularly, its burgeoning HIV epidemic.

There is no conclusive evidence showing that China's experience with SARS changed its attitude toward public health or HIV/AIDS but it does offer a lens into how China has responded to and administered its HIV epidemic and sheds light on those factors that can facilitate development of an appropriate local response to a global pandemic occurring in China. A look into how the government reacted to SARS and HIV will confirm that the themes of informal governance performed through networking, which have run throughout this book, are as important to the response waged against an epidemic as they can be for its generation. I begin with discussion of how international organizations approach global health concerns in local contexts and then go on to describe the response that China sees as appropriate within the context of its own sovereignty. The discussion highlights the value that local solutions offer to global problems.

Global Mobile Sovereigns and Local Needs

I first went to Ruili during the summer of 2002 to explore the possibility of doing ethnographic research on the HIV epidemic in the area. On that trip, I met with the director of the local Bureau of Health (*weisheng bu*). We met in a room on the second floor of an STI and HIV clinic that was established and operated as part of an internationally supported multisectoral project designed to respond to the HIV epidemic in Ruili. The center served as both a clinic and headquarters for the project. We met in the main office for the project, replete with the standard flowchart these types of projects produce to guide and monitor their progress. One wall was covered with pieces of red paper detailing the project's four main areas of focus: advocacy and awareness raising, capacity building, prevention and risk reduction, and treatment and care. They detailed the project timeline and structure, describing how one component of the project would flow into the next. As we sat down, the director of the Bureau of Health looked at the flowchart and said to me, "You see that? We can't do that here."

Accomplishing the goals of this project would require him and a very small staff of four or five people with no training in such technical aspects to provide community-based health education, clinical and psychological support, counseling, telephone information, outreach to both the Chinese and Burmese sex workers in Ruili, life development skills for vulnerable populations, peer education, and condom distribution. The five-year project also included capacity building for local personnel responsible for HIV/AIDS and STD prevention and care. It is often difficult, however, to translate the Western methods of capacity building that have become so popular among international development agencies into reality in local contexts (Milwertz and Wang 2013).

The director of the Bureau of Health was not only concerned about the ambitiousness of conducting such a comprehensive and technical project in his resource constrained area when he said "We can't do this here." He was also concerned about all the other challenges that international organizations do not and cannot take into account when designing programs. It is rare for clear-cut plans like the project this international organization brought to Ruili or even well-designed plans constructed at the provincial or central level of government in China to be simply executed as designed. A government bureau must be incentivized to execute such plans and see the benefit it can accrue from implementation. This requires a lot of negotiation and relationship building between levels of government. Local bureaucracies understand these hurdles, inherent in informal bureaucratic process, that stand between a project's design and its implementation. Even for the local public health bureau, reward comes from merely demonstrating a commitment to a new program mandated from the center. There is little incentive, however, to ensure such programs are effectively implemented. The international organizations bringing global health interventions to China are motivated by different intentions. They truly believe in the international best practices that have been scientifically proven to respond to HIV/AIDS. They too want their organizations to look good. But their ultimate mission is guided by a commitment to reducing HIV transmission. Most, however, do not understand the bureaucratic hurdles that stand between them and their public-health-related goals. In addition, the programs they bring, developed from within Western models and paradigms, are not necessarily appropriate for the local Chinese social and cultural context where they are to be implemented.

The people who staff global health organizations have become what Arjun Appadurai (1996) calls "mobile sovereigns," people who carry a set of skills and knowledge that the scientific and public health community have deemed to be transferrable from one location to another. International interference in public health is a relatively new phenomenon as health has been reconfig-ured as a human right rather than a tool in securing global trade. Aside from introducing the idea of health for all, these mobile sovereigns also bring direct challenges to state sovereignty through calls to adhere to international norms, ethical principles, and standard technical descriptions of how to eradicate poverty and improve health, despite the often unrealistic goals of implement-ing these norms locally (Fidler 2003, Clark 1995, Ferguson and Gupta 2002, Bashford 2006, Brown, Cueto, and Fee 2006, Pandolfi 2003). After all, they are supported by evidence that acts as a modern currency to justify the common measurements and standards used in global public health programs. Such evi-dence is used to create routine paths of connection, which can theoretically be applied in the states that these mobile actors now seemingly supersede. Such a shift has transformed hygiene into a matter of knowledge about bio-logical risk and the scientific evidence and standards that can reduce such risk. Rarely, however, do these sovereigns consider the relationships between the social elements that produce scientific knowledge and standards in one context to those that determine their acceptance and eventual use in another (Pigg 2001). The actors who carry these scientific methods from one coun-try to another epitomize what Giorgio Agamben (1998) describes as a "bare life," stripping the people and communities they work with of their individual identities so they can be viewed from the more efficient level of the popula-tion, where they are aggregated into demographic categories or within neatly labeled subpopulations deemed as most at-risk. Public health is meant to serve the public, but the science that serves as its foundation sits "above and outside the polis" (Patton 1990: 70). This often challenges the effectiveness of pubic health interventions because they must be implemented within a social, cul-tural, and political context that cannot be wholly accounted for in the statisti-cal models that produced the evidence used in their design.

One mobile sovereign that I personally encountered came in the form of a six-and-a-half-foot yellow cartoonlike condom. I worked very closely with a professionally trained Jingpo dancer when I was in Ruili to design perfor-mances that communicated messages to help prevent drug abuse and HIV among local Jingpo people. He had been trained as a dancer in Beijing at the prestigious Central Minorities University Dance Academy (*zhongyang minzudaxue wudao xi*) since the age of eleven and then went on to train as a modern dancer and founder of the first modern dance company in China. He returned to Ruili, just about the same time I arrived, to care for his aging mother and decided it was time to give back to his community, so he started a dance school. The school recruited poor, uneducated Dai and Jingpo youths from rural villages to train them and give them the necessary skills to pursue a career in dance. Such an ambitious plan needed funding, though, which is where I came in. He approached me to help find funding to support his goal. But I was familiar only with HIV funding, and I knew that donors would be open to funding a local program in one of China's most affected regions among the most affected community (the Jingpo). We discussed the seriousness of the HIV epidemic and the drug abuse epidemic in the Jingpo community and decided it would be a great idea to choreograph a performance using traditional Jingpo and Dai music and dance, which could deliver drug abuse and HIV-prevention messages to the ethnic minority villages in Dehong using a culturally compelling format (Panter-Brick et al. 2006) traditionally used to deliver important messages to the community.

This idea for a locally generated prevention program sold like hotcakes to donors. We first pitched the idea to a foreign social marketing organization based in Kunming that regularly sold condoms and conducted harm-reduction trainings in Ruili. They supported the choreography, costumes, and first performance, which happened at the big World AIDS Day celebration in the Ruili town square. There was one small string attached, though. The organization was launching a campaign at that time to encourage people to wear condoms 100 percent of the time with all their sex partners. In Chinese they would say *qing ni meiyici dai shang wo* (please wear me every time). Their ambassador was the giant six-and-a-half-foot yellow cartoon character in the shape of a condom, and the organization made the funding contingent on the character emerging at some point during the performance to deliver his message. The performance, for the most part, was a mixture of traditional Dai and Jingpo dance, music, and poetry written to express a message of danger and concern around drugs. But the happy yellow mobile sovereign of 100 percent condom use always briefly interjected in the middle of each performance. The audience of course noticed the big yellow thing that came out on stage dancing around and spreading its gospel, but they wondered what it was and why it was disturbing the traditional ethnic music and dance they were enjoying. It was called "super baby" (*chaoji baobao*) in the performance because the government prohibited the dance troupe from using the words *condom* and *sex* in the performance. After all, they said, there are children in the audience, so we can't allow you to talk about such things.

This type of campaign grows out of the paradigms of risk and knowledge that international organizations use to prevent HIV infection. They turn this knowledge into a set of acronyms. There is information, education, and communication (IEC), little pamphlets filled with information about HIV that are merely translated from one language to another without consideration of the applicability or feasibility of the terminology used in the pamphlets. The same text written in a Chinese IEC pamphlet in Ruili is translated into Jingpo and Dai, but the caricatures are changed to reflect either a Han, Dai, or Jingpo person, indicated with appropriate clothes and headdress. Aside from the IEC, organizations conduct a PRA (participatory rapid appraisal) to encourage local participation in the initial assessment of community needs before designing a program, and they use KAPB (knowledge, attitudes, perceptions, and beliefs) surveys to evaluate their effects. But the whole alphabet soup of program elements results in programs that rely on international paradigms, representing what one local Yunnanese social scientist described to me as an imperial force imposing its own ideas over the needs and ideas of the local community.

These imperialist influences also cross over boundaries of practice into discourse. Local people affected by and working with HIV/AIDS have not only learned to implement internationally designed programs but also adopted the vernacular that dominates global discussions around HIV/AIDS. They use terms like *advocacy* and *harm reduction* so they can engage in global conversations (and benefit from global sources of funding), but few fully understand the meaning of these terms, which have just recently entered the lexicon in China. The Chinese language does not even inherently include a term for advocacy, a type of action that does not develop in a culture where government is responsible for meeting all public needs. This posed challenges to organizations working to service the HIV positive community. Interaction with the global HIV community taught them about advocacy, but it was difficult to bring these ideas back to China in the absence of even a term to describe the ideas they were hoping to transfer. Those who do speak and understand English have learned to toggle between the global community and their Chinese comrades. They do promote advocacy around HIV in China and have even translated the term into Chinese, but that lexical translation is accompanied by a practical translation of the process into a type of advocacy

PHOTO 6.1 Dancing condom character. Photo by author.

that can be successfully implemented under such a strict authoritarian regime that associates advocacy with activism that can undermine the state.

Global discourse emphasizing the important role that harm reduction can play in reducing HIV infection among injection drug users has assumed a similar hegemonic position in HIV-related vernacular. We rarely hear the term *harm reduction* outside the HIV field, but in fact, the types of practices that help to reduce the harm associated with certain societal risks are critical parts of popular health cultures globally, particularly in Asia and China (Nichter 2003). There is a huge industry around *baojian pin* (health protection products) in China that purports to protect people from all manner of risk to their health. One of the men I knew in Ruili regularly drank a powdered mixture of herbs to protect his liver from the effects of his drinking with government officials. It is also common for sex workers in China and other parts of Asia to take monthly prophylactic injections of penicillin to prevent STIs. So the idea of harm reduction is not new, but it has now been appropriated as new within the HIV field. Harm reduction was integrated into HIV discourse in 2005 when the UN Millennium Project endorsed needle exchange and opiate substitution as a vital control measure for the global HIV pandemic. These measures also promote advocacy for policies that reduce the stigma and discrimination of illicit drug users and promote their human rights as a way to protect their health and the health of others. They also extend to information and education about safe sex, outreach and peer education, and voluntary counseling and testing (VCT) for HIV (Centre for Harm Reduction 2006, IHRD 2006, UN Millennium Project 2005).

The Chinese government initiated its own harm-reduction program in 2004. They first piloted a few clean needle exchange sites with support from the UK Department for International Development (DFID). The government has been much more comfortable supporting methadone maintenance therapy (MMT) as a form of harm reduction, though, because of an ideological opposition to providing people with the equipment necessary for injecting illicit drugs. The Chinese CDC and local bureaus of health opened up approximately eight hundred methadone clinics within a matter of three years beginning in 2005. But global harm-reduction programs have not been successful in China despite the complicity of the local public health workers responsible for their implementation. As one harm-reduction implementer once mentioned, "Harm reduction is not totally suitable for China." Indeed, the program has not been successful despite the hundreds of methadone clinics that are operated around China because of a lack of trained human resources and the grassroots community support that is so crucial to the success of global harm-reduction programs (Sullivan and Wu 2007). Global harm-reduction programs for HIV are also not appropriate ideologically for China. They are founded on the basis of Western individualism, which is hard to sell to a collectivist culture. I had a chance to observe this clash of philosophy when I asked the same organization that spawned the big yellow condom character to come to Ruili to offer some training to the young dancers who were performing to prevent drug abuse and HIV. I thought it would be helpful for them to understand a bit more about the disease they were working to prevent. However, I naïvely did not realize I had set them up for three days of indoctrination into the Western way of thinking about disease prevention.

The training the performers received was the same harm-reduction training this organization offered to incarcerated drug users in Yunnan's compulsory detoxification centers. The trainers arrived with all the standard pre-programmed materials they used with other groups to provide a general introduction to HIV, including a basic scientific presentation of the virus and how it is transmitted. But the three days primarily emphasized harm reduction as a good way for preventing HIV transmission (after all, the training was designed for drug users). They began the discussion of harm reduction by posing a question to the young dancers, "What does harm reduction mean to you?" This prompted responses that drew on the performers' own cultural background, which stressed social order over individual good. The idea of harm reduction, a term that was foreign to them, incited thoughts of reducing harm to society by stopping drug use, rather than protecting the rights of drug users. Instead of working with the students to help them negotiate the space between these two conceptions of harm reduction or to realize what harm reduction means in Chinese society and how it is played out (which would have been very important, given that these students were responsible for translating messages about a global pandemic to the very local audiences that were most severely affected in China), the trainers quickly dismissed the performers' perspectives and dictated the internationally accepted idea of harm reduction as a principle that promotes the reduction of negative health consequences associated with drug use. The trainers saw this as a necessary intervention to help them progress through their schedule, yet it failed to help the students realize how they could use this principle of harm reduction to help people in their community who suffered from the effects of drug abuse and HIV.[3]

The international NGOs that enter China and other developing countries to provide technical support have the power to act as mobile sovereigns because of their convening power and their ability to attract the necessary aid to promote public health and other development projects. But they typically offer technical support that is not appropriate for the local community (Clark 1995, Spires 2012, Milwertz and Wang 2013). They promote messages that give local communities the functional ability to prevent disease through promotion of knowledge, but do not allow them to develop the critical abilities to develop programs that can furnish a culturally compelling reason to work toward prevention (Ruotao Wang 2000, Panter-Brick et al. 2006). It is locally generated responses, though, that prove more effective in changing the behaviors that place people at risk for HIV infection (Parker 2000, Altman 1994). Instead, Western organizations set up drop-in centers where drug users and sex workers can meet and support each other. But as one Chinese employee of an international organization that promoted drop-in centers told me, they don't work because they are so foreign. A better approach, he said, would promote development of a center modeled after an indigenous Chinese institution. But unfortunately, the international powers that have gained ownership over these evidence-based methods shun local adaptations of international practices and discourse. I first noticed this at a training program that a U.S.-based university organized to teach government officials about the common discourses and techniques used in global HIV prevention. The program included information about the ABC (abstinence, be faithful, and condom) discourse that the George W. Bush administration popularized and that was associated with successful reduction of HIV incidence in Uganda. Direct translation into Chinese was difficult, though, and perhaps not wholly appropriate for China. So one of the presenters, who grew up in China but had lived and worked in the U.S. public health field for a long time, modified the saying to a format that a Chinese audience could readily understand and accept. For him, ABC was *tuishi yao* (put off sexual desires), *bu luangao* (literally, don't do anything wild, but it implies don't have sex outside the home), *daishang tao* (wear a condom). This innovative translation rhymed and sounded quite lighthearted in Chinese, even if straying slightly from the original intent of ABC discourse. But it was delivered in a mode that easily communicated with the audience. Yet the American organizer reprimanded the Chinese deliverer of the message for not appropriately representing ABC discourse, despite the fact that it probably would have fallen on deaf ears if he had attempted to translate it literally.

In other instances, I have seen ethnic minority communities draw on indigenous aspects of their culture to develop responses to the drug abuse that threatens their community. With support from an international funder, the anthropologist Zhuang Kongshao (2002) produced a visual ethnography of a shamanistic ritual that the Yi in Xiao Liangshan in Sichuan Province use to detoxify members of the community who have been affected by an evil agent. The film depicts the chanting, animal slaughter, and imbibing of the animal's blood within the community and family that precedes the passing of the harmful humors from the addicted victim to the dead animal. In doing so, it clearly describes the cultural challenges and requirements needed to fight injection drug use in such a community. Such culturally specific messages, however, are difficult to integrate into global public health programs that are designed to respond to scientific and not cultural evidence. Consequently, Xiao Liangshan remains heavily affected by drug use and HIV infection.

I also visited a Jingpo village in Dehong where women joined together to literally beat the men in their village into giving up drugs. Drug use affected almost every household in this village, to the point where the men had become visibly absent. The women, in response, formed what they called the Women's Community Protection and Mutual Assistance Team (WCPMAT). Every night the women involved in the WCPMAT took turns patrolling the village in search of drug users and drug dealers. They even raided people's homes at night if they suspected the presence of a drug user or drug dealer. Jingpo society, as I have noted previously, prioritizes the wellbeing of the collective and these women took it upon themselves to protect that collective nature of the community. The drug users they caught were confined and placed in the WCPMAT self-designed drug rehabilitation program, set up in a local home. At this point, the women reverted from their aggressive role of community protectors back to their revered role in Jingpo society as mothers and caretakers. Their aim was to repair their broken society through combating the harmful effects that had resulted from injection drug use (Xu 2006). They did this by using their respected role as the society's caretakers to repair relationships and heal the community. In the end, the rate of recidivism among drug users remained high, but this village is unique in Dehong in getting drug users into some sort of rehabilitation program. Public health workers who work in Dehong have repeatedly told me about the difficulties in getting ethnic minority drug users (the most affected sector of the population) into methadone clinics. But the men in this village felt more comfortable in a familiar environment where they could speak freely, make jokes, and receive equal treatment with other members of their society, rather than in a punitive government detoxification center, where they are often mistreated, or even in a methadone clinic, where they are still vulnerable to police harassment. I am not advocating blanket use of shamanistic rituals or spousal beating as effective means for HIV prevention, but these local initiatives focus a lens on the types of cultural scenarios required to create functional literacy around HIV prevention in these local areas and are a testament to the value of actively engaging communities in the design of programs that can be culturally compelling (Panter-Brick et al. 2006, Ruotao Wang 2000).

Disease Response with Chinese Characteristics

The Importance of Rhetoric and Propaganda

SARS represented the party's first demonstration during the post-Mao era that health was a crucial element in preserving and promoting the country's goals. In April 2004 the party issued this statement:

> The Party Central Committee and the State Council attach great importance to the serious disease that now confronts the Chinese nation. A string of important measures were adopted at the many meetings they held to study ways and means to deal with the epidemic. On April 17, the CCP Central Committee Political Bureau Standing Committee called an ad hoc meeting to hear some departments' reports and plans about controlling atypical pneumonia. The meeting stressed: Controlling atypical pneumonia has a close bearing on the people's physical health and safety, and also on the country's reform and development as a whole. (Department of Propaganda of the Central Committee of the Chinese Communist Party 2004)[4]

This statement was indicative of the demonstrations of commitment typical of high-level Chinese leaders responding to a party priority. Aside from rhetoric this demonstration manifested itself in visits to the staff of the scientific research institutes working to find a cure for SARS, as well as to the staff at the Chinese CDC, which was responsible for surveillance, and the nurses on the front lines at Beijing's infectious disease hospitals. All were thanked and shown appreciation for their dedication to protecting the country's health and wellbeing. Premier Wen Jiabao showed further concern through visits to universities, middle and primary schools, and kindergartens in order to inspect and understand the health conditions affecting the public at that time. This type of posturing and rhetoric is an important part of the bureaucratic response to any crisis situation in China. For the public it is evidence that the government does care about their welfare, and for the government it is an equally important mechanism for maintaining the social stability (*shehui wending*) and national security (*guojia anquan*) it relies on for China's continued growth and economic development.

The type of rhetoric that blossomed around SARS did not stop after the epidemic ended. Government officials continued uttering similar messages in support of HIV/AIDS, the other and more long-term epidemic the international community had persuaded China to confront in public. It is the sudden rise in rhetoric and propaganda around HIV/AIDS that led to popular beliefs that SARS had catalyzed China's newfound commitment to its HIV epidemic. In June 2004, a year after the SARS epidemic was declared over, Wang Longde, then vice-minister of health, announced: "The government in emphasizing its work to prevent and treat HIV/AIDS has established basic policies of HIV prevention and treatment that prioritize prevention, prioritize education and propaganda, link prevention and treatment, treat the disease by tackling both its root cause and symptoms, and tackle it in a comprehensive way." HIV/AIDS was still a government priority more than a year later, when Wang Longde further emphasized, "The State Council very much prioritizes the work to prevent and control HIV/AIDS. It will be associated with the strategic issues of the country's economic development, social stability, national security, as well as the rise and decline of the nation and must be brought into line with the important agenda of the government's work" (2005). This official rhetoric was accompanied by the official posturing similar to what we saw during the SARS epidemic. Wen Jiabao commemorated World AIDS Day 2003[5] with a visit to HIV-positive patients at the Ditan Hospital. He also acknowledged the serious situation in Henan with a visit to an HIV-affected village during Chinese New Year in 2004. The ultimate statement and demonstration of personal sacrifice, however, came when Hu Jintao shook hands with two AIDS patients at the You'an Hospital's Home of Loving Care (*aixin jiayuan*).[6] The government made it seem as if these events were planned intentionally, but the decision to make these public outpourings of official sacrifice could have been strongly influenced by a serendipitous event that occurred at an International Summit on HIV/AIDS and SARS held at Tsinghua University in November 2003. Former President Bill Clinton, who gave the keynote speech at the seminar, called up the only HIV-positive person in the audience after answering a question from him, which precipitated the photo that made the front pages of both Chinese and American newspapers the next day—something totally unexpected, given that HIV-positive people were expressly not invited to the seminar. This prompted the first handshake, however, between a Chinese official and an HIV-positive person and is thought to have precipitated the gestures on the part of Hu Jintao and Wen Jiabao in the following months.[7]

This also marked the party's firm commitment to ensuring that all levels of government would prioritize HIV/AIDS in their efforts. During his visit to the You'an Hospital, Hu Jintao announced, "Recently under the direction of

PHOTO 6.2 Former U.S. president Bill Clinton met with a Chinese AIDS patient Song Pengfei (right) during his visit to the Tsinghua University for a summit on HIV-AIDS in China November., 2003 [newsphoto/file] [China Daily]

the Central Party and the State Council, the country's leaders have worked tirelessly to achieve positive results in work on the prevention and control of HIV/AIDS. But we must also realize that the country is in an urgent state of need for HIV prevention and control. The entire party and entire society must progress in prioritizing in earnest the completion of its HIV/AIDS prevention and control work." Similar to the high-level commitment demonstrated toward SARS, this type of rhetoric from the party central signaled identification of HIV as a national priority and finally opened up the space for a public health response to the epidemic, which was not possible in the absence of the party's support (Saich 2006a).

Suddenly, HIV, which had been the victim of government cover-ups, was highlighted as a priority necessary for protecting social stability and national security. The State Council formed the State Council AIDS Working Committee, followed by the council's release of a comprehensive policy framework for HIV/AIDS prevention and control called Document 7 (*State Council Notice* . . . 2004), which defined the roles for every sector of government in preventing the spread of HIV. For example, the country's railroad, transportation, and airline systems were expected to promote information to travelers. I noticed this when I flew out of the Kunming airport, which, for about one year between 2004 and 2005, issued boarding passes with red ribbons on the back coupled with the message "We should all work together to prevent HIV" (*yufang aizibing ni wo tong canyu*), followed by two hotline numbers. Bureaus of culture and industry and commerce were responsible for ensuring dissemination of HIV information into the country's entertainment establishments.[8] This directive from the party central transformed the rhetoric and posturing Hu Jintao and Wen Jiabao had demonstrated at AIDS hospitals and villages into concrete evidence of the country's commitment to fighting its HIV epidemic. Suddenly, every Chinese official I met, whether involved in health or not, sputtered the same rhetoric when I mentioned my work. They would say, "AIDS, yes, it is a national priority" (*zhong yang zhengfu hen zhongshi aizibing*). They could also all rattle off the three modes of HIV transmission recognized in official Chinese rhetoric.

Document 7 was followed by a more comprehensive plan specifically addressing necessary measures for HIV prevention among people with high-risk behavior (*gaowei xingwei*; *Guide for Work . . . 2004*). This plan set expectations for the public health apparatus and CDCs at every bureaucratic level to establish working teams (*gongzuo dui*) responsible for conducting comprehensive local surveys designed to promote understanding of people with high-risk behaviors. This plan also included appropriate methods for measures of intervention among specifically designated high-risk groups.

Document 7, and indeed a large proportion of funding for HIV/AIDS in China, stressed the role of the media in disseminating information to society. *Xuanchuan,* or media in the form of propaganda, has been central to the government's goal of educating both party and nonparty members in communist ideology since the CCP came to power in 1949. Mao initiated a series of Patriotic Health Campaigns (*weisheng yundong*), which instructed people to "clean the house before inviting the guests"—clean it of all the flies, rats, and pests that plagued the country (Hanson 2008, Brady 2008, Horn 1969)—and helped to rid China of its image as the Sick Man of Asia.

The Council for Patriotic Health Campaigns (*aiguo weisheng yundong weiyuanhui*), which spearheaded health-related propaganda campaigns during the early communist era, is still active in designing propaganda around crucial public health issues such as SARS and HIV/AIDS. These campaigns not only promote public education (*xuanchuan jiaoyu*) around disease but also maintain face for the party in the wake of such epidemics. The government was implicated in the rise of SARS because of the cover-ups that were tied to its escalation. An aggressive propaganda campaign turned opinions around, however, and the government emerged from SARS as an effective agent for ending the first pandemic of the twenty-first century. In this era of epidemics that are often tied to government culpability, propaganda has become a very useful tool for distilling such opinions and regulating information in a way that once again ensures the public of the government's concern for their wellbeing.

The propaganda of the twenty-first century replaces revolutionary-looking figures with more popular faces that command attention in post-Mao China. The famous actor Pu Cunxin became an early HIV/AIDS ambassador for the Chinese government, urging people to "live and let live" (*huxiang guanai, gongxiang shengming*) and promoting voluntary counseling and testing (VCT). Pu shared his role with actress Xu Fan and the famous singer Peng Liyuan, who is also known as Xi Jinping's wife. Pu's photo was found on HIV prevention propaganda around China, and for a while in 2004 and 2005 billboards of Pu Cunxin and Xu Fan urging people to learn more about HIV/AIDS lined the walls of Beijing's subway tunnels as well as the system's cars. Larger versions of the same billboards appeared throughout China's airports, spreading the gospel about the party's three officially recognized modes of HIV transmission: sexual contact (defined as multiple sexual partners), blood (defined as sharing equipment to inject drugs, using unsanitary injection equipment, or infusing blood that has not been checked), and mother-to-child transmission. These three official modes of HIV transmission were drilled into the minds of the Chinese public. This type of propaganda subsequently helped Wang Longde fulfill his mission of educating the public about HIV, because almost anyone I asked about HIV/AIDS would say to me, "Oh yes, I know about AIDS—there are three modes of transmission: *xing jiechu* (sexual contact), *xueye* (blood), *muyin chuanbo* (mother-to-child transmission)." But knowledge and understanding of HIV did not expand beyond the official propaganda messages.

The government and party propaganda and posturing around HIV/AIDS does little to actually educate the public about the epidemic, but that is not its prime purpose. The party promotes propaganda as a means of ensuring public support through creating a favorable public opinion and public image (Brady 2008). Just as the strong response to SARS ended in a hearty round

PHOTO 6.3 This poster featuring the famous actors Pu Cunxin and Xu Fan was displayed in the Beijing subway and taught people about voluntary counseling and testing (VCT). Photo by author.

of applause, the government's newfound propaganda and rhetoric around HIV/AIDS following the SARS crisis created renewed opinions as to a government that cares about the people and is doing all it can to respond to the HIV epidemic. When I first arrived in Ruili in late 2003, people said to me, "The government doesn't care about AIDS and it doesn't care about protecting us from the disease either; if they cared, there would be propaganda in the streets, on television, on the radio, and in the newspapers." After the government started erecting HIV-related billboards (one occupied the full view of a friend's kitchen window) in March 2004, people appreciated the effort on the government's part to inform them about the dangers of HIV/AIDS.

Suddenly Ruili's lampposts were flanged with banners promoting HIV/AIDS slogans. The government also erected big billboards on roads throughout the prefecture. But the local government was responsible for designing and producing their own billboards, which weren't nearly as flashy as the billboards I saw on display in the Beijing subway. The pictures of Pu Cunxin and Xu Fan were replaced with bucolic beach scenes of purity and young people looking hopefully toward the future. The instructive education on modes of HIV transmission was replaced with standard slogans more reminiscent of traditional Chinese propaganda. Posters with messages in Chinese, Dai, Jingpo (Dehong's three official languages), and English cautioned people to "Preserve Your Purity, Keep Off Drugs, Prevent AIDS" (*jieshen ziai, yuanli dupin, yufang aizibing*) and "Be Concerned for Our Youth, Prevent AIDS" (*guanzhu qingshaonian, yufang aizibing*). The billboards also paid homage to global AIDS slogans such as "Men Make a Difference" (*yufang aizibing, nanshi ze wupang dai*). There was an especially puzzling billboard, though, aimed at promoting condom use. Graphically, it was covered with bronze figures portraying athletic male bodies (see Photo 6.4). Its message read *anquantao fang aizi, "xing" fu you jiankang* (condoms prevent AIDS and allow you to enjoy a healthy sex life). There followed an English translation. I'm not sure why the government felt compelled to translate, but of course, as is typical with English translations on Chinese signage, this one was done cryptically and ended up unintelligible to any native English speaker. The translation read, "Condom Prevents AIDS Happy 'Sex' Life and To Se Healthy."[9] The bottom of the billboard reminded people (in Chinese only) to "use a condom. It is not only a contraceptive, it also prevents HIV transmission" (*shiyong anquantao, ji biyun, you fang aizibing*).[10]

These new campaigns served to show the public that the government now cared about protecting their health. But perhaps even more importantly for the government's image were the accolades that came from the international community, which had been impatiently waiting for the Chinese government to respond to its HIV epidemic. The very public appearances made by China's highest leaders and the strong statements made by their policy arms and health ministers were recognized and applauded by the same international actors who previously reprimanded China for its slow response to the epidemic. In October 2004, I participated in an informal roundtable of local HIV activists and people living with HIV and AIDS held for the benefit of an official Canadian Foreign Affairs delegation. This delegation, which came to China on a human rights mission that included official discussions about HIV/AIDS, was impressed by the government's increased efforts to address the epidemic. From her observations, the head of the delegation believed the Chinese government had placed greater emphasis on its HIV problem, as demonstrated through the heightened commitment of funds dedicated to the problem. Few of the international actors who peer in from Washington, Geneva, or other international home bases have the ability to look beyond the government's rhetoric, though. In the next section, I explore some of the policies at the central level that led to these international accolades, as well as the challenges of truly operationalizing these policies at the local level.

PHOTO 6.4 Billboard from Dehong Prefecture's HIV Prevention Propaganda Campaign. Photo by author.

Getting Beyond the Rhetoric

The government rhetoric and posturing around HIV/AIDS following the SARS crisis was accompanied with concrete policies, but it was a challenge to effectively implement the policies. The State Council announced China's first comprehensive policy in response to HIV, known as the Four Frees and One Care Policy, in late 2003. This policy guaranteed free anti-retroviral treatment to HIV-infected rural residents as well as urban residents facing financial difficulties (*jingji kunnan*), free voluntary counseling and testing, free prophylactic treatment for mother-to-child transmission of HIV and testing of newborn babies, free schooling for AIDS orphans, and care for households affected by HIV/AIDS (in the form of direct financial assistance). The Four Frees and One Care Policy formed the backbone of China's central-level plan to fight HIV/AIDS and represented what Vice-Minister Wu Yi called "the most powerful strategic measure available to China for preventing and treating HIV/AIDS." For many, however, this bold policy represented little more than another level of rhetoric that helped to promote a positive image of a government that now cared about HIV/AIDS. The central government had little authority in ensuring implementation of the new policy at the local levels, where governments often have limited resources and motivation to execute unfunded mandates.

I first heard of the Four Frees and One Care Policy in late 2003, when the State Council publicly announced it. Foreign observers and public health workers applauded the government for creating this initiative, which they saw as China's crossroads in the battle against its HIV epidemic. But while I was discussing the benefits of this new policy with foreign colleagues, many of whom lived and worked at the central level of power in Beijing, the bureaucrats responsible for responding to the epidemic where it occurs (at the local level) had never heard of the policy, at least officially, which is what would allow them to act on the policy. The government bureaucrats in charge of HIV in Dehong Prefecture were first officially informed of the Four Frees and One Care at a provincial-level meeting held in Kunming in August 2004, eight months after the central government announced the policy. They excitedly reported announcement of this new policy to me after they returned from the meeting. Suddenly Dehong would be able to respond to their HIV epidemic, but this response could have come sooner had China's vertical system of bureaucracy functioned in a way that prioritized social policies including those related to health. Challenges still remained, though, because of the fiscal devolution, which has challenged provision of health care since the initiation of market reforms.

From Full Health Care to Fragmented Health Care

The Communist Party fulfilled an ambitious goal of shaking off its reputation as the Sick Man of Asia after its ascent to power in 1949. Much of this is due to the patriotic health campaigns that fought against endemic disease. This sizeable accomplishment is also attributable to the development of a health care system that served 90 percent of the population. The early Communist government developed a Cooperative Medical Scheme (CMS), a three-tiered health care system that provided a broad spectrum of services from basic primary care to more sophisticated tertiary care at the county village and township level. The CMS succeeded in large part because of the financing scheme developed to fund services. Developed under a system of communes and collectivism, the CMS took in a small part of its funds from individual households. Local collectives subsidized the schemes with additional funding from the local finance department. The CMS not only enabled rural access to health care but also established a sound financial basis for operating and maintaining a broad network of health care facilities (Feng et al. 1995, Tang and Squire 2004).

Dismantling of the collectivist system in favor of an individual house-hold registration system decentralized the provision of fiscal outlays for public goods and services. Central government priorities that now focus on developing the market leave little priority for funding health care or health facilities, which has become the responsibility of subnational governments. Township and village governments no longer collect resources from the local community to fund provision of public goods but instead must raise their own resources to support these services. They also depend on outlays from their provincial governments. Unfortunately, discretionary power for trans-ferring resources for health and education to the lowest levels of government frequently deprives local governments of the necessary resources to support the programs and policies they are expected to implement. Provincial govern-ments often retain a disproportionate amount of revenue generated within the province, forcing local governments to restrict their provision of public goods and services. This has created a huge rift among national goals, which serve to protect the image of the country; provincial goals; and lower-level bureau-cratic goals, which have forced local officials to weigh their responsibility to provide public goods against their ability to raise the necessary resources to do so (Brixi et al. 2013, Saich 2008).

This became evident to me when the State Council identified two prefec-tures to represent model AIDS prevention sites (*yufang aizibing zhongdian*) in 2004. The two sites, Dehong and Zhumadian in Henan Province, were the most affected prefectures in the country and, as such, were crucial to dem-onstrating the effectiveness of the country's new plans to combat HIV/AIDS. Their identification came with a direct injection of funds from the State Coun-cil to the prefectural government, effectively bypassing the standard vertically organized fiscal pathway that typically funnels resources through the provin-cial level. This ensured the State Council that all their funds for HIV/AIDS prevention and treatment in these prefectures would reach the prefectural government, thus preventing the provincial government from siphoning off any of the funds. The direct injection of funds also coincided with initiation of USAID's (United States Agency for International Development) HIV/AIDS prevention programs in southwestern China. The agency had negotiated a program with the Yunnan government to provide technical support to both Dehong and Honghe prefectures.[11] But the plan suddenly changed as U.S. gov-ernment officials arrived to sign the MOU in Kunming. Provincial officials said to them, in essence, there is no need to include Dehong Prefecture in the agreement because they have just received a direct injection of funds from the central government. The U.S. officials were perplexed. Their program offered few fiscal resources, and mostly technical support, directed at one of the most affected areas in the country. It was clear, however, that this was done in protest of the State Council's decision, which routed a large fiscal outlay around the province.

Fiscal decentralization, which places responsibility for funding public goods in the hands of provincial and local governments, has created a great imbalance in the provision of health care because there is so much provincial discretion over the distribution of the funds needed to support these services. Demands from higher-level governments carry little authority when they are not coupled with the resources to support implementation of those policies (Lieberthal 1992). This gives local governments the autonomy to decide which services they are willing to provide. This is further complicated by the fact that local governments are no longer accountable to the national government, under a decentralized fiscal system, for their performance related to many national-level policies (Feng et al. 1995, Tang and Squire 2004, Brixi et al. 2013). This occurs in all manner of health care, not just in the highly publicized and politicized field of HIV/AIDS. Tuberculosis patients entitled to free testing and treatment are often uninformed of their rights, which allows doctors and hospitals to charge them for drugs and send them for unnecessary tests. This is the result of a system that requires hospitals to make available government-guaranteed services but also support themselves financially. A similar story occurred with local implementation of the Four Frees and One Care Policy. The central government designed a comprehensive policy that demonstrated its care and concern for those affected by HIV/AIDS. But local levels of government were both operationally and fiscally responsible for supporting implementation of the policy. They had little ability to implement the policy without the financial resources to do so, particularly provision of financial aid to families affected by HIV/AIDS. Implementation was further complicated because the Four Frees and One Care is designated as a policy. The central government has the authority to enforce only legal statutes, not policy. There was little incentive for local governments to implement the policy beyond the outlays furnished by the central government. Free treatment was offered through the central CDC, but procurement was dependent on local efforts. Consequently, only twenty thousand people were taking the anti-retroviral medications needed to control the level of HIV in their blood two years after announcement of the Four Frees and One Care Policy. The government also provided free testing, but hospitals often prescribed other unnecessary tests and services that could command a fee. HIV testing has suffered as well because local governments are responsible for maintaining the testing facilities built under the policy (Saich 2008).

As these situations demonstrate, provision of public goods, including health services, is much more dependent on China's incentive mechanism than on the announcement of policy or even national priorities. Hu Jintao and Wen Jiabao's public appearances with HIV-infected people brought national attention to the epidemic, assigning it a privileged position within bureaucratic discourse at every level of government, but they did not assign it the level of importance that would sway local officials into creating results. Chinese officials primarily act in response to a target responsibility system (*mubiao guanli zeren zhi*), which evaluates them on the basis of a set of hard and soft priority targets. The political and performance contracts that set these targets prioritize maintenance of social order, which is often viewed as success in controlling the threat of heterodox groups and meeting family-planning quotas. The contracts place almost equal importance on an official's ability to meet hard targets like economic growth and expectations for tax revenue. Success in meeting these targets earns an official promotion and economic reward, so it is little wonder they expend most of their efforts in these areas and relatively little in ensuring provision of public goods (Saich 2002).

This system has resulted in very imbalanced provision of services from one locale to another. I often asked employees of the local CDC in Ruili why a prefecture in another part of the province seemed better equipped to offer more HIV/AIDS services despite the fact that Dehong had a much more mature and prevalent epidemic with a longer history of international assistance. They explained to me the discrepancy was not caused by need or experience but by variations in the local power structure. Governments with a stronger industrial base, which can contribute to the overall economic strength of the province, have historically had more leverage and power to supply services to the local populace in China (Huang 2004, Remick 2003, Saich 2006b). Other less-powerful governments respond more to the bureaucratic responsibility system, which does not reward officials for providing social goods and services. Their assessment of whether to implement a policy or program takes into account what they can gain from expending such effort and whether the effort is needed to satisfy evaluation from higher up in government (Huang

2004, Tang and Squire 2004). In the absence of such incentives, officials can receive positive evaluations for their work by demonstrating their commitment to a particular policy, but the government uses no specific measures to evaluate its outcomes.

Kate Mason (2011) illustrates this beautifully in her ethnography of the Shenzhen CDC. She shows how the CDC carefully reviews any directive from the Bureau of Health that comes in the form of a *wenjian* (official document) to determine if it is "crucial" to carry it out. The decision, she argues, is based on how much priority leaders at the level above the given CDC place on the project and partially on how much benefit the CDC receiving the *wenjian* can gain from implementing the directive. What is clear, she says, is that the decision to implement the directive bears little relation to its potential for producing an effective public health intervention. Both my examination of the design and implementation of measures to combat HIV in Yunnan and Mason's ethnographic portrayal of the Shenzhen CDC illustrate, however, that it is also quite simple for local CDCs and health-related bureaucracies to satisfy higher levels of government without actually producing results. Mason speaks of a measles vaccination campaign that the Shenzhen CDC undertook at the behest of the WHO. Any directive from the WHO had become a national priority at the time because of the international embarrassment China suffered at the hands of the WHO during the SARS epidemic, so the Shenzhen CDC made sure the campaign was carried out at all levels within the city. Shenzhen knew it could succeed in producing adequate results because they had already greatly reduced the number of measles cases in the city, by 60 percent during the year preceding this campaign. At the end they reported 100 percent compliance with their vaccine campaign, which is difficult to achieve in the best of situations. But, as in many cases, producing the data that met the expectations of the authority releasing the directive (in this case an international governing body capable of issuing extreme embarrassment) was more important than producing data about what was actually done. Production of data in China is not, as Susan Blum (2007) reminds us, about truth but rather about a "sincere attempt to please and meet the expectations of the receiver" (68). The importance here lay in "producing" the data that could satisfy the WHO because of the potential for embarrassment that could ensue. There was little incentive to rigorously carry out a campaign that could actually reduce the incidence of measles.

Following the State Council's prioritization of HIV, the Yunnan government similarly issued a directive that served to guide HIV prevention projects throughout the province. The "Notice from the General Office of the People's Government of Yunnan Province on Implementing Six Projects on HIV Prevention" (*yunnan renmin zhengfu banggongting guanyu shishi fangzhi aizibing liu xiang gongcheng de tongzhi,* hereafter referred to as the Notice) expected local governments to independently design projects that could (1) purify society and prevent and treat HIV/AIDS, (2) educate all people about HIV prevention and treatment, (3) promote condom use, (4) promote harm-reduction measures such as needle exchange and methadone replacement therapy, (5) establish care centers for people living with HIV/AIDS, and (6) conduct medical research and strengthen surveillance for prevention activities (*Yunnan renmin . . .* 2004). Not only did the Notice specify the types of projects it expected local governments to design, but it also instructed them in the methods for implementing these six types of projects by detailing the general and specific objectives of each, the appropriate government units for undertaking the implementing strategies and activities associated with each one, the action plan the unit should pursue while progressing toward the project's strategic goal, and the evaluation measures necessary for monitoring progress of the project. For example, implementation for Project One, which includes "cracking down on the high-risk behaviors that transmit HIV," is primarily assigned to the Public Security Bureau (PSB). The Notice identifies several objectives related to this project, among them a decline in the number of new drug users and growth in the number of former drug users who have not used in three or more years. This strategy, which is the responsibility of the Drug Enforcement Department (*jindu ban*), should be implemented through a widely publicized antidrug and HIV/AIDS prevention (*jindu fangai*) campaign, whose main activities include organization and expansion of antidrug and HIV/AIDS prevention campaigns and public education.

The expectations of Project Two, which encourages condom use, is designed in a similar manner, clearly stipulating the strategic, action, and evaluation components important for the project's implementation. However, a seemingly incomplete plan for implementation causes the project to fall short of its goal of encouraging condom use as an effective means of HIV prevention. This project, which promotes distribution of condoms in hotels, entertainment establishments, medical facilities, and drugstores through product placement and vending machines, is the primary responsibility of a condom promotion subgroup headed by the local family-planning committee and the PSB, in addition to the bureaus of culture, health, industry and commerce, drug supervision (similar to the American FDA), and tourism. Under this plan each cooperating bureau is assigned duties associated with its own function. The project is evaluated through nine key measures, including the number of condoms sold or distributed in each county and the number of condom dispensers or condoms placed in key areas.

The Notice represented a turning point in Yunnan and Dehong's response to HIV, ushering in what officials in charge of health in Ruili and Dehong described to me as "the Spring of HIV in Dehong Prefecture" (*Dehong zhou aizibing de chuntian*). Issuance of a directive from a higher level of government finally gave them the authority to launch what they perceived as an aggressive response to the epidemic, and the provincial government even gave them a framework to structure the program, which was funded by the direct injection of funds the prefecture had received from the State Council. Dehong's response began immediately following the announcement of the Notice with erection of all the various billboards and lamppost banners mentioned earlier. They also piloted three needle-exchange sites, opened a methadone clinic within a year, and designed a response to satisfy the requirements outlined by the provincial government, including a multisectoral condom promotion project coordinated between the seven requisite bureaus stipulated in the provincial Notice.[12] The local Family Planning Bureau (*jihua shengyu ju*) was placed in charge of coordinating the project because of its role as the only government bureau officially associated with condoms and condom distribution.[13] All the condoms had to undergo a process of quality control, though, which was the responsibility of the Bureau of Drug Supervision (*yaowu jiandu ju*).[14] They also organized social marketing of condoms to pharmacies, which they regularly monitored as part of their standard bureaucratic role. The project also involved the Bureau of Health (*weisheng ju*), which was tasked with training people in condom use and supplying free condoms to people living with HIV and AIDS. The Bureau of Industry and Commerce (*gongshang ju*) was responsible for supervising the placement and usefulness of the program in local entertainment and establishments, while the Bureaus of Culture (*wenhua ju*) and Tourism (*luyou ju*) were given responsibility for supporting, negotiating, and supervising implementation and usefulness of the condom promotion program in hotels and entertainment establishments. This was all performed under the oversight of the PSB (*anquan ju*), which was responsible for ensuring coordination between the Bureaus of Health and Family Planning and providing necessary information for the project's success (*Dehong Zhou renmin zhengfu bangongshi . . .* 2004).

The Dehong government designed a beautiful plan for distributing condoms, drawing on the roles and responsibilities of all the bureaus with authority over all the local places and mechanisms that governed condom distribution. Planning is easy in a country that is governed on the basis of well-crafted plans. Implementation, however, is a much larger challenge, particularly in a vertically structured bureaucratic environment that dissuades horizontal communication between bureaucratic units. But really the government needed to demonstrate its work only during the initial evaluation of the plan's implementation. The provincial- and national-level officials who came to inspect Dehong's work saw satisfactory evidence that Dehong was working to prevent HIV. They saw propaganda lining the streets (in fact, Dehong spent most of its direct injection of State Council funds on propaganda). They also saw one hundred condom vending machines installed in hotels throughout the prefecture. One of the high-level officials in the Dehong government took me to a hotel in the prefectural capital to proudly show me the brand new vending machine. The inspecting officials left with a positive impression of Dehong's work, and the Dehong officials in charge of the plan received positive evaluation of their work, which is what they sought. Despite the positive reviews, though, implementation of the plan was wrought with challenges that would preclude it from having any measurable impact. To begin, the condom vending machines that the Dehong official so proudly showed me were all installed in conspicuous locations in hotels, often near the main entrance. The condom machines, which were purchased from a company based in another part of China, also required a one yuan coin, which is rarely used in Dehong.[15] Stories quickly emerged as well about the many men who were reluctant to use condoms, whose purchase often incurred a fee posted on the hotel bill. Other men who were long-term residents in certain hotels did not want to reveal "abnormal" (*bu zhengchang*) activities to the women who cleaned the rooms, for fear of rumors that could sully their reputation. In addition, insufficient support for the hotel and entertainment establishment managers created problems for sustainability of the project because they were responsible for replenishing the supply of condoms once the initial supply was depleted. Meanwhile, the government made available neither a central distribution channel for quality assured condoms nor the funding to purchase them. Emphasis on supervision of condom promotion in hotels also allowed managers of entertainment establishments to ignore their responsibilities in this project. Many hotels did comply with the new regulations, but most entertainment establishments did not participate in condom promotion for fear it would associate them with illegal provision of sexual services inside their "entertainment" related business. Managers of entertainment establishments refused to attend training programs. Enforcing their participation wasn't necessary either, because the officials who came to inspect the local work entered only hotels and not entertainment establishments in order to avoid official recognition of the illegal activities conducted in such venues.

Dehong's plan served the Dehong officials; it improved their public image and earned them positive evaluation of their work. But there is little incentive to ensure effective implementation of a program unless its related outcomes are tied to an official's promotion or other benefits that can accrue to a government official. This was the case with Project One of Yunnan's Notice, which aimed to fulfill antinarcotic and HIV-prevention goals. Responsibility for this project within the Bureau of Drug Prohibition (*jindu ban*), which is governed under the PSB, connected this aspect of HIV prevention with protection of public security, which is essential to the country's goals of social harmony. *Jindu fangai* was thus carried out with the political fervor and dedication of the Patriotic Health Campaigns conducted during the 1950s. The campaign mobilized three thousand people from thirty-nine government work units around Dehong to once again "wage a people's war," as the government had done with SARS, but this time on drugs and HIV (*dupin he fang aizibing renmin zhanzheng*). Many government workers were relieved of their daily responsibilities for three months and organized into volunteer work teams (*gongzuo dui*) similar to those used in the Patriotic Health Campaigns, to go into the country side to conduct comprehensive local surveys that gave the government an understanding of people with high-risk behaviors. They collected information about poverty, incidence of drug use, and HIV infection. They also obtained public education about the dangers of drug use, drug trafficking, and HIV prevention. The program's true intention, though, was to purify the social environment (*jinghua shehui huanjing*), which is very important for reaching the party's goals. Government workers who were sent into the villages to carry out the work of the *jindu fangai* campaign told me they were really only expected to catch drug users.

Implementation of national-level policies, in the absence of official incentives, is often dependent more on complex interactions that structure elaborate deals and bureaucratic bargaining than on public interest (Saich 2002, Lieberthal 1992, Wang 1995). Political analysis speaks of bureaucratic bargaining, which can of course mean many things, but oftentimes *guanxi* making through *yingchou* is the most basic type of bureaucratic bargaining taking place between two levels of government or between bureaucratic agencies. I often saw members of the Bureau of Health at a karaoke bar with members of the Bureau of Quarantine, or other bureaus or levels of government whose cooperation they needed in implementing a program. Mason (2011) also closely observed the *guanxi* making necessary for motivating local public health officials to commit any effort to a public health program in her investigation of the Shenzhen CDC. She recounts routine inspections of a hospital malaria program that begin in the morning and last until late at night, when the members of the Shenzhen parasitology department are toasting the local hospital and vowing to work together to fight malaria. Nothing she witnessed during her fieldwork in Shenzhen, from a vaccine campaign to an HIV awareness event or a routine malaria inspection, happened without the necessary practices of *yingchou*, which allowed the people involved to build up the necessary *guanxi* to work together. Good *guanxi* networks, as she observed, were the only way local CDC officials could implement any public health directive issued by the local Bureau of Health, and thus most of the CDC employees she met viewed the *yingchou* practices necessary to build the *guanxi* required to complete their work as one of the most critical parts of their jobs. What Mason points out is that the public health system she observed was driven more by dyadic interactions between individuals than by a concern to produce public health results. From what I observed in Ruili and Dehong as well, it is power structures and the personal relations forming these structures that influence implementation of effective public health interventions much more than the national-level or even international-level goals to prevent or reduce disease incidence. Those looking to understand the administration of an epidemic in China, particularly the HIV epidemic, thus need look no further than the very mechanisms responsible for its generation.

Finding a Space for Nongovernmental Organizations in the Response to China's HIV Epidemic

Finally, no discussion of a response to an HIV epidemic can be complete without attention to the role of nongovernmental actors. Nongovernmental organizations (NGOs) have been crucial to the fight against HIV, shaping the initial social and political responses in almost every country and community that has confronted an HIV epidemic and often forcing governments, including the Chinese government, out of an initial stage of denial of their epidemic. NGOs have also been very effective in mobilizing around health care policies and programs to ensure their proper implementation (Parker 2009). Although there is equal need for these types of organizations globally, their role is limited in countries where "political society" is stronger than "civil society," leaving little space for development of community-level organizations (Altman 1994). China saw a huge spike in organizations outside the formal government sector that provide services related to education, prevention, and treatment of HIV/AIDS, following the government's recognition of its epidemic and subsequent entrance of foreign donors who uphold a model of HIV response informed by Western neoliberal traditions. The survival of many of these organizations has been threatened by the subsequent exit of many foreign donors and increasingly restrictive attitudes that have developed around civil society under the Xi regime. Funding for nongovernmental activities targeted at HIV/AIDS is now increasingly administered by the government. This underscores a need to reconceptualize our definition of NGO in China and the expectations for how these organizations respond to the local HIV epidemic in a society that has not yet developed the social or political culture to support the types of organizations that meet the international definitions and expectations of NGOs and civil society (Ma 2002).

Initiating discussion of NGOs in China is challenging, for many reasons. To begin, NGO is still a very sensitive term in China because of the government's skepticism of organizations that can subvert the party's goals. Consequently, organizations that operate outside the formal government structure register in various ways and are referred to by various terms. Organizations refer to themselves as *minjian zuzhi* (an organization of the people), *caogen zuzhi* (grassroots organization, also referred to as community-based organizations or CBOs),[16] *fei yingli zuzhi* (nonprofit organization), *shehui zuzhi/shehui tuanti* (social organization),[17] and *renmin tuanti* (people's organization). There is little understanding, however, of the variation between these categories, knowledge of which would be very helpful in clarifying the roles and abilities of each type. It is also difficult, however, to speak of NGOs in China because few organizations are truly nongovernmental. Many of the larger organizations can be referred to as GONGOs, government-operated NGOs. These organizations are typically operated by retired government officials and rely heavily on government funding. Nongovernmental HIV/AIDS work in much of China is overseen by the

China STD and AIDS Prevention Foundation, an organization legally registered as an NGO and run by a retired government official who was previously
responsible for China's HIV response. The organization has subordinate NGOs
in several provinces, among them Yunnan, where the former head of the Yunnan AIDS Working Group runs the Yunnan STD and AIDS Association. These
organizations receive most of their support from the government and so must
first meet government expectations. But once their work for the government is
finished, they can work with CBOs. The woman who runs the China STD and
AIDS Prevention Foundation very deliberately distinguishes between NGOs
and CBOs. NGOs are registered with the government as such, but CBOs can
be registered in various ways (as nonprofit organizations, or organizations of
the people). Some are even registered as businesses to avoid certain restrictions
on nongovernmental organizations, which are required to register under the
umbrella of an official sponsoring organization (*guakao danwei*), sometimes
referred to as a mother-in-law; and some are not registered at all. NGOs, as the
retired officials in charge of the China and Yunnan STD and AIDS Associations
told me, are legal and valuable organizations even in the eyes of the Chinese
government. In their perspective, other organizations such as CBOs are often
renegades that haphazardly develop overnight, operate with no mission to guide
them, and have few resources. People in official capacities have little tolerance
for such organizations.

This intermediate type of organization, presented in the form of a GONGO,
offers comfort to a government afraid of organizations that can subvert state
authority. The Chinese government has not outlawed organizations that exist
outside the state, but it has created a structure that asserts state control over
their operation. In the case of the China STD and AIDS Prevention associations, the government created a structure that could simultaneously satisfy
international donors who require their funds be transferred to local NGOs and
exert control over community organizations. These are safe organizations in the
eyes of the government, run by individuals who are still loyal to the party by virtue of their former career yet in a new role where they can legally interact with
organizations outside the government. But although this kind of arrangement
satisfied the Chinese government, foreign organizations eventually decided they
were not comfortable with the virtual government interception of funds that
were earmarked for nongovernmental organizations. Of the 172 projects that
the Global Fund to Fight AIDS, Tuberculosis and Malaria supported in Yunnan, only two were awarded to true independent NGOs.[18] The rest of their funds

supported GONGO-operated programs. This initially angered the Global Fund in 2010 and caused them to suspend funds for several months, before they eventually ceased operation in China at the end of 2013.

Support from the Global Fund and other international organizations that require direct funding to local CBOs or NGOs is further reminder that standard approaches to global health are not necessarily effective in the Chinese context. Most international organizations want to work within a familiar framework that they believe represents democracy and human rights. Only one senior international representative, who I spoke with in 2011, realized that international organizations must change their conception of the definition of NGO or CBO in order to work effectively in China because NGOs operate on a different basis and are often controlled by the government.

Unlike Europe, where state and society operate independently and often in opposition to one another, civil society in China can operate only as a "third realm" in an intermediate space between state and society, where the two can interact symbiotically with one another (Huang 1993, Chamberlain 1993). This intermediate state, also described as "consultative authoritarianism" (Teets 2013) or "contingent symbiosis" (Spires 2011), creates a system of social management where the state can assert control over organizations but also exist alongside them in a way that benefits the government.

The most successful organizations in this system work in a way that serves the party and avoids any appearance of working in opposition to the government. They also find ways to build strong relations with government and perform the tasks that government may otherwise not be able to accomplish. In this way, community and social organizations are neither wholly autonomous nor completely bound to the limitations of state agencies but can truly operate within a realm that proves beneficial to their government sponsors without posing any type of threat to their image (Mertha 2009, Hildebrandt 2013, Saich 2000). Many governments and community organizations have developed symbiotic relationships, much like those that political scientists have described between government and corporate entities, where businesspeople rely on government to accomplish their goals in exchange for some benefit to the officials as well. Local community organizations often serve an important role for government in carrying out unfunded central-level mandates or serving in a capacity that may conflict with the standard government roles accepted under Leninist philosophy. For example, organizations outside the government can provide services and interact with illicit populations like sex workers, which the government cannot legally recognize or approach within its official capacity. This offers government officials the opportunity to receive positive evaluations for their work without having to commit resources. It also benefits many grassroots organizations whose goals converge with government expectations, even those that operate illegally, because the government is willing to support the operation of any organization that is cooperative and can improve its image (Saich 2000, Spires 2011, Teets 2013, Gallagher 2004, Dickson 2002, Wank 1999).

The nature of this structure once again demonstrates the importance of relationships. Success, as Timothy Hildebrandt (2013) shows in his comparative study of social organizations in China, comes to those who know how to take advantage of political, economic, and personal opportunities. Just as the businessman does with government officials who offer him access to the needed resources for his operations, successful NGOs massage their relationships with local government officials over meals. Some argue that these personal relationships are the most essential part of NGO work in China for getting approvals for registration, protection from potential government annoyances, access to state financial personnel, and informational resources (Economy 2004, Ma 2006). Friends of Nature, the first and perhaps most successful NGO in China to date, was founded by a man named Liang Congjie, who was not only the grandson of the late Qing reformer Liang Qichao but also a member of the Standing Committee of the Chinese People's Consultative Conference. Many of the successful NGOs I have seen, however, also work hard to build and maintain relationships with the government. One NGO I visited has its own restaurant (a small one with just two tables), supposedly to provide safe food for its employees, but they also have a good supply of liquor to serve to government officials who visit. The director also serves in the local district government. Other organizations I have observed are registered as civil nonprofit organizations (*fei yingli minjian zuzhi*), under the direction of a local work unit (*danwei*) but still dependent on good relations (*guanxi*) with the government through relatives or services they can offer to the government, often with only the promise for compensation but frequently accepting no compensation in exchange for the ability to operate.

In the end, any organization outside the government, whether it be a business or a nongovernmental organization, finds more success if it has stronger relations with government to the extent where both reach a point of embedding themselves into the state to accomplish their goals (Dickson 2002, Hildebrandt 2013). In her examination of civil society, Jude Howell demonstrates

(2004b) the reliance on government of some organizations in Yunnan that have been instrumental to the HIV response. The Yunnan Reproductive Health Research Institute[19] was the first NGO established in Yunnan, with support from the Ford Foundation. They are a network of medical and social scientists who have done research on maternal and child health and HIV and STIs around Yunnan, but they rely on a strong government network to access research sites and participants. Very savvy operators of NGOs work quietly to demonstrate their benefit to the government.

Howell (2004b) presents the example of Li Jianhua, the psychiatrist who is deputy director of the Yunnan Institute on Drug Abuse (YIDA). Dr. Li is responsible for training the doctors, nurses, and social workers who staff all of the methadone clinics around China. He also supports much of the research on drug users in Yunnan. Dr. Li is a hard-working, soft-spoken man who daily demonstrates his benefit to the government in carrying out its anti-narcotic work. This allowed him to change policy by introducing the first therapeutic community model of drug rehabilitation in Yunnan. More recently, he has helped to change a policy that discriminates against both current and former drug users. The Dynamic Surveillance System (DSS), which tracks drug users in China, records the names of every convicted drug user—a badge that previously followed drug users around for the rest of their life under this system. A drug user's presentation of his or her national identity card at a hotel or ticketing agency automatically alerted the local police station, who could come to perform a random urine test and often harass the person as well. This deterred many former drug users from reentering society. With support from an international organization, one former drug user who runs an NGO in Yunnan received help from Li Jianhua in designing a study to survey former drug users about the impact of the DSS on their livelihood. The report he authored with Li Jianhua demonstrated the negative effects of the DSS on their ability to reintegrate to society. Li Jianhua was able to deliver the report to Beijing and modify the policy to remove the names of former drug users from the DSS once they have had three consecutive years of negative drug tests. This type of accomplishment is incredible in an environment that generally has only a punitive attitude toward drug users, but relationships (*guanxi*) must have played an integral role in this change. A lone former drug user would have little chance of effecting such change. But in this case, the same types of networks that carry the potential to promote HIV transmission have worked to benefit those who are at risk.

Conclusion

Going Beyond the Evidence

KONG CHUIZHU, FORMER VICE-GOVERNOR OF YUNNAN Province from 2003–2013, died as the result of suicide on July 12, 2014. He was likely the victim of Xi Jinping's severe anti-corruption measures, afraid that he would be implicated for his own corrupt practices. It was not Kong's suicide that was most surprising. Suicide among government officials has become a more common occurrence as Xi Jinping's efforts to "swat flies and hunt down tigers" (*pai cangying da laohu*)[1] escalates. Officials who foresee their fate may choose to end their life rather than endure the torture and humiliation that could befall them as the result of an accusation of corrupt practices. The bigger surprise was discovery of Kong's HIV-positive status. He died after his third attempt at suicide, the first occurring several months earlier while attending the National People's Congress in Beijing. One night during the meeting Kong went back to his hotel room and cut his wrist, arms, and neck with a broken wine glass. He was admitted to a hospital, where doctors performed a routine HIV test that revealed his status.

News of an elite HIV-positive member of society or government is surprising from the perspective of the public-health-focused discourse that dominates research and programming targeted at HIV/AIDS. Global paradigms have long painted a picture of HIV/AIDS as a disease that primarily affects the most marginalized members of society. Even within that paradigm, we expect HIV-positive people to carry identities of commercial sex workers, injection drug users, or men who have sex with men. Notice of a heterosexual

HIV-positive man automatically brands him as a "client of a sex worker," an epidemiologic appellation that places these men within the standard public health paradigms that govern global HIV/AIDS discourse. However, few of these men, if any, would willingly respond to this type of constructed identity.

More than a decade of experience conducting research on the relationship between elite male sexual practices and HIV in China taught me to not be surprised at the report of an HIV-positive government official. News of such officials is rarely made public and is extremely protected for fear of marring Party legitimacy, but my research revealed that these powerful men can also be extremely vulnerable to HIV infection because of the role commercial sex plays in the work that promotes their economic and career advancement. Despite this experience, I was surprised to hear of Kong Chuizhu's positive HIV status. I had met Kong several times ten years before his untimely death, and we met each time on a tennis court in Kunming. I had always held him up in my mind as a pioneer who was accomplishing his career advancement on the tennis court rather than in the brothel. I had obviously only seen one side of Kong Chuizhu. The other side of him shared a tight sexual network with Shen Peipeng,[2] another former vice-governor from Yunnan, which at once promoted their careers while exposing them to HIV. This network also extends throughout the province and results in HIV infections among other government officials, which has further expanded the epidemic of sexually transmitted HIV in a place like Ruili, where Wang Yantao is no longer the only government official known to be HIV-positive.

Perhaps I was naïve in thinking that Kong Chuizhu had risen to such a high level of bureaucracy on a tennis court. Few Chinese officials can climb that high in the system without engaging in the risky behaviors that characterize the *yingchou* rituals I have discussed in this book. Xi Jinping's anti-corruption campaign is turning this hearsay into fact, with frequent allegations of high-level officials who exchanged political favors for sex, and the reports of economic slowdown caused by government officials who are dragging their feet approving investment projects or implementing national policy in the absence of some sort of incentive (Wong 2015, Denyer 2015).

I cannot claim that Kong's HIV infection is representative of men in his political or economic class; nor can I claim that men like Kong occupy any nominal proportion of HIV cases in China because there are no statistics that identify people infected with the virus on the basis of their political or economic status. Globally, statistics on HIV infection are divided into standard categories of risk and vulnerability, defined by commercial sex workers, injection drug users, men who

have sex with men, and pregnant women. Neither Kong nor any government official would fit into these marginalized categories of identity, and in fact the Chinese government probably works hard to cover up infections among officials to
protect its legitimacy and moral authority. Reports of HIV-infected government
officials, even in *zhong nanhai*,[3] do exist, but they are merely rumor and not supported in evidence. There are thus no statistics to support my argument that businessmen and government officials are at risk for STIs or HIV. But this book has
been less a presentation of epidemiologic evidence and more a narrative used to
explain the silent risks these men incur as a result of the contemporary structures
that promote and support them in their social, economic, and political positions.
Unlike the most at-risk populations,[4] which are neglected by society, these men
control economic and political structures of power. Yet they are neglected, from
a public health perspective, because they do not fit into the neat categories that
public health uses to define risk. Furthermore, these men incur risk collectively,
which is also difficult to address within the individual-level responses that guide
many public health interventions.

What we do know is that the narrative I tell in this book is not unique to
Ruili. Men throughout China realize the need to engage in rituals of *yingchou*
as part of their aspirations to build the *guanxi* necessary for climbing the
political and economic ladders of success. Anthropologists who have conducted research from Chengdu to Dalian and Shenzhen have documented
these practices throughout China (Mason 2011, Osburg 2013, Zheng 2009).
But these practices, which help men achieve success through a culturally specific form of networking, also have serious public health implications that
often go unnoticed because public health is shaped by paradigms of individual behavior. Many people tell me they never thought about the public health
implications of the practices related to rituals of *yingchou*, which always sur-
prises me given the rate at which such men drink, smoke, banquet, and frequent entertainment venues that are also associated with commercial sex. The
focus is often on the process, though, and not its ancillary implications. The
neglect is deepened because few public health studies consider men's influence
on HIV infection. The researched burden of heterosexual infection is most
frequently attributed to women. There is a glut of research and programs that
target female commercial sex workers. Those that do focus on men sample
marginalized populations of men who are commonly associated with infection in the global HIV literature, like migrants, truck drivers, and miners.
But the one representative national survey on STIs in China, which was based

on Edward Laumann and John Gagnon's 1992 National Health and Life Survey (Laumann et al. 1994), points out the significant role that men with high incomes who socialize and travel for business play in STI transmission. The authors found that these men were more likely than other Chinese men to engage in unprotected sex with a sex worker (Parish et al. 2003).

This book has acted as a necessary interlocutor between the social science and public health literature that examines the men who fuel China's commercial sex industry. These types of interdisciplinary conversations are crucial to providing the theoretical analysis that can help to develop effective solutions to the contemporary social problems that also influence public health. This helps to uncover the social structures that can promote the development, spread, and administration of a disease like HIV. In China, as I have discussed, much of the social analysis needed to unravel the HIV epidemic relates to how the country has been governed in the post-Mao period.

"Good governance" is an essential part of responding to the HIV pandemic, creating transparent and accountable governing officials who will dedicate resources to alleviating local epidemics. This book has taken the relationship between governance and HIV infection one step further because of the additional role governance plays in transmitting the virus. Governance is not merely a public concern in China. It is also a private concern because of the authority that the Chinese state has over the supposed "private sector." This has transformed governance from a purely institutional mechanism into one that also influences private lives because of the modes of operation it has assumed in China. Governance, of course, is officially conducted through the official bureaucratic channels. But the informal modes of governance required to influence many of the decisions that occur within the competing models governing China's political and economic system work through more individualistic channels of person-to-person contact. The men in these positions have assumed the burden of a set of often unspoken and unofficial work requirements obligating them to engage in practices that are socially, politically, and economically beneficial, but biologically very risky.

These requirements, even though they are unofficial, have reframed the nature of work in post-Mao China to include a set of activities typically framed as individually motivated and risky behaviors in the West. This includes the risky sexual behaviors that can expose individuals to STIs or HIV. Western culture and discourse distinguishes between activities that qualify as work and those that qualify as leisure. Worker evaluation and promotion in the West is typically determined on the basis of merit, although a certain amount of social networking is sometimes used to build rapport among colleagues. For the most part, however, work occurs within an institution defined by professional and occupational roles and can be distinguished from leisure, which occurs in settings outside of such boundaries. The distinction can often be much blurrier in China, where, as I have argued in this book, work is defined by position rather than by a particular occupational role. The work done to maintain that position often assumes an arbitrary format more suitable to the cultural and political expectations of the definition of work within the Chinese context. Consequently, not only have eating and drinking become a part of work in China, but massage, foot reflexology, sauna, karaoke, and soliciting the services of commercial sex workers are also often part of work, in addition to the standard office-related duties that are most readily associated with work. As so many men demonstrated and articulated to me, the behaviors associated with these practices are not individually motivated; they are "occupational hazards" related to their positions at work. Men do not go to the sauna on their way home from work, much as a Western man may stop by the gym on his way home from work. The trip to the sauna is a logical extension of the workday for many Chinese men, following a trip to the banquet and preceding a trip to a brothel—all before they even think of "going home."

Addressing any epidemic related to these behaviors in China thus requires reframing discussions of risk, work, and even the stigma-laden term *sex work*. Risk does not happen only individually. In China, it also happens collectively, within the shared rituals that support the social networks structuring Chinese society. In addition, these behaviors do not necessarily occur within an aberrant or marginalized framework outside the standard structures and organizations associated with everyday life. Many of the men who are most vulnerable to disease in China are incurring risk *within* their standard work environment. In this context, sex is not only work for women; it is also part of a man's job.

Mention of the terms *sex work* or *sex worker* invokes images of dirty, marginalized women at risk for STIs or HIV infection. But sex work was developed as a functional category meant to legitimize the use of sex as an occupational activity (Farley 2004, Kampadoo and Doezma 1998, Weitzer 2009). This makes it a useful category for understanding the behaviors of men or women who engage in sex as part of their work-related duties. Sex work reverted to a socially disdained category after public health advocates saw the potential for it to help identify a population category considered "vulnerable" to HIV infection. Expanding this framework back to a functional role that views sex as a legitimate part of work could help to broaden the paradigms used to examine and respond to diseases transmitted through acts of sex work. Globally, sex serves a recognized occupational role for women, but it also serves an unrecognized occupational role *for men* in many Asian countries.

The ideas I have put forth in this book do not fit well into the dominant public health paradigms that have been used to respond to HIV, and it is difficult to translate them into the individual types of interventions global and public health practitioners envision as part of a response to the pandemic. They are appropriate, however, for understanding how HIV and other diseases are transmitted in China. From a biomedical perspective, the sexually transmitted infections and HIV that I discuss in this book result from discrete etiologies facilitated through individual behaviors. The same is true for the chronic diseases that are transforming China's burden of disease. From the perspective I put forward in this book these diseases all stem from a related cause rooted in the sociocultural and politico-economic fabric of post-Mao China. In the coming years, many Chinese men suffering from tobacco-related illnesses will find their way to a thoracic surgeon, and men suffering from alcohol-related illnesses may consult a liver specialist, while those affected by sexually transmitted infections and HIV/AIDS may find solace in various courses of antibiotics and anti-retroviral therapies. But even though these illnesses all require distinct biomedical treatments, clues into their causes can often be found within a singular cultural and politico-economic phenomenon linked to the unofficial work requirements that ensure success for many of China's urban businessmen and government officials. Alternatively, we may suddenly see a precipitous drop in the rates of STIs and chronic disease, at least among China's economic and political elite, as Xi Jinping's anti-corruption campaign fulfills the ideals of an unintended public health campaign. It turns out the ongoing purge of officials is also an effective public health deterrent that targets a collective political aim and not an individual one. Men are suddenly terrified to engage in all of these expected yet prohibited practices related to *yingchou*. The text messages I once watched for signs of off-color jokes are now being replaced with We Chat posts from men who are losing their love handles, seeing their blood pressure drop, and spending more time with their families. That could all end if Xi's anti-corruption campaign gives way to the economic pains occurring because it has removed the basis of trust that facilitates economic growth in China. In the meantime, Xi's campaign has opened up a lens into effective public health interventions in China. Perhaps he should also be appointed minister of health.

Notes

Introduction

1. There was only one hospital ward in China (the one in Beijing) that accepted and treated HIV-positive people on an in-patient basis at the time.

2. This term (*fangyi zhan* in Chinese) was adopted from the old Soviet system of health. Anti-epidemic stations were responsible for monitoring disease in China. The Chinese government has now adopted the model and name of the Centers for Disease Control (CDC) from the United States.

3. It is difficult to assess the impact of the HIV epidemic on this class of men because the government does not keep statistics on infections within this sector of the population. Doing so would reveal the weaknesses of the state. In 2012, however, the Chinese CDC did announce that men over the age of fifty are now accounting for the fastest rise in new cases of HIV (Shan 2012). The cause is not known, but it could be related to retiring men who spent their careers engaging in *yingchou* practices and soliciting commercial sex.

4. Global sales of Remy Martin fell by 17 percent following Xi Jinping's announcement of his austerity measures.

5. The first case of HIV was detected in China in 1985, in a foreign tourist. The first domestic outbreak was detected in 1989, among injection drug users. Until 2003, approximately 70 percent of all recorded infections were detected among injection drug users.

6. MSM is a behavioral category designed to fit men who engage in sex with other men but do not identify as gay or homosexual. It has quickly developed into its own category of constructed identity. For more on the construction of MSM identity, see Boellstorff (2011).

7. My analysis of masculinity in this book focuses on the type of masculinity valued in Han society. I do, at times, discuss ethnic minority men, particularly men of the Jingpo ethnicity. But even my discussion of Jingpo masculinity is used to highlight the particularities of Han masculinity.

8. The use of the name Burma in this book refers to the country now officially named Myanmar. Myanmar is the name given to the country by its ruling military junta, but I will discuss it as Burma throughout the text except in instances when I refer to official accounts.

9. In 2007 the UN Office on Drugs and Crime (UNODC) declared that opium and heroin production had been greatly reduced in Burma. But opium production has at least tripled since that time, indicating a strong comeback for the industry. For more on the situation see Fuller (2015).

10. China has a relatively small HIV epidemic in comparison to its population. Estimated cases of HIV have remained between 650,000 and 800,000 since 2001 and reported cases rise incrementally every year, representing a fairly constant 0.05 percent prevalence rate of infection.

11. Several studies of private lives in China have noted the relative openness of people in remote or rural areas, particularly as they relate to sexual attitudes and discourses. In particular, see Honig (2003), Yungxiang Yan (2003), and Diamant (2000).

12. The practices I discuss in this book are prevalent throughout China among businessmen and government officials. For further discussion, see Osburg (2013) and Mason (2011).

13. This same man was part owner of a casino based in Laiza, the capital of the Kachin State. He offered me an opportunity that could have been a huge turning point in my research, but I declined for reasons of personal security. He and his Hong Kong partners thought I could have represented a valuable aspect of social capital if they could be seen alongside an American woman in their casino. They offered to hire me at 30,000 RMB per month just to act as a translator when needed. They would let me come back to Ruili once every few weeks and even allow me access to their patrons for the purposes of my research. The offer was tempting because of its ethnographic value, but I declined because it would have meant traveling into the Kachin State undocumented because I was legally prohibited from entering that part of Burma as an American citizen. These types of offers from wealthy Chinese men to Chinese-speaking foreigners are not uncommon because of the ability to transmit social capital onto the Chinese partner. John Osburg speaks of a similar arrangement with a wealthy informant during his research in Chengdu. I was primarily concerned with my safety, though, which is often something that ethnographers can overlook when faced with such a lucrative ethnographic prospect.

14. According to Bruce Dickson, this type of scenario is quite common in post-Mao China as it allows the government to easily co-opt and benefit off of businessmen. This particular businessman traveled between Kunming and Dehong quite often because much of his business of course centered and depended on his relationships there.

15. In fact, one of the reasons why I reveal Ruili's identity in this book, rather than veiling it as other anthropologists have done with locations that engage in politically sensitive activities, is to demonstrate the merit of Ruili.

16. Ruili is home to many Burmese, Pakistani, and even Afghani migrants, but not Westerners.

17. A minor wife in China is a woman with whom a man shares a marital relationship aside from his primary wife, who he is legally married to. Men share households with their minor wives and have children with them but may not be legally married to them. This trend derives from the imperial Chinese tradition of a man who had a First Wife (*yi taitai*), who was the most powerful and dominant wife in his household, and his lesser wives, who bore children for him but were more marginalized in the home.

Chapter 1

1. *Zimei dui* is equivalent to a card game called Tractor in English.

2. These girls only accompanied the men in singing, dancing, and drinking and were not requested to provide sexual services.

3. Scott Kennedy and Deng Guosheng discuss the presence of local chambers of commerce (*yidi shanghui*) around China in their 2010 article, according to which local Fujianese chambers of commerce are among the most prevalent in China.

4. These were often large celebrations filled with pageantry that included performances, floats, and speeches from all the major local government officials. This was one way of showing the state's presence in a sensitive area that could be considered a threat to China's harmonious society.

5. *Yan* (cigarette) *jiu* (wine) is a homophone for the word *yanjiu*, which means to research.

6. The very public case of the mining town of Lüliang in Shanxi Province is a good example of the important role *guanxi* with government officials plays in corporate success. It is also a good example of the close relationships government officials have with local corporate partners. For more on this case, see Johnson (2014) and Tian, Ouyang, and Guo (2014).

7. Private business was once illegal in China. Increasingly, however, businessmen are gaining entry to Party membership as the result of state cooptation. For more on this see Dickson (2008) and Tsai (2007).

8. I say men. These practices were originally reserved for men but do not exclude women in contemporary China. Women participate in these rituals to a much lesser extent and can often be excused but are equal participants in certain parts of China. On a trip to Guizhou Province, I saw women participate in the drinking and banqueting characteristic of *yingchou* and was told by one man that his wife is a better drinker than he is.

9. Drinking rituals in many parts of China also dictate the height of one's glass in relation to one's partner. People of lower status should clink their glass on a lower

portion of that of their higher-status drinking partner. Some will even clink below their drinking partner's glass in the event of a large status differential. I did not observe this custom in Ruili, but Eileen Otis saw it during research in Kunming. For a more complete explanation, see Otis (2012).

10. I found this to be true in my own fieldwork as well.

11. Zhu Rongji served as mayor and party secretary of Shanghai in the late 1980s and then eventually went on to become premier under Jiang Zemin from 1998 to 2003. Zhu was best known as a pragmatist with a strong work ethic who took a tough stance toward corruption.

12. This procedure, which had become popular among businessmen in the prefecture, drew a patient's blood out of the body, stripped it of the fatty deposits, and then reinfused the clean blood.

13. This is an allusion to the sexual activities that are included as part of *yingchou* and *jiedai keren*.

Chapter 2

1. I will discuss Jingpo culture more in Chapter Six. The Jingpo are one of the five ethnic minorities that inhabit Dehong Prefecture and are historically a nomadic culture.

2. Robert Connell's discussion of hegemonic masculinity borrows from Gramsci's definition of hegemony in which he describes "a cultural dynamic by which a group claims and sustains a leading position in social life."

3. Confucian Chinese culture is centered on five important relationships, between ruler and subject, father and son, husband and wife, older brother and younger brother, and friend and friend.

4. A new law promulgated in January 2013 allows the wives of gay-identified men to annul their marriage. This allows them to seek a suitable marriage partner without the stigma attached to a divorced woman.

5. I apparently could have also helped to strengthen ties and improve his image with the partners for this new venture, a casino located in the Kachin State. At one point, A Rong asked if I would spend some time inside the new venture because I offered a way to communicate with some Hong Kong Chinese partners who could speak English but not Mandarin. He offered me full access to the wealthy men who would visit the casino as a resource for research. Tempting as the offer was, my safety as an American woman who would have to enter the Kachin State illegally was more important to me.

6. Liu Dun's daughter is, consequently, now a graduate student at an Ivy League business school.

7. I met an older anthropologist from the United States in Kunming before I began fieldwork in Ruili. He too had just completed some fieldwork on another topic in Ruili. I eagerly spoke with him as a blind naïve doctoral student, not knowing what was in store for me. When I told him I was going to Ruili to study HIV/AIDS, he assured me

I had chosen the right place. He said, "there's got to be a lot of AIDS there because there are so many gay men." Knowing how hidden homosexuality is in China (it was even more hidden at that time and much more so in a remote ethnic minority area), I asked how he knew there were so many gay men there. He said because he always saw the men, especially the hairdressers, holding hands and hanging all over each other. Such culturally irrelevant remarks from an anthropologist were surprising but were testament to the fact that homosocial relations in China can easily be mistaken for homosexual relations when seen through the eyes of a Western observer. Indeed, many friends of the same sex are beginning to adopt terms from local homosexual discourse to refer to their relationships. The term *jiyou*, which is usually used to refer to a relationship between two gay people, is more and more being used by straight people to refer to their closest friends.

8. In another interview, a man referred to one's closest friends as "steel" (*tiegang*). He said *zhiji* is only used by well-educated and erudite men.

9. This is the general attitude toward businessmen, although the Chinese Communist Party opened up membership to entrepreneurs and "capitalists" following the 2002 party congress. This benefits both the entrepreneurs, who gain the political capital necessary for their success, and the party, which gains control over otherwise independent entrepreneurs who are now critical to the progress of China's economy.

10. This popular slogan was first uttered by Deng Xiaoping in 1984 as a way of promoting his new policy of economic reform throughout China.

11. Jingpo in China and the Kachin in Burma were instrumental in fighting off the Japanese invasion of China during World War II because of their ability to navigate and survive in the thick jungles that dominate the region's geography.

12. These types of tattoo are common among men belonging to Chinese triad societies.

13. Most of the Jingpo men I saw with such tattoos were either Kachin or Jingpo who had spent a considerable amount of time in the Kachin State.

14. Although some television programming is becoming slightly more progressive and experimental, all programs aired are still approved by the party's propaganda division. Inclusion of the word "Comrade" (*tongzhi*) in the title of the program is also indicative that it addresses the lives of people either within the party or friendly with the Party.

15. In this case he was open with her about his plans. Although she did not agree with such a plan, she really had no choice but to go along with it.

16. In some instances when people spoke to me about minor wives, they were secret from the man's primary wife; in other cases minor wives and primary wives are good friends. One woman told me her father has four wives, who play mahjong together every day. In another I was told of a man who has three wives; two are sisters and the third is their cousin. I have also heard of cases of out-of-town businessmen who establish a relationship with a minor wife in the town where they do business and move the minor wife out of the house when the primary wife comes to visit.

Chapter 3

1. The shops used to bill themselves as products-for-sexual-use shops (*xing yong-pin*), but new regulations in 2004 mandated that they all change their names to reflect that they sell health-related products (*baojian pin*).

2. I put "community" in quotes here because of the definition it assumes in China. We take a community in the West to refer to a natural grouping of people who share an identity or mission. It is an unstructured and informal entity. Community or *shequ* in post-Mao China is a formal administrative unit, governed under the party structure, that has been established to provide social services and monitor the actions of people living within a certain defined residential area. For more, see Bray (2006).

3. The work unit (*danwei*) was also the social nexus for urban residents. It provided housing, education, a common dining hall, and health care for all its employees. It also served as a surveillance mechanism for the government. For more on the *danwei* system, see Lu and Perry (1997).

4. The campaign resulted in 2,290 disciplinary actions in just the first few months, as well as a slowdown in business for some expensive cigarette manufacturers, alcohol producers, and high-end restaurants. *The South China Morning Post* ("2,290 party members disciplined . . . " 2013) reported, however, that many businessmen had just hired their own chefs and converted their homes into banquet halls to avert the policy.

5. This was how Deng Xiaoping defended his reformist vision, by saying, "If you open the window for fresh air you have to expect some flies to blow in."

6. These shops originally called themselves sexual-use product shops (*xing yong-pin dian*) but were mandated to change their names to either health-protection-use product shops (*baojian yongpin dian*) or adult-use product shops (*chengren yongpin dian*) in 2004. This was obviously a move to cover up their purpose, but the shops themselves did not change at all beyond the characters on the awning or window. They remained the same shops that sold sex toys and aphrodisiacs and remained just as open to the street.

7. A hairwash in a Chinese salon is an experience of its own and not just a precursor to a haircut. It involves a thickening agent massaged into the hair without water, which results in a stiff mountain of suds that are then scooped off and rinsed out. The hairwash includes basic massage of head, neck, shoulders, and arms as well. The whole process takes about half an hour.

8. *Zouhun* is translated as walking marriage but is not an institutionalized form of marriage. Women and men in the matriarchal Mosuo culture do not marry; rather, they pair up for liaisons at night. Any child born to a couple stays with the mother's household, of course. By not marrying, men are able to stay in their matriarchal home in order to help out with the heavy agricultural work. Han culture has interpreted *zouhun* as a very lax sexual practice that allows women and men to have sexual liaisons with a different person every night. Urban Han myths also purport that many children do not know their true father because the father does not live in the mother's

home. This type of fabricated cultural structure has led the transformation of the Mosuo region into an area exploited for prostitution.

9. Men often told me that 90 percent of the men in their networks had lovers or mistresses. Journalistic accounts also report that 95 percent of government officials keep mistresses. Some say no official is considered a real man without his own *ernai* (mistress). Even the housing bubble in Beijing has been associated with the explosion of Chinese mistresses, whose men have been buying up expensive apartments for the women to live in. See Timmons (2013).

10. The CCP operates on a tenet of *wei renmin fuwu* (for the service of the people).

11. The title for this revolutionary song, "If there were no Communist Party, there would be no new China," drew off an editorial published in the *Liberation Daily* (*jiefang ribao*) in 1943 that was written as criticism in response to a book by Chiang Kai-shek called *China's Destiny* (*zhongguo zhi mingyun*), which argued if there were no Kuomintang there would be no China. The editorial argued that if there were no Communist Party, there would be no China. The slogan was then lyricized by the song writer Cao Huoxing, only to be eventually edited by Mao, who added the word "new" to make "If there were no Communist Party there would be no new China."

12. The environment is much different from the West, where sexual transgressions are more subject to moral rather than political code. Although many Western men are morally shamed into leaving public office after committing some sort of sexual transgression, the legal system has little say in the cause for their resignation. In China, government officials are almost celebrated socially for their sexual exploits, but legally they are prohibited from engaging in such activities. This requires them to cover up their actions as a way to protect their status.

13. *Danweis* were first created before implementation of the one-child policy but still had the authority to determine how many children a family could bear. This function of managing births is now managed by the State Family Planning Commission.

14. The government originally took this approach to drug control in the 1990s (see Zhou 1999).

15. Prior to 2008 the Public Security Bureau was responsible for administering compulsory detoxification centers, which subjected first-time drug offenders to six months of unassisted detoxification. Repeat offenders were sentenced to two to three years of compulsory labor through reeducation, which was administered by the Ministry of Justice. Labor through reeducation for drug offenders is not officially prohibited, and compulsory detoxification centers have been placed under the administration of the Ministry of Justice.

16. Lisa Tran offers an interesting analysis of the one-husband, one-wife system (*yifu yiqi zhi*), showing that it was included in legal code as early as the late Qing (very late—it was used in the Draft Civil Code of the Great Qing, completed in 1911) but that it referred only to one man and one woman being married to each other at a time and did not refer to monogamy or outlaw relationships with concubines. Understanding of *yifu yiqi zhi* as monogamy began in the Republican era because Republican law required marital fidelity between husbands and wives. But fundamentally, she argues,

yifu yiqi zhi refers only to the restriction of one man and one woman being married to each other at a time and does not refer to monogamy. Many people in contemporary China refer to *yifu yiqi zhi*; but a culture of mistresses and lovers and minor wives also seems to have been normalized, perhaps because of the original sentiment of *yifu yiqi zhi*. China's Marriage Law has subsequently been updated in 1980 and 2001. For a more complete discussion on China's marriage laws, see Friedman (2000), Watson and Ebrey (1991), Wong (1997), and Yang (1988).

17. The state required premarital health exams until October 2003.

18. Young people from urban areas were often sent to live and work in the countryside during the Cultural Revolution in order to appreciate the life of the peasants. They are referred to as *zhiqing* in Chinese, or sent-down youth in English.

19. There is now space for such discussion on Chinese microblogs like Sina Weibo (Chinese Twitter) and Weixin (We Chat).

20. When taken literally, this character has multiple meanings, including "to be," "therefore," "only then," or "your," but in this instance it is defined merely by the allusion implied in its shape.

21. Chinese people are often surprised to hear that we publicly criticize our public officials, including our president, in the United States because of the potential ramifications they could face for publicly criticizing their public officials. Any criticism of public officials in China must be in veiled discourse.

22. A post on the Chinese microblog Sina Weibo in July 2013 revealed that bribing local officials (the post referred to officials in a city in Ningxia Province) can indeed be quite inexpensive. The post released a list of bribes ranging around 2,000–3,000 RMB for various favors, permits, and allowances.

23. An inexpensive type of liquor.

24. Refers to telling dirty jokes and speaking about pornography, something that is scorned in official discourse and really only possible at the lowest and most peripheral levels of government.

25. A butterfly refers to a woman, and here a "yellow butterfly" refers to a sex worker, a low-level woman who is accessible to low-level officials.

26. *Baijiu* or white liquor (a clear liquor made from sorghum) is the most common liquor in China, which of course is available in varying qualities and degrees of strength.

27. White skin is considered a privilege of beauty in China.

28. Red wine, symbolic of more developed foreign culture, is becoming a status symbol among Chinese officials.

29. Red envelopes containing money are typically exchanged at holidays and special occasions like weddings.

30. Another symbol of a beautiful woman.

31. A provincial-level cadre is elite enough to access the exotic foreign resources that are now available in China. VSOP cognac is a symbol of wealth and power in contemporary urban China. He enjoys listening to foreign music, and can enjoy the

company of a foreign prostitute. Russian prostitutes are especially coveted in large urban centers.

32. All references to the most expensive and elite items made available to China's most powerful government officials, and finally the reference to the famous movie stars, alludes to Jiang Zemin's lover, suggesting that only a powerful government official would have access to such a desirable woman.

33. It was explained to me that in Jingpo culture once a woman takes her shoes off it means she will be taking the rest of her clothes off too, and the process cannot be reversed. This also clarified for me why this same official begged me not to take my shoes off in a karaoke bar several months prior to this event. After resisting urges from his friends in the karaoke bar to invite me to a dance because he was embarrassed at being so much shorter than me, I took off my high-heeled shoes as a way of being polite and bringing myself closer to his height, but he insisted that I not do so.

34. Those who can afford used to go to Macao (before the anti-corruption campaign limited this type of travel), but China's borders are surrounded by gambling houses owned and operated by Chinese businessmen just across the border like Ruili, or border towns in Guangxi province.

35. The Great Wall Sheraton (*changcheng fandian*) was the first joint venture hotel in Beijing and for a long time the nicest hotel in Beijing. It is partially owned by the People's Liberation Army. The disco/karaoke club affiliated with the hotel was known as a very upscale club, so its closure made a strong statement.

Chapter 4

1. Sad because my husband could not get to know all these people himself; but also because it was always difficult to sustain a long conversation when everyone around the table depended on my translation.

2. These condoms are usually provided for a fee, though, which in itself is a barrier to HIV prevention.

3. Sandra Hyde argues in her book *Eating Spring Rice* that the government deliberately structured a picture of HIV/AIDS that blamed ethnic minority communities. Although this did occur, particularly in a place like Ruili where ethnic minority communities make up the majority of the population and hence HIV infections, I do not agree that the government conspired in this way to portray the epidemic as a minority epidemic.

4. I heard of instances of relationships with lovers among many strata of men, including my higher-class informants as well as taxi drivers and even migrants. A Western friend in Beijing once told me of a tense situation that developed between him and his wife and another Western couple living in their expatriate complex. My friend's migrant nanny's husband had started a relationship with the other couple's migrant nanny, a situation that had to cross cultural and class boundaries for resolution.

5. It is often said that SARS restricted people's movement so much that men were even found at home with their wives and children.

6. Nine, which was regarded as the highest number in imperial China, is associated with the emperor and is symbolic of imperial power. The emperor often had nine consorts in addition to his empress. The number nine was also associated with male energy. Polygamy is legal in Burma, but unfortunately her uncle died one year before I started fieldwork.

7. A Rong and several other informants also told me that nine is the ideal number of wives for a Chinese man.

8. Unlike Western massage, where the client is disrobed and covered during the treatment, the typical Burmese, Thai, or Chinese massage provided in the average Chinese massage parlor is performed while the client is clothed.

9. Mosuo men and women do not marry or form permanent committed relationships, as is common in patriarchal cultures. They do form committed relationships in which the woman remains part of her natal household and the man part of his. The man comes to the woman's household at night to sleep and then returns to his mother's home during the day to help with work in the fields. This arrangement is crucial for preservation of a matriarchal culture that is dependent on an agricultural economy. As a result, they maintain a custom referred to in Chinese as "walking marriage" (*zouhun*), which does not require marriage commitment between a man and woman. The Han Chinese interpretation of the Mosuo culture, however, portrays the women as sexually loose and men as furtive agents who sneak in and out of a window in the dead of night in order to have sex with the woman.

10. This type of marriage helps to fulfill a national goal of Sinicizing ethnic minority areas in China.

11. Chinese people often distinguish between standard (*zhengui*) and nonstandard (*bu zhengui*) massage parlors and beauty salons when referring to those establishments that specialize in sexual services versus those that truly offer only massage and hair-dressing services. However, I found that among the expatriate community, particularly the expatriate HIV/AIDS community whose programs target commercial sex workers as a "high-risk" group, all hair salons and massage parlors were stereotyped as "brothels." Expatriates, who saw all the massage parlors, often asked me if there was somewhere in town where they could actually get a massage for their fatigued backs and muscles. And a female employee of one of the international HIV/AIDS NGOs in Kunming excitedly boasted to me that she and several other colleagues were once treated by a local government to a "hair washing by a real prostitute." I'm not sure why she was so positive the girl washing her hair was a prostitute.

12. The first character of the Chinese word for prostitute, "*jinu*," is a homophone for the word for chicken "*ji*." As a result, female prostitutes can be referred to as "chickens" (to make chicken—"*zuoji*"—colloquially means to work as a female prostitute). In a similar vein, male prostitutes who service women are referred to as "ducks" (*yazi*). Male prostitutes who service men are referred to as "money boys" (MB).

13. This influence could be stronger yet under Xi Jinping's anti-corruption campaign, although there is no evidence to support such a claim. Many people I speak with, however, do note an association between the anti-corruption campaign and a reduction in other *yingchou*-related activities.

Chapter 5

1. In Ruili at the time, 70–80 percent of all injection drug users were infected with HIV. All of those infected were from Dai or Jingpo ethnic minority communities.

2. These are the primary routes of transmission that most HIV prevention programs target. Transmission via blood transfusion is also a large driver of HIV transmission. Many hemophiliacs contracted HIV through blood transfusions at the beginning of the HIV epidemic before measures were implemented to protect blood supplies. Blood-borne transmission was also a major cause of HIV infection in China up to the first decade of the current century because of an illegal underground industry that bought blood plasma from rural peasants in central China, an industry centered around Henan Province. For more on this aspect of China's HIV epidemic, see Shao (2007).

3. The majority of heroin imported into China originates in Burma.

4. The capital of Dehong Prefecture and the closest airport to Ruili.

5. Three of the five ethnic minorities that inhabit Dehong Prefecture.

6. Ethnic minority areas of China that have been developed into tourist destinations often exude a sense of false ethnicity fabricated for tourists. This is not the case in Dehong Prefecture. Dehong has not been popularized as a tourist destination and consequently preserves the natural ethnic minority lifestyle that I describe here. Many women wear the same types of sarongs their ethnic kin wear in southeast Asia, and the men wear the same *longyi* (a long piece of fabric similar to a sarong that is draped around the waste like a skirt) typically worn by men in Burma.

7. Rice is also plentiful in Dehong, where two crops are harvested every year. As a result, Dehong was a popular escape for many Han people from other parts of Yunnan during the Great Famine of 1958–1961.

8. The Dai people are one of China's fifty-five ethnic minority communities. They live primarily in Xishuangbanna and Dehong Prefectures and make up almost half the population in Dehong Prefecture. The Dai people of Xishuangbanna are known as *shuidai* and are closely related to the Thai people. The Dai people of Ruili are known as the *handai* and are from the same ethnicity as the Shan people who live in northern Burma. To learn more about the Dai of Xishuangbanna, see Hyde (2007) and Davis (2007).

9. This is quickly changing. The government buys land from rural peasants to transform into residential and commercial space on its march toward economic growth and development.

10. The majority population in Burma is Burman. Burma is also occupied by many ethnic minority populations. Most of northeast Burma is divided into seven independent states governed by ethnic minorities, some of which also have armies: the Kachin State, which is situated on Ruili's northern border with Burma; the Shan State, situated on Ruili's southern border with China; the Chin State; the Independent State of Wa; Kayin State; Karen State; and the Mon State.

11. For obvious reasons, this is an important part of history for China, Yunnan, and Ruili. The airfields are still untouched and people in Ruili daily recount the name of General Stillwell and Claire Chennault, who led the Flying Tigers. The section of the Burma Road that goes through Ruili is now the southwestern terminus for national road 320, which connects Ruili with Shanghai. But local residents call this part of the road "Stillwell Road" (*shidiwei lu*). For a complete descriptive account of the Burma Road and General Stillwell's direction of the China-Burma-India theater, see Webster (2003).

12. The Rakhine State is home to the Rohingya people, who have been the subject of extreme oppression from the government of Myanmar.

13. These pipelines were completed and put into use by the end of 2014. The gas pipeline extends all the way to Guizhou.

14. Many of these projects are very controversial because they inflict cultural and environmental harm on ethnic land and communities and offer no benefit to those same communities. The Myitsone dam project in the Kachin State is a prime example of such controversy. Much of the controversy is over the placement of the dam, which will threaten the existence of some of the foundational elements of the Kachin culture when it floods certain pivotal villages along this important point on the Irrawady River. There is also controversy over the fact that the Chinese government negotiated directly with the Burmese junta for construction of the dam, with no benefit going to the Kachin people, even though the dam is being constructed on their land. Still others have said that Burmese engineers purposely planned the dam for its location (which is not optimal, from an engineering perspective) in order to affect Kachin culture. This could be a symptom of the continuing tension between the SLORC and the KIO, which has resulted from SLORC's suspected attempt to neutralize what it believes to be one of Burma's best-organized independent rebel groups. For more on this, see Smith (1994a).

15. This was the case until the announcement of democratic reforms in Burma. Relations between China and Burma have changed since the announcement because of their renewed relationship with the United States and a sudden influx of investment and international aid.

16. A prime example is construction of the controversial Myitsone Dam, designed for a section of the Irrawady River in the Kachin State. The dam is part of a deal signed between the Chinese government and the Burmese junta (SLORC), with little economic benefit returning to the Kachin Independence Organization (KIO), the governing body of the Kachin State. Ongoing controversy over the dam, though, led President Thein Sein to suspend construction of the dam in 2011.

17. Burma was once the largest producer of poppies and heroin in the world. It is now the second-largest producer behind Afghanistan but is also a major producer of methamphetamines.

18. Much of this came to an end as Burma began to institute democratic reforms in 2012.

19. The State Law and Order Council (SLORC) changed its name to the State Peace and Development Council (SPDC) in 1997, which ruled until the Thein Sein government took over following political reforms in 2012.

20. Indeed, the Chinese government did provide the CBP with extensive support from the late 1960s until the late 1970s and then on a smaller scale through the 1980s.

21. This was founded on five principles: (1) mutual respect for each other's territorial integrity and sovereignty, (2) nonaggression, (3) noninterference in each other's internal affairs, (4) equality and mutual benefits, and (5) peaceful coexistence. For further details, see Liang (1997).

22. The Burmese government has maintained peace with its ethnic states through cease-fire agreements, including an agreement with the Kachin State. Peace between the Burmese government and the Kachin State was maintained through a cease-fire agreement signed in 1994. The agreement ended in 2011, and they have not been able to renegotiate another one. This has caused an ongoing war and extensive refugee situation in the area, where many refugees escape over the border to China. This concerns China as well because it threatens stability in this strategically important region. China has been so concerned that it violated its own policy of nonintervention in February 2013 to host peace talks between the Burmese and Kachin governments. The talks took place in Ruili but resulted in nothing.

23. Although China's economy is still technically controlled under a centralized plan, market reforms placed the onus on individual governments to finance their social development and welfare systems. Officials of individual governments are also now evaluated on the amount of economic growth that takes place in their jurisdiction. For more on fiscal decentralization in China's market reform era, I refer you to Saich (2008), Sargeson and Zhang (1999), and Tsui and Youqiang (2004).

24. Arnott argues that substantial trade already existed before the legalization enabled through this agreement.

25. Although Jiegao technically sits inside China's borders, it is privileged to an extraterritorial type of status that affords implementation of economic rules not officially recognized under Chinese law.

26. This is also a way to encourage legal trade in gems and jade.

27. Poppy cultivation is also popular among local Kachin and Shan farmers because it is a cash crop that can yield more revenue than any other.

28. Burma is home to the highest-quality jade in the world and supplies more than 70 percent of the world's quality jade, much of which is sold in China. Like many lucrative mining industries though, this industry is exploitative of the people whose land houses the resource.

29. Some jade may be imported legally, but large amounts are also smuggled into China.

30. The casino industry in Ruili is very cyclical—vulnerable to closure when the central government feels it poses a threat to national security. The casinos that operate across the border in Burma (primarily in the Kachin State) were closed when I first arrived in Ruili. I heard various stories about the causes of the closure. Some told me they were closed because of increased loan shark activity. Others told me it was after the daughter of a Beijing official was killed in one of the casinos. They open and close frequently.

31. The KIO governs only a portion of the Kachin State. The rest of the state, including the capital of Myitkyina, is in central government hands.

32. The owner of the hotel also owned and operated one of the casinos built just across the border.

33. Shenzhen is one of the first Special Economic Zones (SEZ) developed under China's export-oriented market economy in the 1980s.

34. In 1956 Mao wrote a treatise titled *On the Ten Major Relationships,* which stressed the need to overcome ten basic problems in order to strengthen the nation. Included among them was the need to improve relationships between the Han nationality and the national minorities. He stressed the need to reduce Han chauvinism and improve relations between all nationalities so that socialist construction could benefit from the resources available in minority areas.

35. The Kachin State is one of seven independently governed ethnic states in Burma. The Kachin State is ruled by the Kachin Independence Organization (KIO) and protected by the Kachin Independent Army (KIA)

36. There are currently fifty-five officially recognized ethnic minority communities in China. The fifty-fifth (the Jinuo) was identified in 1979. Added to the Han majority, this means China officially recognizes fifty-six ethnicities within its populace. Ethnic minorities make up a mere 8 percent of the population.

37. There are also Kachin/Jingpo communities in India and Thailand.

38. The Lisu are categorized as a separate ethnicity in China.

39. A small percentage of Kachin in Burma believe in Catholicism.

40. This shutdown resulted in the immediate layoff of eight thousand casino workers. See "44 Gambling Houses . . . " (2003).

41. Briefly, the *gumlao* system can be characterized as anarchistic and egalitarian. The *gumsa* tradition does not believe in social stratification by lineage, chiefdom, etc. *Gumsa* tradition is characterized by complicated, hierarchical relations between clans/lineages. *Gumsa* societies have a chief. The structure of these societies is given in much more detail in Leach's book.

42. The last two are certainly not official parts of the Jingcheng enterprise but do attract a lot of revenue for its owner. Shuttle vans from the hotel to the casinos ran frequently while I was conducting fieldwork.

43. Dehong is one of 155 autonomous areas in China, included among 5 provincial-level autonomous regions, 30 prefectural-level autonomous regions, and 120 autonomous counties nationwide.

44. Water Splashing Festival (*poshuijie*), often referred to as the Dai New Year, is celebrated annually on April 11, 12, and 13. For more details on the history and customs related to *poshui jie*, see Komlosy (2004).

45. The *munaos* can also be danced during special events to celebrate someone in the community who has succeeded in business, the death of an important elder or noblewoman, infertile couples, building a new home, going into or winning a battle, movement of a village, and solving differences among family members. See Wu and Yang (1996) and Lintner (1997).

46. Jingpo folklore attributes its origins to one hundred species of birds.

47. The totem sits on a horizontal beam that has the head of a condor at one end and a tail on the other. Atop the beam sit four pillars with circuitous designs that represent the possible routes from the Tibetan Plateau to the current Kachin homeland. There are sun and moon representations that signify male and female, and a sword and sheath in between two of the beams to represent gender division. The horizontal beam also depicts friezes of two, four, and six teats representing female cows, pigs, and humans in order to denote the important position of women in the culture.

48. I describe government control over the Jingpo *munaozongge* celebration here. Celebration of the Dai *poshuijie* (Water Splashing Festival) has assumed the same government control.

49. The Chinese government had designated three national holiday weeks as Golden Weeks (*huangjin zhou*) in 1999, including National Day (*guoqin jie*), Spring Festival (*chunjie*), and May Day (International Labor Day). Golden Week was so named because the government declared three days of national holiday and rearranged the rest of the work week so government employees could have seven days of continuous vacation. This was done to promote domestic tourism. The National Day Golden Week was suspended in 2003 due to SARS, and in 2007 the government ended the Golden Week around May Day.

50. This is a different word from the *yingchou* I speak about in other parts of the book, referring to social entertaining.

51. Chen Duxiu was one of the cofounders of the Chinese Communist Party in 1921. Feng Yuxiang was an important Warlord during the period of rule of the Republic of China (1911–1949). Hu Shih was an important revolutionary figure in China's May Fourth Movement and the New Culture Movement (1919–1921), both student-led movements, which advocated a move away from feudalism and development of a modern vernacular. Hu received his Ph.D. in philosophy from Columbia in 1919. He later became the first president of Peking University and then served as consul general to the United States in San Francisco. Lu Xun, known as the father of modern Chinese literature, as well as an important revolutionary figure in China, also promoted the use of vernacular and the need to abandon China's feudal past.

52. Zhang Zhidong and Li Hongzhang were major forces behind the Self-Strengthening Movement at the end of the Qing dynasty. Along with other reformers in the movement, they aimed to strengthen China through adoption of Western technologies.

53. Yenan is known as the birthplace of the Chinese communist revolution. Located in northern China in Shaanxi Province, Yenan was near the end of the Long March (1937–1948) and thus became the focal point of the Chinese communist revolution in 1949.

54. There are currently some 1.5 million registered drug users in China. Approximately two-thirds are categorized as injecting drug users, and the other third use so-called new drugs or amphetamine-type stimulants.

55. 1 *mu* = 1.6 acres.

56. Burma produced thirty tons of opium annually when it gained independence from Britain in 1948. Opium was used in Burma, Laos, and Thailand to trade for bars of pure gold, which resulted in the region's appellation as the Golden Triangle. This continued to increase. In 1996–1997 it was estimated that annual output had increased by 8,000 percent to at least 2,500 tons of raw opium (Linter 1999).

57. Drug suppression was more difficult in Dehong because of its remote location and also because it was not "liberated" until 1953.

58. Restaurants in Dehong serve cold poppy leaves with a spicy tomato-based dipping sauce. It is euphemistically called "green" food (*lü si shipin*).

59. A popular dish in Ruili is *yanzi doufu* (tofu cooked with raw poppy seeds). The raw poppy seeds are illegal in China. I innocently tried to carry a bag to a friend in Beijing who had visited Ruili and enjoyed eating *yanzi doufu*. I was stopped at the airport in Mangshi, where my poppy seeds were confiscated as contraband.

60. I put the word *borders* in quotes here because, as Chao-Tzang Yawnghwe notes in his article, borders are basically meaningless and inconsequential in this situation. I too noticed during my fieldwork that borders were easily traversed and made invisible if a businessman had relationships with the right government officials on either side.

61. An inordinate amount of attention was focused on Ruili and Dehong Prefecture after flooding and mudslides killed ninety people (including the director of the Bureau of Transportation of Yinjiang, one of five counties in Dehong Prefecture) on July 5, 2004. Representatives of several central-level ministries traveled to the area within one or two days of the disaster, as well as one of Yunnan's vice-governors along with representatives from provincial-level bureaus that assisted in the disaster response.

62. Workers who were in the casinos at the time the border was shut down remained at the casinos until the border was reopened.

63. Officials stay in his hotels, and if they go across the border to gamble, they gamble in his casino. They are entertained by singers and dancers in his local ethnic village (*minzu cun*). As of 2012 they can even play eighteen holes on his golf course.

Chapter 6

1. Requirements for reporting a disease outbreak to the WHO are governed by the International Health Regulations (IHR). At the time, the IHR required reports of

outbreaks of only six infectious diseases: cholera, plague, yellow fever, typhus, small-pox, and recurring fever. SARS served as a catalyst for modification of the IHR.

2. The Chinese government instituted a series of radical but successful public health campaigns, following the communist revolution of 1949, to eradicate diseases like cholera, leprosy, STDs, and schistosomiasis. For more on these campaigns, see Horn (1969).

3. The trainers were a young college-educated woman working in public health and a former drug user who was now devoting his life to preventing drug abuse. They themselves had been "trained" in this method and program of HIV prevention training. Most likely they regurgitated back to their trainees the information they had been fed. Lacking any understanding of the concept of harm reduction, or any analytic capacity to help people work through the meaning of harm reduction within their own cultural landscape, is a big handicap, I believe, to training programs that train people about harm reduction. Such programs can only hope to train people to think in the ways they are trained but cannot give them the skills to critically assess and respond to the unique aspects of global situations that affect their locales.

4. This excerpt is taken from a translation of an official document from the People's Superior Court of Beijing City, eds. *Banli she 'feidian' angjian fali, guifan, wen-jian xuanbian* (Selected collection of laws, regulations, and documents for dealing with cases related to atypical pneumonia), Beijing, May 2003.

5. World AIDS Day is celebrated annually on December 1, so this visit followed the end of the SARS epidemic by just a few months.

6. Ditan Hospital and the You'an Hospital are the two infectious disease hospitals in Beijing; they house the only two AIDS wards in China. Ditan is much more research-oriented, while You'an houses an active ward.

7. The decision for Hu Jintao to visit the You'an Hospital may also have been prompted by Clinton's visit to the hospital during his trip to Beijing during November 2003.

8. All organizations in China must be registered under the government bureau responsible for their sector of work. Entertainment establishments, which fall under the category of a business and can also be considered culturally related, are normally registered under the Bureau of Culture or the Bureau of Industry and Commerce. As a result, these governmental units are responsible for regulating the operations of such businesses.

9. "Se" here is not a typo. I imagine they meant to write "Be."

10. The HIV epidemic resulted in a change in terminology for the word *condom* in Chinese. Condoms, which were regularly provided through the birth planning campaign, were known as contraceptive sheaths (*biyun tao*). But when referring to HIV prevention, they are now known as safety sheaths (*anquan tao*).

11. USAID initiated small programs to target HIV prevention on Chinese border areas at the time, which was funded through its Bangkok mission, since USAID does not have a mission in China. Dehong, of course, shares a border with Burma, and Honghe Prefecture, located to the southeast of Kunming, extends down to the

Vietnamese border. The project also later extended into Guangxi Province, whose southern border also adjoins Vietnam.

12. This in itself is a sign of political posturing. Multisectoral collaboration is nearly impossible in China's vertically organized bureaucratic system.

13. This is a role assigned to the Family Planning Bureau because of the importance of condom distribution to achieving the goals of China's family planning policy (the one-child policy).

14. Thousands of brands of condoms are sold in China, many of questionable quality. Only two are certified according to WHO standards, so quality control is an important part of an effective condom promotion program in China.

15. The one yuan denomination is issued in both coin and paper forms, but I rarely, if ever, see the coins used in Dehong, which would make it difficult to use the condom machines.

16. Of all the terms used to refer to NGOs in China, this is the one that most closely draws from Western discourse. It is used by very local organizations that operate on small budgets close to the grass roots of society.

17. I have most often seen this term used by organizations that have a close association with some sort of government unit and operate very carefully to avoid posing any threat to the government.

18. This information comes from personal communication with a local academic in Yunnan who was contracted to evaluate Global Fund work in Yunnan.

19. The organization changed its name in 2007 to the Yunnan Health and Development Research Association.

Conclusion

1. A reference to Xi Jinping's approach to stamping out official corruption in China, where he vowed to go after officials at both higher and lower municipal levels of government.

2. Shen Peipeng is a native of Baoshan in Western Yunnan Province and became mayor of the city of Pu'er (known for its famous tea) in 2007. He was vice-governor of Yunnan for one year before investigations into his corrupt practices began. Shen and Kong had a long relationship that included visiting high-end brothels together while Kong was vice-governor of the province. Kong decided to commit suicide after interrogations of Shen Peipeng began, during which it is believed he exposed some of Kong's own political transgressions.

3. *Zhong nanhai* is the central headquarters for the Communist Party and the State Council, situated adjacent to the Forbidden City. Aside from its physical existence, though, *zhong nanhai* is often synonymous with Chinese leadership at large.

4. Global health organizations usually use the term *most-at-risk-populations* (MARPs) to refer to the categories of people thought to be most at risk for HIV infection, among them commercial sex workers (CSWs), injection drug users (IDUs), and men who have sex with men (MSM).

References

"44 Gambling Houses Shut Down along Sino-Burmese Border." *Ming Pao*, Dec. 2, 2003.

Paper read at National Comprehensive AIDS Response Experience Sharing Conference, at Zhengzhou, Henan. 2005

Adegbola, O., and O. Babatola. 1999. "Premarital and Extra-marital Sex in Lagos, Nigeria." In *The Continuing HIV/AIDS Epidemic in Africa: Responses and Coping Strategies*, edited by O. Orubuloye et al. Canberra: Health Transition Center, National Center for Epidemiology and Population Health.

Agamben, Giorgio. 1998. *Homo Sacer: Sovereign Power and Bare Life*. Translated by Daniel Heller-Roazen. Stanford: Stanford University Press.

Allison, Anne. 1994. *Nightwork : Sexuality, Pleasure, and Corporate Masculinity in a Tokyo Hostess Club*. Chicago: University of Chicago Press.

Altman, Dennis. 1994. *Power and Community: Organizational and Cultural Responses to AIDS*. London: UCL Press.

———. 2001. *Global Sex*. Chicago: University of Chicago Press.

Anagnost, Ann. 1995. "A Surfeit of Bodies: Population and the Rationality of the State in Post-Mao China." In *Conceiving the New World Order: The Global Politics of Reproduction*, edited by Faye Ginsburg and Rayna Rapp. Berkeley: University of California Press.

———. 1997. *National Past-times: Narrative, Representation, and Power in Modern China*. Durham, NC: Duke University Press.

Appadurai, Arjun. 1996. "Sovereignty without Territoriality: Notes for a Postcolonial Geography." In *The Geography of Identity*, edited by Patricia Yaeger. Ann Arbor: University of Michigan Press.

Armajo-Hussein, Jacqueline, and Allan Beesey. 1998. *Young People and Social Change in China: A Survey on Risk Factors for HIV/AIDS in Yunnan Province*. Report of the HIV/AIDS Youth Survey conducted by the Australian Red Cross. Kunming: Yunnan Center for AIDS Care, Prevention, and Research and Yunnan Red Cross.

Arnott, David. 2001. "China-Burma Relations." In *Challenges to Democratization in Burma: Perspectives of Multilateral and Bilateral Responses*, edited by International Institute for Democracy and Electoral Assistance. Stockholm, Sweden: International Institute for Democracy and Electoral Assistance.

Ball, Desmond. 1999. *Burma and Drugs: The Regime's Complicity in the Global Drug Trade*. Canberra: Australian National University, Strategic & Defense Studies Center.

Barry, Andrew, Thomas Osborne, and Nikolas Rose, eds. 1996. *Foucault and Political Reason: Liberalism, Neo-liberalism and Rationalities of Government*. Chicago: University of Chicago Press.

Bashford, Alison. 2006. "Global Biopolitics and the History of World Health." *History of the Human Sciences* no. 19 (1): 67–88.

Baud, Michael, and Willem Van Schendel. 1997. "Toward a Comparative History of Borderlands." *Journal of World History* no. 8 (2): 211–242.

Bauman, Zygmunt. 1998. "On Postmodern Uses of Sex." *Theory, Culture, and Society* no. 15 (3–4): 215–242.

Baumler, Alan. 2000. "Opium Control Versus Opium Suppression: The Origins of the 1935 Six-Year Plan to Eliminate Opium and Drugs." In *Opium Regimes: China, Britain, and Japan, 1839–1952*, edited by Timothy Brook and Bob Tadashi Wakabayashi. Berkeley: University of California Press.

Bazzano, Lydia, Dongfeng Gu, Kristi Reynolds, Xiqui Wu, Chiung-Shiuan Chen, Xiufang Duan, Jing Chen, Rachel Wildman, Michael Klag, and He Jiang. 2007. "Alcohol Consumption and Risk of Stroke Among Chinese Men." *Annals of Neurology* no. 62 (6): 569–578.

Bernstein, Elizabeth. 2001. "The Meaning of the Purchase: Desire, Demand and the Commerce of Sex." *Ethnography* no. 2 (3): 389–420.

Bernstein, Elizabeth, and Laurie Shaffner. 2005. *Regulating Sex: The Politics of Intimacy and Identity*. New York: Routledge.

Beyrer, Chris. 2003. "Hidden Epidemic of Sexually Transmitted Diseases in China." *JAMA* no. 289 (10): 1303–1305.

Blum, Susan. 2001. *Portraits of "Primitives": Ordering Human Kinds in the Chinese Nation*. Walnut Creek, CA: Rowman & Littlefield.

———. 2007. *Lies That Bind: Chinese Truth, Other Truths*. Lanham, MD: Rowman & Littlefield.

Boellstorff, Tom. 2003. "Dubbing Culture: Indonesian *gay* and *lesbi* Subjectivities and Ethnography in an Already Globalized World." *American Ethnologist* no. 30 (2): 225–242.

———. 2011. "BUT DO NOT IDENTIFY AS GAY: A Proleptic Genealogy of the MSM Category." *Cultural Anthropology* no. 26 (2): 287–312.

Bond, Katherine, Thomas Valente, and Carl Kendall. 1999. "Social Network Influences on Reproductive Health Behaviors in Urban Northern Thailand." *Social Science and Medicine* no. 49 (12): 1599–1614.

Bourdieu, Pierre. [1980] 1990. *The Logic of Practice*. Stanford: Stanford University Press.

———. 1991. *Language and Symbolic Power*. Translated by John B. Thompson. Cambridge: Polity, in association with Basil Blackwell.

———. 2001. *Masculine Domination*. Translated by Richard Neice. Stanford: Stanford University Press.

Bovingdon, Gardner. 2004. *Autonomy in Xinjiang: Han Nationalist Imperatives and Uyghur Discontent*. Washington, DC: East-West Center.

Brady, Anne-Marie. 2008. *Marketing Dictatorship: Propaganda and Thought Work in Contemporary China*. New York: Rowman & Littlefield.

Brautigam, Deborah. 2009. *The Dragon's Gift: The Real Story of China in Africa*. New York: Oxford University Press.

Bray, David. 2006. "Building 'Community': New Strategies of Governance in Urban China." *Economy and Society* no. 35 (4): 530–549.

Bray, Francesca. 1997. *Technology and Gender: Fabrics of Power in Late Imperial China*. Berkeley: University of California Press.

Brixi, Hana, Yan Mu, Beatrice Targa, and David Hipgrave. 2013. "Engaging Sub-national Governments in Addressing Health Equities: Challenges and Opportunities in China's Health System Reform." *Health Policy and Planning* no. 28: 809–824.

Brown, Jill, James Sorrell, and Marcela Raffaelli. 2005. "An Exploratory Study of Constructions of Masculinity, Sexuality, and HIV/AIDS in Namibia, Southern Africa." *Culture, Health, and Sexuality* no. 7 (6): 585–598.

Brown, Theodore, Marcus Cueto, and Elizabeth Fee. 2006. "The World Health Organization and the Transition from International to Global Health." In *Medicine on the Border: Disease, Globalization and Security 1850 to the Present*, edited by Alison Bashford. New York: Palgrave.

Brownell, Susan, and Jeffrey Wasserstrom. 2002. *Chinese Femininities/Chinese Masculinities: A Reader*. Berkeley: University of California Press.

Burchell, Graham, Colin Gordon, and Peter Miller, eds. 1991. *The Foucault Effect: Studies in Governmentality*. Chicago: University of Chicago Press.

Butler, Judith. 1990. *Gender Trouble: Feminism and the Subversion of Identity*. New York: Routledge.

Campbell, Carole. 1995. "Male Gender Roles and Sexuality: Implications for Women's AIDS Risk and Prevention." *Social Science and Medicine* no. 41 (2): 197–210.

Cao, Yunzhen. 2004. Speech. In *Inauguration of the Tsinghua-Bayer Public Health and HIV/AIDS Media Studies Program*. Beijing.

Carrigan, Tim, Robert Connell, and John Lee. 1985. "Toward a New Sociology of Masculinity." *Theory and Society* no. 14 (5): 551–604.

Carrillo, Hector. 2002. *The Night Is Young: Sexuality in Mexico in the Time of AIDS, Worlds of Desire*. Chicago: University of Chicago Press.

Castells, Manuel. 1991. *The Informational City: A New Framework for Social Change*. Toronto: Center for Urban and Community Studies, University of Toronto.

———. 1998. *End of Millennium*. Malden, MA: Blackwell.

Centre for Harm Reduction. 2006. "Understanding Harm Reduction Fact Sheet." Melbourne: Burnett Institute.

Chamberlain, Heath. 1993. "On the Search for Civil Society in China." *Modern China* no. 19 (2, Symposium: "Public Sphere/Civil Society in China? Paradigmatic Issues in Chinese Studies III"): 199–215.

Chan, Anita, and Jonathan Unger. 1983. "The Second Economy of Rural China." In *Studies in the Second Economy of Communist Countries*, edited by G. Grossman. Berkeley: University of California Press.

Chang, Wen-Chin. 2004. "Guanxi and Regulation in Networks: The Yunnanese Trade Between Burma and Thailand, 1962–1988." *Journal of Southeast Asian Studies* no. 35 (3): 479–501.

Chen, Qingliang. 1992. *Saohuang: Shensheng de shiming* (The Anti-Pornography Campaign: A Sacred Mission). Beijing: Zhonggong zhongyang dangxiao chubanshe.

Chen, Xiangsheng, Xiangdong Gong, Guojun Liang, and Cheng Guo. 2000. "Epidemiologic Trends of Sexually Transmitted Diseases in China." *Sexually Transmitted Diseases* no. 27 (3): 138–142.

Chen, Yungfa. 1995. "The Blooming Poppy under the Red Sun: The Yan'an Way and the Opium Trade." In *New Perspectives on the Chinese Communist Revolution*, edited by Tony Saich and Hans Van de Ven. New York: Sharpe.

Chen, Zhengming, Liming Lee, Junshi Chen, Rory Collins, Fan Wu, Yu Guo, Pamela Linksted, and Richard Peto. 2005. "Cohort Profile: The Kadoorie Study of Chronic Disease in China (KSCDC)." *International Journal of Epidemiology* no. 34: 1243–1249.

Chen, Zhiqiang, Guocheng Zhang, Xiangdong Gong, Charles Lin, Xing Gao, Guojun Liang, Xiaoli Yue, Xiangsheng Chen, and Myron S. Cohen. 2007. "Syphilis in China: Results of a National Surveillance Program." *The Lancet* no. 369: 132–138.

Cheng, Sea-ling. 2000. "Assuming Manhood: Prostitution and Patriotic Passions in Korea." *East Asia: An International Quarterly* no. 18 (4): 40–78.

"China's Myanmar Dilemma." 2009. In *Asia Report No. 177*. Washington, DC: International Crisis Group.

"China's Relations with Myanmar: Welcome, Neighbor." 2010. *The Economist*, Sept. 11.

Chodorow, Nancy. 1978. *The Reproduction of Mothering: Psychoanalysis and the Sociology of Gender*. Berkeley: University of California Press.

Ch'ü, T'ung-tsu 1965. *Law and Society in Traditional China*. Paris: Mouton.

Ci hai (Sea of Words). *1979*. Shanghai: Shanghai cishu chubanshe.

Clark, Anne Marie. 1995. "Non-governmental Organizations and Their Influence on International Society." *Journal of International Affairs* no. 48 (2): 507–525.

Cochrane, Johanne, Hanhui Chen, Katherine Conigrave, and Wei Hao. 2003. "Alcohol Use in China." *Alcohol and Alcoholism* no. 38 (6): 537–542.

Cohen, Abner. 1974. *Two-dimensional Man: An Essay on the Anthropology of Power and Symbolism in Complex Society*. Berkeley: University of California Press.

Cohen, Myron, et al. 1996. "Successful Eradication of Sexually Transmitted Diseases in the People's Republic of China: Implications for the 21st Century." *Journal of Infectious Diseases* no. 174 (Suppl. 2): S223–S229.

———. 2000. "Sexually Transmitted Diseases in the People's Republic of China in Y2K." *Sexually Transmitted Diseases* no. 27 (3): 143–145.

Connell, R. W. 1993. "The Big Picture: Masculinites in Recent World History." *Theory and Society* no. 22 (5): 597–623.

———. 1995. *Masculinities*. Berkeley: University of California Press.

———. 2000. *The Men and the Boys*. St. Leonards, NSW: Allen and Uwin.

———. 2002. *Gender: Short Introductions*. Malden, MA: Polity Press.

———. 2005. "Hegemonic Masculinity: Rethinking the Concept." *Gender and Society* no. 19: 829–859.

Connell, Robert, and James Messerschmidt. 2005. "Hegemonic Masculinity: Rethinking the Concept." *Gender and Society* no. 19 (6): 829–859.

Constable, Nicole. 2003. *Romance on a Global Stage: Pen Pals, Virtual Ethnography, and "Mail-Order" Marriages*. Berkeley: University of California Press.

Cornwall, Andrea. 1997. "Men, Masculinity, and 'Gender in Development.'" In *Men and Masculinity*, edited by Caroline Sweetman. London: Oxfam.

Cornwall, Andrea, and Nancy Lindesfarne. 1994. "Dislocating Masculinity: Gender, Power, and Anthropology." In *Dislocating Masculinities: Comparative Ethnographies*, edited by Adrea Cornwall and Nancy Lindesfarne, 1–10. New York: Routledge.

Courtenay, Will H. 2000. "Constructions of Masculinity and Their Influence on Men's Well-being: A Theory of Gender and Health." *Social Science and Medicine* no. 50: 1385–1401.

Curtis, Valierie, Michael de Barra, and Robert Aunger. 2011. "Disgust as an Adaptive System for Disease Avoidance Behaviour." *Philosophical Transactions of the Royal Society of Biological Sciences* no. 366: 389–401.

Davis, Sara. 2007. *Song and Silence: Ethnic Revival on China's Southwest Borders*. New York: Columbia University Press.

de Carteau, Michel. 1984. *The Practice of Everyday Life*. Translated by Steven Rendall. Berkeley: University of California Press.

de Zalduondo, Barbara. 1991. "Prostitution Viewed Cross-culturally: Toward Recontextualizing Sex Work in AIDS Intervention Research." *Journal of Sex Research* no. 28 (2): 223–248.

Dean, Mitchell. 1999. *Governmentality: Power and Rule in Modern Society*. London: Sage.

Dehong Zhou renmin zhengfu bangongshi guanyu yinfa "Dehong zhou aizibing fanghzhi gongzuo fangan" de tongzhi (Notice of the Office of Dehong Prefecture People's Government Distribution of the "Dehong Prefecture Plan for HIV/AIDS Prevention and Treatment Work"). 2004. Edited by Office of the Government of the Dehong Dai Jingpo Autonomous Prefecture.

Dehong Zhou renmin zhengfu hongpai guanli gonggao (A Public Announcement on the Administration of Red Plates from the Dehong Prefecture People's Government). 2005.

Denyer, Simon. 2015. "Without Corruption, Some Ask, Can the Chinese Economic System Function?" *Washington Post*, Feb. 11.

Department of Propaganda of the Central Committee of the Chinese Communist Party. 2004. "SARS Related Propaganda (yu feidian youguan de xuanchuan)." *Chinese Law and Government* no. 37 (1): 28–42.

Diamant, Neil Jeffrey. 2000. *Revolutionizing the Family: Politics, Love, and Divorce in Urban and Rural China, 1949–1968*. Berkeley: University of California Press.

Dickson, Bruce. 2002. "Do Good Businessmen Make Good Citizens? An Emerging Collective Identity Among China's Private Entrepreneurs." In *Changing Meanings of Citizenship in Modern China*, edited by Merle Goldman and Elizabeth Perry. Cambridge, MA: Harvard University Press.

———. 2008. *Wealth into Power: The Communist Party's Embrace of China's Private Sector*. New York: Cambridge University Press.

Dietler, Michael. 1990. "Driven by Drink: The Role of Drinking in the Political Economy and the Case of Early Iron Age France." *Journal of Anthropological Archaeology* no. 9: 352–406.

———. 2006. "Alcohol: Anthropological/Archaeological Perspectives." *Annual Review of Anthropology* no. 35: 229–249.

Dikötter, Frank. 2008. *The Age of Openness: China before Mao*. Berkeley: University of California Press.

Dikötter, Frank, Lars Laamann, and Xun Zhou. 2004. *Narcotic Culture: A History of Drugs in China*. Chicago: University of Chicago Press.

Douglas, Mary. 1992. *Risk and Blame: Essays in Cultural Theory*. Edited by Mary Douglas. New York: Routledge.

Dowsett, Gary. 2001. "HIV/AIDS and Constructs of Gay Community: Researching Educational Practice with Community-Based Health Promotion for Gay Men." *International Journal of Social Research Methodology* no. 4 (3): 206–223.

Dupont, Alan. 2001. *East Asia Imperiled: Transnational Challenges to Security*. New York: Cambridge University Press.

Dworkin, Shari. 2005. "Who Is Epidemiologically Fathomable in the HIV/AIDS Epidemic? Gender, Sexuality, and Intersectionality in Public Health." *Culture, Health, and Sexuality* no. 7 (6): 615–623.

Dworkin, Shari, Abigail M. Hatcher, Chris Colvin, and Dean Peacock. 2013. "Impact of a Gender-Transformative HIV and Antiviolence Program on Gender Ideologies and Masculinities in Two Rural South African Communities." *Men and Masculinities* no. 16 (2): 181–202.

Ebrey, Patricia. 1993. *The Inner Quarters: Marriage and the Lives of Chinese Women in the Sung Period*, Berkeley: University of California Press.

Economy, Elizabeth. 2004. *The River Runs Black: Environmental Challenges in China's Future*. Ithaca: Cornell University Press.

Elvin, Mark. 1985. "Between the Earth and Heaven: Conceptions of the Self in China."

In *The Category of the Person*, edited by Steven Collins, Michael Carrithers, and Steven Lukes. New York: Cambridge University Press.

Entwistle, Barbara, and Gail Henderson, eds. 2000. *Re-drawing Boundaries: Work, Households, and Gender in China*. Berkeley: University of California Press.

Ewald, François. 1991. "Insurance and Risk." In *The Foucault Effect: Studies in Governmentality*, edited by G. Burchell, C. Gordon, and P. Miller. London: Harvester/ Wheatsheaf.

"Experts Urge Men to Care for Health." 2004. *Shanghai Daily News*, Oct. 29.

Farley, Melissa. 2004. "'Bad for the Body, Bad for the Heart': Prostitution Harms Women Even If Legalized or Decriminalized." *Violence Against Women* no. 10: 1087–1125.

Farmer, Paul. 1992. *AIDS and Accusation: Haiti and the Geography of Blame*. Berkeley: University of California Press.

Farquhar, Judith. 2002. *Appetites: Food and Sex in Postsocialist China, Body, commodity, text*. Durham, NC: Duke University Press.

Farrer, James. 2002. *Opening Up: Youth Sex Culture and Market Reform in Shanghai*. Chicago: University of Chicago Press.

Fei, Xiaotong. 1980. "Ethnic Identification in China." *Social Sciences in China* no. 1 (1).

———. [1947] 1992. *From the Soil: The Foundations of Chinese Society*. Translated by Gary Hamilton and Wang Zheng. Berkeley: University of California Press.

Feng, Xueshan, Tang Shenglan, Gerald Bloom, Malcolm Segall, and Gu Xingyuan. 1995. "Cooperative Medical Schemes in Contemporary Rural China." *Social Science and Medicine* no. 41 (8): 1111–1118.

Ferguson, James, and Akhil Gupta. 2002. "Spatializing States: Toward an Ethnography of Neoliberal Governmentality." *American Ethnologist* no. 29 (4): 981–2002.

Fidler, David. 2003. "SARS: Political Pathology of the First Post-Westphalian Pathogen." *Journal of Law Medicine and Ethics* no. 31 (4): 485–505.

Field, Andrew. 1999. "Selling Souls in Sin City: Shanghai Singing and Dancing Hostesses in Print, Film, and Politics, 1920–49." In *Cinema and Urban Culture in Shanghai, 1922–1943*, edited by Yingjin Zhang. Stanford: Stanford University Press.

Fordham, Graham. 1995. "Whiskey, Women, and Song: Men, Alcohol, and AIDS in Northern Thailand." *Australian Journal of Anthropology* no. 6 (3): 154–177.

Foreman, Martin. 1999. *AIDS and Men: Taking Risk or Taking Responsibility*. London: Panos, Zed.

Foucault, Michel. 1978. *The History of Sexuality: An Introduction*. New York: Random House.

———. 1991. "Governmentality." In *The Foucault Effect: Studies in Governmentality*, edited by Graham Burchell, Colin Gordon, and Peter Miller. Chicago: University of Chicago Press.

———. 1995. *Discipline and Punish: The Birth of the Prison*. Translated by Alan Sheridan. 2nd ed. New York: Vintage Books.

Friedman, Sara. 2000. "Spoken Pleasures and Dangerous Desires: Sexuality, Marriage, and the State in Rural Southeastern China." *East Asia: An International Quarterly* no. 18 (4): 13–39.

———. 2005. "The Intimacy of State Power: Marriage, Liberation, and Socialist Subjects in Southeastern China." *American Ethnologist* no. 32 (2): 312–327.

Fuller, Thomas. 2015. "Myanmar Returns to What Sells: Heroin." *New York Times*, Jan. 4.

Furth, Charlotte. 1988. "Androgynous Males and Deficient Females: Biology and Gender Boundaries in Sixteenth- and Seventeenth-Century China." *Late Imperial China* no. 9 (2): 1–30.

———. 1994. "Rethinking Van Gulik: Sexuality and Reproduction in Traditional Chinese Medicine." In *Engendering China: Women, Culture, and the State*, edited by Christina K. Gilmartin, Gail Hershatter, Lisa Rofel, and Tyrene White. Cambridge, MA: Harvard University Press.

———. 1999. *A Flourishing Yin: Gender in China's Medical History, 960–1665.* Berkeley: University of California Press.

Gallagher, Mary. 2004. "China: The Limits of Civil Society in a Leninist State." In *Civil Society and Political Change in Asia: Expanding and Contracting Democratic Space*, edited by Muthiah Algappa, 419–454. Palo Alto, CA: Stanford University Press.

Gardiner, Judith Kegan. 2002. *Masculinity Studies and Feminist Theory: New Directions.* New York: Columbia University Press.

Giddens, Anthony. 1992. *The Transformation of Intimacy: Sexuality, Love, and Eroticism in Modern Societies.* New York: Polity Press.

Gil, Vincent. 1996. "Prostitutes, Prostitution, and STD/HIV Transmission in Mainland China." *Social Science and Medicine* no. 42 (1): 141–152.

Gilmore, David. 1990. *Manhood in the Making: Cultural Concepts of Masculinity.* New Haven, CT: Yale University Press.

Gladney, Dru. 1994. "Representing Nationality in China: Refiguring Majority/Minority Identities." *Journal of Asian Studies* no. 53 (1): 92–123.

Goodman, Bryna. 1995. *Native Place, City, and Nation: Regional Networks and Identities in Shanghai, 1853–1937.* Berkeley: University of California Press.

Greenhalgh, Susan. 2008. *Just One Child: Science and Policy in Deng's China.* Berkeley: University of California Press.

Greenhalgh, Susan, and David Winkler. 2005. *Governing China's Population: From Leninist to Neoliberal Biopolitics.* Stanford: Stanford University Press.

Grosz, E. A. 1994. *Volatile Bodies: Toward a Corporeal Feminism.* St Leonards, NSW, Australia: Allen & Unwin.

Gu, Dongfeng, Xigui Wu, Kristi Reynolds, Xiufang Duan, Xue Xin, Robert Reynolds, Paul Whelton, and Jiang He. 2009. "Cigarette Smoking and Exposure to Environmental Tobacco Smoke in China: The International Collaborative Study of Cardiovascular Disease in Asia." *American Journal of Public Health* no. 94 (11): 1972–1976.

A Guide for Work Related to Intervention for High-Risk Behavior (gaowei xingwei ganyu gongzuo zhidao fangan). 2004. State Council.

Guo, Xiaolian. 2010. "Boom on the Way from Ruili to Mandalay." In *Myanmar/Burma*

Inside Challenges, Outside Interests, edited by Lex Rieffel. Washington, DC: Brookings Institution.

Gutmann, Matthew. 1996. *The Meanings of Macho: Being a Man in Mexico City*. Berkeley: University of California Press.

———. 1997a. "The Ethnographic (G)ambit: Women and the Negotiation of Masculinity in Mexico City." *American Ethnologist* no. 24 (4): 833–855.

———. 1997b. "Trafficking in Men: The Anthropology of Masculinity." *Annual Review of Anthropology* no. 24 (4): 833–855.

———. 2007. *Fixing Men: Sex, Birth Control, and AIDS in Mexico*. Berkeley: University of California Press.

Hanson, Marta. 2008. "The Art of Medicine: Maoist Public Health Campaigns, Chinese Medicine, and SARS." *Lancet* no. 372: 1457–1458.

Hao, Wei, Zhonghua Su, Binglun Liu, Kui Zhang, Hanqing Yang, Shaozhong Chen, Meizi Biao, and Chun Cui. 2004. "Drinking and Drinking Patterns of Health Status in the General Population of Five Areas of China." *Alcohol and Alcoholism* no. 39 (1): 43–52.

Harrell, Stevan. 1995. "Introduction: Civilizing Projects and the Reaction to Them." In *Cultural Encounters on China's Ethnic Frontiers*, edited by Stevan Harrell. Seattle: University of Washington Press.

Harrison, Abigail, Lucia O'Sullivan, Susie Hoffman, Curtis Dolezal, and Robert Morrell. 2006. "Gender Role and Relationship Norms among Young Adults in South Africa: Measuring the Context of Masculinity and HIV Risk." *Journal of Urban Health* no. 83 (4): 709–722.

Hart, Angie. 1995. "Risky Business? Men Who Buy Heterosexual Sex in Spain." In *Culture and Sexual Risk: Anthropological Perspectives on AIDS*, edited by Han ten Brummelhuis and Gilbert Herdt. Amsterdam: Gordon & Breach.

Hastings, Donnan, and Thomas Wilson. 2001. *Borders: Frontiers of Identity, Nation, and State*. New York: Berg.

He, Jiang, Dongfeng Gu, Xigui Wu, Kristi Reynolds, Xiufang Duan, Chonghua Yao, Jialiang Wang, Chung-Shiuan Chen, JIng Chen, Rachel Wildman, Michael Klag, and Paul Whelton. 2005. "Major Causes of Death among Men and Women in China." *New England Journal of Medicine* no. 353: 1124–1134.

Heimke, Gretchen, and Steven Levitsy. 2005. "Informal Institutions and Comparative Politics: A Research Agenda." *Perspectives on Politics* no. 2 (4): 725–740.

Henriot, Christian. [1997] 2001. *Prostitution and Sexuality in Shanghai*. Translated by Noel Castelino. New York: Cambridge University Press.

Herdt, Gilbert. 1994. *Third Sex, Third Gender: Beyond Sexual Dimorphism in Culture and History*. New York: Zone Books.

———. 1997. "Sexual Cultures and Population Movement: Implications for AIDS/ STDS." In *Sexual Cultures and Migration in the Era of AIDS: Anthropological and Demographic Perspectives*, edited by G. Herdt, 3–22. Oxford: Clarendon Press.

Hershatter, Gail. 1997. *Dangerous Pleasures: Prostitution and Modernity in Twentieth-Century Shanghai*. Berkeley: University of California Press.

Hertz, Ellen. 1998. *The Trading Crowd: An Ethnography of the Shanghai Stock Market.* New York: Cambridge University Press.

Hildebrandt, Timothy. 2013. *Social Organizations and the Authoritarian State in China.* New York: Cambridge University Press.

Hill, Ann Maxwell. 1998. *Merchants and Migrants: Ethnicity and Trade Among Yunnanese Chinese in Southeast Asia.* New Haven, CT: Yale University Press.

Hirsch, Jennifer, Holly Wardlow, Daniel Jordan Smith, Harriet Phinney, Shanti Parikh, and Constance Nathanson. 2010. *The Secret: Love, Marriage, and HIV.* Nashville, TN: Vanderbilt University Press.

H'o, Ts'ui-p'ing. 2007. "Rethinking Kachin Wealth Ownership." In *Social Dynamics in the Highlands of Southeast Asia: Reconsidering Political Systems of Highland Burma* by E. R. Leach, edited by Francois Robinne and Mandy Sadan. Boston: Brill.

Hoang, Kimberly. 2014. "Flirting with Capital Negotiating Perceptions of Pan-Asian Ascendancy and Western Decline in Global Sex Work." *Social Problems* no. 61 (4): 1–23.

———. 2015. *Dealing in Desire: Asian Ascendancy, Western Decline, and the Hidden Currencies of Global Sex Work.* Berkeley: University of California Press.

Hoffman, Lisa. 2006. "Autonomous Choices and Patriotic Professionalism: On Governmentality in Late-Socialist China." *Economy and Society* no. 35 (4): 550–570.

Honig, Emily. 2003. "Socialist Sex: The Cultural Revolution Revisited." *Modern China* no. 29 (2): 143–175.

Horn, Joshua. 1969. *Away with All Pests: An English Surgeon in People's China 1954–1969.* New York: Monthly Review Press.

Howell, Jude. 2004a. *Governance in China.* New York: Rowman & Littlefield.

———. 2004b. "New Directions in Civil Society: Organizing around Marginalized Interests." In *Governance in China*, edited by Jude Howell, 143–171. New York: Rowman & Littlefield.

Hu, Chi-hsi. 1974. "The Sexual Revolution in the Jiangxi Soviet." *China Quarterly* no. 59: 477–490.

Hu, Hsien Chin. 1944. "The Chinese Concept of Face." *American Anthropology* (46): 45–64.

Huang, Philip. 1993. "Public Sphere/Civil Society in China? The Third Realm between State and Society." *Modern China* no. 19 (2): 216–240.

Huang, Yanzhong. 2004. "Bringing the Local State Back In: The Politcial Economy of Public Health in Rural China." *Journal of Contemporary China* no. 13 (3): 367–390.

Hwang, Kwang-kuo. 1987. "Face and Favor: The Chinese Power Game." *American Journal of Sociology* no. 92 (4): 944–974.

Hwang, Shu-Ling. 1996. "Taiwan tezhong hangye funu" (Taiwanese Women of Special Professions). *Taiwan shehui yanjiu jikan* (Taiwan Annals of Social Research) no. 22.

Hyde, Sandra. 2007. *Eating Spring Rice: The Cultural Politics of AIDS in Southwest China, Department of Anthropology.* Berkeley: University of California Press.

IHRD. 2006. *Harm Reduction Developments 2005: Countries with Injection Driven Epidemics*. New York: International Harm Reduction Development Program of the Open Society Institute.

International IDEA. 2001. *Challenges in Democratization in Burma: Perspectives on Multilateral and Bilateral Perspectives*. Stockholm, Sweden: International Institute for Democracy and Electoral Assistance.

Jeffreys, Elaine. 2004. *China, Sex and Prostitution*. New York: Routledge Curzon.

Jin, Liyan. 2003. "Qianshi ershi shiji wushi niandai qian dehong jingpozu hunyin zhidu zhong de shehui xingbie guanxi" (A Preliminary Analysis of Early 1950s Gender Relations in the Dehong Jingpo Marriage System). In *Shehui xingbie minzu shequ fazhan yanjiu wenji* (A Collection of Studies on Gender, Ethnicity, and Regional Development), edited by Xiao Zhang, Wu Xu, Zhonghua Xu and Ma Linying. Guiyang: Guiyang renmin chubanshe.

Jing, Jun. 2011. "From Commodity of Death to Gift of Life." In *Deep China: The Moral Life of the Person, What Anthropology and Psychiatry Tell Us about China Today*, edited by Yunxiang Yan Arthur Kleinman, Jing Jun, Sing Lee, Everett Zhang, Pan Tianshu, Guo Jinhua. Berkeley: University of California Press.

Jobson, Geoffrey. 2010. "Changing Masculinities: Land-use, Family Communication, and Prospects for Working with Older Men Towards Gender Equity in a Livelihoods Intervention." *Culture, Health, and Sexuality* no. 12 (3): 233–246.

Joffe, Alexander. 1998. "Alcohol and Social Complexity in Ancient Western Asia." *Current Anthropology* no. 39 (3): 297–322.

Johnson, Ian. 2014. "In Limbo, a City in China Faces Life After Graft." *New York Times*, Dec. 27.

Jones, Rose. 1999. "Husbands and Lovers: Gender Construction and the Ethnography of Sex Research." In *Sex, Sexuality, and the Anthropologist*, edited by Fran Markowitz and Michael Ashkenazi. Urbana: University of Illinois Press.

Kampadoo, Kamala, and Jo Doezma, eds. 1998. *Resistance Global Sex Workers: Rights, and Redefinition*. New York: Routledge.

Kaufman, Joan, and Jun Jing. 2002. "China and AIDS: The Time to Act Is Now." *Science Magazine*, June 28: 339–340.

Kazer, William, and Rose Yu. 2012. "Bottoms Up, Profits Up: Moutai Defies China Slump." *Wall Street Journal*, Sept. 4.

Kennedy, Scott, and Guosheng Deng. 2010. "Big Business and Industry Association Lobbying in China: The Paradox of Contrasting Styles." *China Journal* no. 63: 101–125.

Kipnis, Andrew. 2007. "Neoliberalism Reified: Suzhi Discourse and Tropes of Neoliberalism in the People's Republic of China." *Journal of the Royal Anthropologic Institute* no. 13: 383–400.

Kleinman, Arthur. 1981. *Patients and Healers in the Context of Culture*. Berkeley: University of California Press.

———. 1999. "Experience and Its Moral Modes: Culture, Human Conditions, and Disorder." In *The Tanner Lectures on Human Values*, edited by Grethe Peterson, 357–420. Salt Lake City: University of Utah Press.

———. 2006. *What Really Matters: Living a Moral Life Amidst Uncertainty and Danger*. New York: Oxford University Press.

Klovdahl, Alan. 1985. "Social Networks and the Spread of Infectious Diseases: The AIDS Example." *Social Science and Medicine* no. 21 (11): 1203–1216.

Ko, Dorothy. 1994. *Teachers of the Inner Chambers: Women and Culture in Seventeenth Century China*. Stanford: Stanford University Press.

Komlosy, Analouska. 2004. "Procession and Water Splashing: Expressions of Locality and Nationality During Dai New Year in Xishuangbanna." *Journal of the Royal Anthropologic Institute* no. 10 (2): 351–373.

Kuhn, Philip. 1990. *Soulstealers: The Chinese Sorcery Scare of 1768*. Cambridge, MA: Harvard University Press.

Kutcher, Norman. 2000. "The Fifth Relationship: Dangerous Friendships in the Confucian Text." *American Historical Review* no. 105 (5): 1615–1629.

Lai, Gina. 1995. "Work and Family Roles and Psychological Well-Being in Urban China." *Journal of Health and Social Behavior* no. 36 (Mar.): 11–37.

Lam, T. H., Y. He, S. L. Li, S. F. He, and B. Q. Liang. 1997. "Mortality Attributable to Cigarette Smoking in China." *JAMA* no. 278 (278): 1505–1508.

Laumann, Edward, and John Gagnon. 1995. "A Sociological Perspective on Sexual Action." In *Conceiving Sexuality: Approaches to Sex Research in a Postmodern World*, edited by Richard Parker and John Gagnon. New York: Routledge.

Laumann, Edward, John Gagnon, R. T. Michael, and S. Michaels. 1994. *The Social Organization of Sexuality: Sexual Practices in the United States*. Chicago: University of Chicago Press.

Leach, Edmund. 1959. *Political Systems of Highland Burma: A Study of Kachin Social Structure*. London: Athlone Press.

Lemke, Thomas. 2001. "'The Birth of Bio-politics': Michel Foucault's Lecture at the College de France on Neo-liberal Governmentality." *Economy and Society* no. 30 (7): 190–207.

Leung, A. K. 2000. "Prostitution in Modern Shanghai: Two Recent Studies." *Nan Nu Men, Women, and Gender in Early and Imperial China* no. 2 (1): 180–187.

Lewis, Oscar. 1951. *Life in a Mexican Village: Tepoztlan Restudied*. Urbana: University of Illinois Press.

Li, Chenyang. 2010. "The Policies of India and China toward Myanmar." In *Myanmar/Burma: Inside Challenges, Outside Interests*, edited by Lex Rieffel. Washington, DC: Brookings Institution.

Li, Xiaojiang. 1999. "With What Discourse Do We Reflect on Chinese Women? Thoughts on Transnational Women in China." In *Spaces of Their Own: Women's Public Sphere in Transnational China*, edited by Mayfair Mei-Hui Yang. Minneapolis: University of Minnesota Press.

Liang, Chi-shad. 1990. *Burma's Foreign Relations: Neutralism in Theory and Practice*. New York: Praeger.

———. 1997. "Burma's Relations with the People's Republic of China: From Delicate Friendship to Genuine Co-operation." In *Burma: The Challenge of Change in a Divided Society*, edited by Peter Carey. New York: St. Martin's Press.

Liao, Susu, Jean Schensul, and Ivan Wolffers. 2003. "Sex Related Health Risks and Implications for Interventions with Hospitality Women in Hainan, China." *AIDS Education and Prevention* no. 15 (2): 109–121.

Lieberthal, Kenneth. 1992. "Introduction: The Fragmented Authoritarianism Model and Its Limitations." In *Bureaucracy, Politics, and Decision Making in Post-Mao China*, edited by Kenneth Lieberthal and David Lampton, 1–32. Berkeley: University of California Press.

Linge, G. J. R., and Doug Porter, eds. 1997. *No Place for Borders: The HIV/AIDS Epidemic and Development in Asia and the Pacific*. New York: St. Martin's Press.

Link, Perry, and Kate Zhou. 2002. "*Shunkouliu*: Popular Satirical Sayings and Popular Thought." In *Popular China: Unofficial Culture in a Globalizing Society*, edited by Perry Link, Richard Madsen, and Paul Pickowicz. Lanham, MD: Rowman & Littlefield.

Lintner, Bertil. 1997. *The Kachin: Lords of Burma's Northern Frontier*. New Zealand: Sollo Development.

———. 1999. *Burma in Revolt: Opium and Insurgency since 1948*. Chiang Mai, Thailand: Silkworm Books.

———. 2002. *Blood Brothers: The Criminal Underworld of Asia*. New York: Palgrave Macmillan.

Litzinger, Ralph. 2000. *Other Chinas: The Yao and the Politics of National Belonging*. Durham, NC: Duke University Press.

Louie, Kam. 2002. *Theorising Chinese Masculinity: Society and Gender in China*. New York: Cambridge University Press.

Lu, Lin, Manhong Jia, Yanling Ma, Li Yang, Zhiwei Chen, David Ho, Yan Jiang, and Linqi Jiang. 2008. "The Changing Face of HIV in China." *Nature* no. 455 (2): 609–611.

Lu, Xiaobo, and Elizabeth Perry. 1997. *The Danwei: Changing Chinese Workplace in Historical and Comparative Perspective (Socialism and Social Movements)*. Armonk, NY: Sharpe.

Lu, Xing. 1998. "An Interface between Individualistic and Collectivist Orientations in Chinese Cultural Values and Social Relations." *Howard Journal of Communication* no. 9: 91–107.

Lupton, Deborah. 1999. *Risk*. New York: Routledge.

Lynch, Ingrid, P. W. Brouard, and M. J. Visser. 2010. "Constructions of Masculinity among a Group of South African Men Living with HIV/AIDS: Reflections on Resistance and Change." *Culture, Health and Sexuality* no. 12: 15–27.

Lyttleton, Chris, and Amorntip Amarapibal. 2002. "Sister Cities and Easy Passage: HIV, Mobility and Economies of Desire in a Thai/Lao Border Zone." *Social Science and Medicine* no. 54 (4): 505–518.

Ma, Qiushi. 2002. "Defining Chinese Nongovernmental Organizations." *Voluntas: International Journal of Voluntary and Nonprofit Organizations* no. 13 (2): 113–130.

———. 2006. *Non-Governmental Organizations in Contemporary China*. New York: Routledge.

Ma, Y. 1990. "HIV Was First Discovered among IDUs in China." *Chinese Journal of Epidemiology* no. 21 (6): 184–185.

Mackerras, Colin. 1994. *China's Minorities: Integration and Modernization in the Twentieth Century*. Oxford: Oxford University Press.

Madsen, Richard. 1984. *Morality and Power in a Chinese Village*. Berkeley: University of California Press.

Mane, Purnima, and Peter Aggleton. 2001. "Gender and HIV/AIDS: What Do Men Have to Do with It?" *Current Sociology* no. 49 (6): 23–37.

Mann, Susan. 2000. "The Male Bond in Chinese History and Culture." *American Historical Review* no. 105 (5): 1600–1614.

Marcus, George. 1998. *Ethnography Through Thick and Thin*. Princeton, NJ: Princeton University Press.

Markus, Francis. 2005. "Chinese City Eyes Official Affairs." BBC News, Shanghai 2005 [accessed June 1, 2005]. Available from http://news.bbc.co.uk/2/hi/asia-pacific/4565291.stm.

Mars, Gerald, and Yochanan Altman. 1987. "Alternative Mechanism of Distribution in a Soviet Economy." In *Constructive Drinking: Perspectives on Drink from Anthropology*, edited by Mary Douglas. New York: Cambridge University Press.

Mason, Katherine. 2011. "After SARS: The Rebirth of Public Health in China's 'City of Immigrants.'" Diss., Harvard University, Cambridge, MA.

———. 2013. "To Your Health! Toasting, Intoxication, and Gendered Critique Among Banqueting Women." *China Journal* (69): 108–113.

Mauss, Marcel. 1985. "A Category of the Human Mind: The Notion of the Person, the Notion of Self." In *The Category of the Person*, edited by Steven Collins, Michael Carrithers, and Steven Lukes. New York: Cambridge University Press.

McGirk, Tim, and Susan Jakes. 2002. "Stalking a Killer." *Time Asia*, Sept. 30.

McMahon, Keith. 1995. *Misers, Shrews, and Polygamists: Sexuality and Male-Female Relationships in Eighteenth Century Chinese Fiction*. Durham, NC: Duke University Press.

———. 2002. *The Fall of the God of Money: Opium Smoking in Nineteenth-Century China*. New York: Rowman & Littlefield.

Meisner, Maurice. 1999. *Mao's China and After: A History of the People's Republic of China*. 3rd ed. New York: Free Press.

Mertha, Andrew. 2009. "Fragmented Authoritarianism 2.0: Political Pluralization in the Chinese Policy Process." *China Quarterly* no. 200: 995–1012.

Messersmith, Lisa, et al. 2000. "Who's at Risk? Men's STD Experience and Condom Use in Southwest Nigeria." *Studies in Family Planning* no. 31 (3): 203–216.

Micollier, Evelyne. 2004. "Social Significance of Commercial Sex Work: Implicitly Shaping a Sexual Culture?" In *Sexual Cultures in East Asia: The Social Construction of Sexuality and Sexual Risk in a Time of AIDS*, edited by Evelyne Micollier, 3–22. New York: Routledge Curzon.

Milwertz, Cecilia, and Fengxian Wang. 2013. "Masculine Modernity Trumps

Feminine Tradition: A Gendered Capacity Building Operation in China." *Gender Technology and Development* no. 17: 259–280.

Mitchell, James Clyde. 1969. "The Concept and Use of Social Networks." In *Social Networks in Urban Situations: Analyses of Personal Relationships in Central African Towns*, edited by James Clyde Mitchell. Manchester, UK: Manchester University Press.

Morrell, Robert. 1998. "Of Boys and Men: Masculinity and Gender in Southern African Studies." *Journal of South African Studies* no. 24 (4): 605–630.

Morris, Martina. 2004. *Network Epidemiology: A Handbook for Survey Design and Data Collection*. New York: Oxford University Press.

Mueggler, Erik. 2001. *The Age of Wild Ghosts: Memory, Violence, and Place in Southwest China*. Berkeley: University of California Press.

Murphy, Rachel. 2004. "Turning Peasants into Modern Chinese Citizens: 'Population Quality' Discourse, Demographic Transition and Primary Education." *China Quarterly* no. 177 (March): 1–20.

Murray, Diane. 1994. *The Origins of the Tiandihui: The Chinese Triads in Legend and History*. Stanford: Stanford University Press.

Nader, Laura. 1974. "Up the Anthropologist: Perspectives Gained from Studying Up." In *Reinventing Anthropology*, edited by Dell Hyme. Ann Arbor: University of Michigan Press.

Narcotic Control Law of the People's Republic of China (jiedu tiaoli). 2008. Edited by Legal Office of the State Council.

Neagius, Alan, Samuel Friedman, Thomas Ward, Jerome Wright, Richard Curtis, and Don Desjarlais. 1994. "The Relevance of Drug Injectors' Social and Risk Networks for Understanding and Preventing HIV Infection." *Social Science and Medicine* no. 38 (1): 67–78.

Nichter, Mark. 2003. "Harm Reduction: A Core Concern for Medical Anthropology." In *Risk, Culture, and Health Inequality: Shifting Perceptions of Danger and Blame*, edited by Barbara Herr Harthorn and Laury Oaks. New York: Praeger.

Nonini, Donald. 2008. "Is China Becoming Neoliberal?" *Critique of Anthropology* no. 28 (2): 145–176.

North, Douglas. 1990. *Institutions, Institutional Change, and Economic Performance*. Cambridge: Cambridge University Press.

Oboler, Regina Smith. 1986. "For Better or for Worse: Anthropologists and Husbands in the Field." In *Self, Sex, and Gender in Cross-Cultural Fieldwork*, edited by Tony Whitehead and Mary Ellen Conaway. Urbana: University of Illinois Press.

Oi, Jean. 1985. "Communism and Clientelism: Rural Politics in China." *World Politics* no. 37 (2): 238–266.

Ortner, Sherry. 1972. "Is Female to Male as Nature Is to Culture?" *Feminist Studies* no. 1 (2): 5–31.

Orubuloye, I. O., John Caldwell, and Pat Caldwell. 1991. "Diffusion and Focus in Sexual Networking: Identifying Partners and Partners' Partners." *Studies in Family Planning* no. 23 (6): 343–351.

Osburg, John. 2013. *Anxious Wealth: Money and Morality Among China's New Rich*. Stanford: Stanford University Press.

Otis, Eileen. 2012. *Markets and Bodies: Women, Service Work, and the Making of Inequality in China*. Stanford: Stanford University Press.

Padilla, Mark. 2007. *Caribbean Pleasure Industry : Tourism, Sexuality, and AIDS in the Dominican Republic, Worlds of Desire*. Chicago: University of Chicago Press.

Paiva, Vera. 2000. "Gendered Scripts and the Sexual Scene: Promoting Sexual Subjects among Brazilian Teenagers." In *Framing the Sexual Subject: The Politics of Gender, Sexuality, and Power*, edited by Richard Parker, Regina Maria Barbosa, and Peter Aggleton. Berkeley: University of California Press.

Palmer, James. 2013. "Kept Women." *Aeon*, October.

Pan, Suiming. 2004. "Three Red Light Districts." In *Sexual Cultures in East Asia: The Social Construction of Sexuality and Sexual Risk in a Time of AIDS*, edited by Evelyne Micollier, 23–53. New York: Routledge Curzon.

———. 2006. *Sex Revolution in China: Its Origins, Expressions, and Evolution (zhongguo xing geming zonglun)*. Taiwan: Wangyou.

Pandolfi, Mariella. 2003. "Contract of Mutual (In)Difference: Governance and the Humanities Apparatus in Contemporary Albania and Kosovo." *Indiana Journal of Global Legal Studies* no. 10: 369–381.

Panter-Brick, Catherine, Sian E. Clark, Heather Lomas, Margaret Pinder, and Steve Lindsay. 2006. "Culturally Compelling Strategies for Behavior Change: A Social Ecology Model and Case Study in Malaria Prevention." *Social Science and Medicine* no. 62: 2810–2825.

Parish, William, Edward Laumann, Myron Cohen, Suiming Pan, Heyi Zheng, Irving Hoffman, Tianfu Wang, and Kwai Hang Ng. 2003. "Population Based Study on Chlamydial Infection in China." *Journal of the American Medical Association* no. 289 (10): 1265–1273.

Parish, William, and Suiming Pan. 2004. "Sexual Partners in China: Risk Patterns for Infection by HIV and Other Sexually Transmitted Diseases." Paper read at Social Policy and HIV/AIDS in China, May 6–8, at Center for Business and Government, Kennedy School of Government, Harvard University.

Parker, Richard. 1987. "Acquired Immunodeficiency Syndrome in Urban Brazil." *Medical Anthropology Quarterly* no. 1 (2): 155–175.

———. 1991. *Bodies, Pleasures, and Passions: Sexual Culture in Contemporary Brazil*. Boston: Beacon Press.

———. 1995. "The Social and Cultural Construction of Sexual Risk, or How to Have (Sex) Reserach in an Epidemic." In *Culture and Sexual Risk: Anthropological Perspectives on AIDS*, edited by H. T. Brummelhuis and G. Herdt, 257–270. Amsterdam: Gordon and Breach.

———. 1999. *Beneath the Equator: Cultures of Desire, Male Homosexuality, and Emerging Gay Communities in Brazil*. New York, London: Routledge.

———. 2000. "Administering the Epidemic: HIV/AIDS Policy, Models of Development, and International Health." In *Global Health Policy, Local Realities: The*

Fallacy of the Level Playing Field, edited by Linda Whiteford and Lenore Manderson. London: Lynn Rjenner.

———. 2009. "Civil Society, Political Mobilization, and the Impact of HIV Scale-up on Health Systems in Brazil." *Journal of Acquired Immune Deficiency Syndrome* no. 52 (Suppl 1): S49–S51.

Parker, Richard, and Peter Aggleton. 2002. *HIV and AIDS-related Stigma and Discrimination: A Conceptual Framework and Implications for Action*. Rio de Janeiro: ABIA.

Parreñas, Rhacel Salazar. 2011. *Illicit Flirtations: Labor, Migration, and Sex Trafficking in Tokyo*. Stanford: Stanford University Press.

Patton, Cindy. 1985. *Sex and Germs: The Politics of AIDS*. Boston: South End Press.

———. 1990. *Inventing AIDS*. New York: Routledge.

———. 2002. *Globalizing AIDS*. Minneapolis: University of Minnesota Press.

Peterson, Willard. 1979. *Bitter Gourd: Fang I-Chih and the Impetus for Intellectual Change*. New Haven: Yale University Press.

Pigg, Stacey Leigh. 2001. "Languages of Sex and AIDS in Nepal: Notes on the Social Production of Commensurability." *Cultural Anthropology* no. 16 (4): 481–541.

Porter, Doug. 1997. "A Plague on the Borders: HIV, Development, and Traveling Identities in the Golden Triangle." In *Sites of Desire, Economies of Pleasure: Sexualities in Asia and the Pacific*, edited by Lenore Manderson and Margaret Jolly. Chicago: University of Chicago Press.

Prestage, Garrett, and Roberta Perkins. 1994. "Introduction." In *Sex Work and Sex Workers in Australia*, edited by G. Prestage, R. Perkins, R. Sharp, F. Lovejoy. Sydney: University of South Wales Press.

Pye, Lucian. 1981. *The Dynamics of Chinese Politics*. Cambridge, MA: Oelgeschlager, Gunn & Hain.

———. 1991. "The State and the Individual: An Overview Interpretation." *China Quarterly* no. 127 (Special Issue: The Individual and State in China): 443–466.

Rabinow, Paul. 1996. *Essays on the Anthropology of Reason*. Princeton, NJ: Princeton University Press.

Raw, Seng. 2004. "The Role of Minorities in the Transitional Process." In *NBR Analysis Reconciling Burma/Myanmar: Essays on US Relations with Burma*. Washington, DC: National Bureau of Asian Research.

Remick, Elizabeth. 2003. "Prostitution Taxes and Local State Building in Republican China." *Modern China* no. 29 (1): 38–70.

———. 2014. *Regulation Prostitution in China: Gender and Local Statebuilding 1900– 1937*. Stanford: Stanford University Press.

Robinne, François, and Mandy Sadan. 2007. *Social Dynamics in the Highland of Southeast Asia: Reconsidering Political Systems of Highland Burma by E. R. Leach*. Boston: Brill.

Rofel, Lisa. 2007. *Desiring China: Experiments of Neoliberalism, Sexuality, and Public Culture*. Durham, NC: Duke University Press.

Rosaldo, Michelle. 1974. "Woman, Culture, and Society: A Theoretical Overview." In

Woman, Culture, and Society, edited by Michelle Rosaldo and Louise Lamphere. Stanford: Stanford University Press.

Rose, Nikolas, and Peter Miller. 1992. "Political Power beyond the State: Problematics of Governmentality." *British Journal of Sociology* no. 43: 173–205.

Ruan, F. F. 1991. *Sex in China: Studies in Sexology in Chinese Culture*. New York: Plenum Press.

Saich, Tony. 2000. "Negotiating the State." *China Quarterly* no. 161: 124–141.

———. 2001. *Governance and Politics of China*. New York: Palgrave.

———. 2002. "The Blind Man and the Elephant: Analyzing the Local State in China." In *East Asian Capitalism: Conflicts, Growth and Crisis*, edited by Luigi Tomba, 75–101. Milan: Fondazione Giangiacomo Feltrinelli.

———. 2006a. "Is SARS China's Chernobyl or Much Ado About Nothing?" In *SARS in China: Prelude to Pandemic*, edited by Arthur Kleinman and James Watson. Stanford: Stanford University Press.

———. 2006b. "Social Policy Development in the Era of Economic Reform." In *AIDS and Social Policy in China*, edited by Joan Kaufman, Arthur Kleinman, and Tony Saich. Cambridge, MA: Harvard University Asia Center.

———. 2008. *Providing Public Goods in Transitional China*. New York: Palgrave Macmillan.

Saich, Tony, and David Apter. 1994. *Revolutionary Discourses in Mao's Republic*. Cambridge, MA: Harvard University Press.

Sanderson, Henry. 2007. "Report: Sex Main Cause of HIV in China." *Associated Press*, Nov. 30.

Sargeson, Sally, and Jian Zhang. 1999. "Reassessing the Role of the Local State: A Case Study of Local Government Interventions in Property Rights Reform in a Hangzhou District." *China Journal* no. 42: 209–231.

Schein, Louisa. 2000. *Minority Rules: The Miao and the Feminine in China's Cultural Politics, Body, Commodity, Text*. Durham: Duke University Press.

Scheper-Hughes, Nancy. 1994. "An Essay: AIDS and the Social Body." *Social Science and Medicine* no. 39 (7): 991–1003.

Scheper-Hughes, Nancy, and Margaret Lock. 1987. "The Mindful Body: A Prolegomenon to Future Work in Medical Anthropology." *Medical Anthropology Quarterly* no. 1 (1): 6–41.

Scott, James C. 1985. *Weapons of the Weak: Everyday Forms of Peasant Resistance*. New Haven: Yale University Press.

———. 2009. *The Art of Not Being Governed: An Anarchist History of Upland Southeast Asia*. New Haven: Yale Univerisity Press.

Sedgwick, Eve. 1985. *Between Men: English Literature and Male Homosocial Desire*. New York: Columbia University Press.

Shan, Juan. 2012. "HIV Rises Sharply among Chinese 50 and Older." *China Daily*, Aug. 23.

Shao, Jing. 2007. "Fluid Labor and Blood Money." *Cultural Anthropology* no. 21 (4): 535–569.

Shirk, Susan. 1982. *Competitive Comrades: Career Incentives and Student Strategies in China.* Berkeley: University of California Press.

———. 1984. "The Decline of Virtuocracy in China." In *Class and Social Stratification in Post-Revolution China*, edited by James Watson, 56–83. New York: Cambridge University Press.

Sigley, Gary. 2001. "Keep It in the Family: Government, Marriage, and Sex in Contemporary China." In *Borders of Being: Citizenship, Fertility, and Sexuality in Asia and the Pacific*, edited by Margaret Jolly and Kalpana Ram. Ann Arbor: University of Michigan Press.

———. 2004. "Liberal Despotism: Population Planning, Subjectivity, and Government in Contemporary China." *Alternatives* no. 29: 557–575.

Silverstein, Josef. 1997. "The Civil War, the Minorities and Burma's New Politics." In *Burma: The Challenge in a Divided Society*, edited by Peter Carey. New York: St. Martin's Press.

Simon, Scott. 2011. "Between China and India Lies Myanmar's Future: An Interview with Thant Myint-U." On *Weekend Edition Saturday*, National Public Radio, Sept. 24.

Simon, William, and John Gagnon. 1984. "Sexual Scripts." *Society* no. 22 (1): 53–60.

Singh, Teshu. 2013. *China and Myanmar: The Great Game of the Gas Pipeline.* Institute of Peace and Conflict Studies, New Dehli.

Skinner, William. 1977. "Introduction: Urban Social Structure in Ch'ing China." In *The City in Late Imperial China*, edited by William G. Skinner. Stanford: Stanford University Press.

Slack, Edward, Jr. 2000. "The National Anti-opium Association and the Guomindang State, 1924–1937." In *Opium Regimes: China, Britain, and Japan, 1839–1952*, edited by Timothy Brook and Bob Tadashi Wakabayashi. Berkeley: University of California Press.

Smart, Josephine. 2005. "Cognac, Beer, Red Wine or Soft Drinks? Hong Kong Identity and Wedding Banquets." In *Drinking Cultures: Alcohol and Identity*, edited by Thomas Wilson. New York: Berg.

Smith, Martin. 1994a. *Ethnic Groups in Burma: Development, Democracy, and Human Rights.* Human Rights Series. London: Anti-Slavery International.

———. 1994b. "The Question: Humanitarian and Development Aid in Burma?" *Burma Debate.*

Sommer, Matthew Harvey. 1997. "The Penetrated Male in Late Imperial China: Judicial Construction and Social Stigma." *Modern China* no. 23 (2): 140–180.

———. 2000. *Sex, Law, and Society in Late Imperial China.* Law, Society, and Culture in China. Stanford: Stanford University Press.

Spence, Jonathan. 1992. "Opium." In *Chinese Roundabout*, edited by Jonathan Spence. New York: Norton.

Spires, Anthony. 2011. "Contingent Symbiosis and Civil Society in an Authoritarian State: Understanding the Survival of China's Grassroots NGOs." *American Sociological Review* no. 117 (1): 1–45.

————. 2012. "Lessons from Abroad: Foreign Influences on China's Emerging Civil Society." *China Journal* no. 68: 125–146.

State Council Notice on Earnestly Strengthening HIV/AIDS Prevention and Treatment Work (guowu yuan guanyu qieshi jiaqiang aizibing fangzhi gongzuo de tongzhi). 2004. Beijing.

Steinberg, David. 2001. *Burma: The State of Myanmar*. Washington, DC: Georgetown University Press.

Sturgeon, Janet. 2004. "Borders, Practices, Boundaries, and the Control of Resource Access: A Case from China, Thailand, and Burma." *Development and Change* no. 35 (3): 463–484.

Sullivan, Sheena, and Zunyou Wu. 2007. "Rapid Scale up of Harm Reduction in China." *International Journal of Drug Policy* no. 18: 118–128.

Sun, Yan. 2004. *Corruption and Market in Contemporary China*. Ithaca, NY: Cornell University Press.

Taleb, Nassim Nicholas, and Mark Blyth. 2011. "The Black Swan of Cairo: How Suppressing Volatility Makes the World Less Predictable and More Dangerous." *Foreign Affairs* no. 90 (3): 33–39.

Tang, Shenglan, and Stephen Bertel Squire. 2004. "What Lessons Can Be Drawn from Tuberculosis (TB) Control in China in the 1990s: An Analysis from a Health System Perspective." *Health Policy* no. 72: 93–104.

Tatlow, Didi Kirsten. 2013. "Play Tests China's Sexual Limits." *New York Times*, July 16.

Teets, Jessica. 2013. "Let Many Civil Societies Bloom: The Rise of Consultative Authoritarianism in China." *China Quarterly* no. 213: 19–38.

Tian, Yuan, Yanqin Ouyang, and Qingyuan Guo. 2014. "Rise and Fall of a Coal Boomtown in Shanxi Province." *Caixin online*, Oct. 24. http://english.caixin.com/2014–10–24/100743023.html.

Timmons, Heather. 2013. "The Secret Factor in China's Housing Bubble? Mistresses." *Atlantic*, Oct. 10.

Tran, Lisa. 2011. "The ABCs of Monogamy in Republican China: Adultery, Bigamy, and Conjugal Fidelity." *Twentieth-Century China* no. 36 (2): 99–118.

Treichler, Paula. 1999. *How to Have Theory in an Epidemic: Cultural Chronicles of AIDS*. Durham, NC: Duke University Press.

Tsai, Kellee. 2007. *Capitalism without Democracy: The Private Sector in Contemporary China*. Ithaca, NY: Cornell Univeristy Press.

Tsui, Kai-yuen, and Wang Youqiang. 2004. "Between Separate Stoves and a Single Menu." *China Quarterly* no. 177: 71–90.

"2,290 Party Members Disciplined over Graft." 2013. *South China Morning Post*, Aug. 1.

UN Millennium Project. 2005. *Combating AIDS in the Developing Worlds*. Task Force on HIV/AIDS, Malaria, TB and Access to Essential Medicines, Working Group on HIV/AIDS.

Uretsky, Elanah. 2015. "'Sex'—It's Not Only Women's Work: A Case for Refocusing on the Functional Role That Sex Plays in Work for Both Women and Men." *Critical Public Health* no. 25 (1): 78–88.

Van Gulik, R. H. 1974. *Sexual Life in Ancient China: A Preliminary Survey of Chinese Sex and Society from Ca. 1500 B.C. till 1644 A.D.* Leiden: E. J. Brill.

van Kerkwijk, Carla. 1995. "The Dynamics of Condom Use in Thai Sex Work with *Farang* Clients." In *Culture and Sexual Risk: Anthropological Perspectives on AIDS*, edited by Han ten Brummelhuis and Gilbert Herdt. Amsterdam: Gordon and Breach.

Vance, Carole. 1991. "Anthropology Rediscovers Sexuality: A Theoretical Comment." *Social Science and Medicine* no. 33 (8): 875–884.

Walder, Andrew. 1986. *Communist Neo-traditionalism: Work and Authority in Chinese Industry.* Berkeley: University of California Press.

———. 1995. *The Waning Communist State: Economic Origins of Political Decline in China and Hungary.* Berkeley: University of California Press.

Wang, Hongying. 2000. "Informal Institutions and Foreign Investment in China." *Pacific Review* no. 13 (4): 525–556.

Wang, Longde, Lingzhi Kang, Fan Wu, Yimin Bai, and Robert Burton. 2007. "Preventing Chronic Diseases in China." *Lancet* no. 366: 1821–1824.

Wang, Ruotao. 2000. "Critical Health Literacy: A Case Study from China in Schistosomiasis Control." *Health Promotion International* no. 15 (3): 269–274.

Wang, Shaoguang. 1995. "The Rise of the Regions: Fiscal Reform and the Decline of Central State Capacity in China." In *The Waning of the Communist State: Economic Origins of Political Decline in China and Hungary*, edited by Andrew Walder. Berkeley: University of California Press.

Wang, Xiaoying. 2002. "The Post Communist Personality: The Spectre of China's Capitalist Markets." *China Journal* no. 47: 1–17.

Wang, Zhusheng. 1997. *The Jingpo: Kachin of the Yunnan Plateau.* Tempe, AZ: Program for Southeast Asian Studies, ASU.

Wank, David. 1999. *Commodifying Communism: Business, Trust, and Politics in a Chinese City.* New York: Cambridge University Press.

———. 2000. "Cigarettes and Domination in Chinese Business Networks: Institutional Change during the Market Transition." In *The Consumer Revolution in Urban China*, edited by Deborah Davis. Berkeley: University of California Press.

Warner, Michael. 1999. *The Trouble with Normal: Sex, Politics, and the Ethics of Queer Life.* New York: Free Press.

Watson, James L. 1997. *Golden Arches East: McDonald's in East Asia.* Stanford: Stanford University Press.

Watson, Rubie, and Patricia Ebrey, eds. 1991. *Marriage and Inequality in Chinese Society.* Berkeley: University of California Press.

Webster, Donovan. 2003. *The Burma Road: The Epic Story of the China-Burma-India Theater in World War II.* New York: Farrar, Straus, and Giroux.

Wedel, Janine, Chris Shore, Gregory Feldman, and Stacy Lathrop. 2005. "Toward an Anthropology of Public Policy." *Annals of the American Academy of Political and Social Science* no. 600 (1): 30–51.

Wehrfritz, G. 1996. "Unbuttoning a Nation." *Newsweek*, Apr. 15: 8–11.

Weitzer, Ronald. 2009. "Sociology of Sex Work." *Annual Review of Sociology* no. 35: 213–234.

Wellman, Barry, Wenhong Chen, and Weizhen Dong. 2002. "Networking Guanxi." In *Social Connections in China: Institutions, Culture, and the Changing Nature of Guanxi*, edited by Tom Gold, Doug Guthrie and David Wank. New York: Cambridge University Press.

Wong, Edward. 2015. "Suddenly Strict, Beijing Slaps Its Mouthpiece." *New York Times*, Feb. 14.

Wong, Yuk-Lin Renita. 1997. "Dispersing the 'Public' and the 'Private': Gender and the State in the Birth Planning Policy of China." *Gender and Society* no. 11 (4): 509–525.

Wu, Zhixiang, and Yongsheng Yang. 1996. *Dehong shizhi ziliao* (Materials for the Dehong Gazetteer). Dehong Ethnic Press.

Wu, Zunyou, Keming Rou, and Haixia Cui. 2004. "The HIV/AIDS Epidemic in China: History, Current Strategies, and Future Challenges." *AIDS Education and Prevention* no. 16: 7–17.

Xiao, Suowei. 2011. "The 'Second-Wife' Phenomenon and the Relational Construction of Class-Coded Masculinities in Contemporary China." *Men and Masculinities* no. 14 (5): 607–627.

Xin, Ren. 1999. "Prostitution and Economic Modernization in China." *Violence Against Women* no. 5: 1411–1436.

Xu, Jun. 1995. *Jinu Shi* (The History of Prostitution). Shanghai: Shanghai wenyi chuban she.

Xu, Zhixiang. 2006. *Healing from Social Suffering: Women's Experience in a Drug Afflicted Jingpo Community in Yunnan, China*. Faculty of Graduate Studies, Mahidol University, Bangkok, Thailand.

Yan, Hairong. 2003. "Neoliberal Governmentality and Neohumanism: Organizing Suzhi/Value Flow through Labor Recruitment Networks." *Cultural Anthropology* no. 18 (4): 493–523.

Yan, Ming. 1992. *Zhongguo mingji yishu shi* (A History of the Art of Courtesanship in China). Taibei: Wenjin chubanshe.

Yan, Yunxiang. 1996. *The Flow of Gifts: Reciprocity and Social Networks in a Chinese Village*. Stanford: Stanford University Press.

———. 2003. *Private Life Under Socialism: Love, Intimacy, and Family Change in a Chinese Village 1949–1999*. Stanford: Stanford University Press.

———. 2011. "The Changing Moral Landscape." In *Deep China, The Moral Life of the Person: What Anthropology and Psychiatry Tell Us About China*, edited by Yunxiang Yan Arthur Kleinman, Jing Jun, Sing Lee, Everett Zhang, Pan Tianshu, and Guo Jinhua. Berkeley: University of California Press.

Yang, Gonghuan, Lingzhi Kong, Wenhua Zhao, Xia Wan, Lincoln Chen, and Jeffrey Koplan. 2008. "Emergence of Chronic Non-communicable Diseases in China." *Lancet* no. 372 (9650): 1697.

Yang, Mayfair Mei-hui. 1988. "The Modernity of Power in the Chinese Socialist Order." *Cultural Anthropology* no. 3 (4): 408–427.

———. 1994. *Gifts, Favors, and Banquets: The Art of Social Relationships in China.* Ithaca, NY: Cornell University Press.

———. 2002. "The Resilience of Guanxi and Its New Deployments: A Critique of Some New Guanxi Scholarship." *China Quarterly* no. 170: 459–476.

Yawnghwe, Chao-Tzang. 1993. "The Political Economy of the Opium Trade: Implications for the Shan State." *Journal of Contemporary Asia* no. 23 (3): 306–326.

Young, Allan. 1981. "The Creation of Medical Knowledge: Some Problems in Interpretation." *Social Science and Medicine* no. 15B: 379–386.

Yunnan renmin zhengfu bangongting guanyu shishi fangzhi aizibing liu xiang gongcheng de tongzhi (The Notice from the General Office of the People's Government of Yunnan Province on Implementing Six Projects on HIV Prevention). 2004. Edited by General Office of the People's Government of Yunnan Province.

Zamperini, Paola. 1999. "But I Never Learned to Waltz: The 'Real' and Imagined Education of a Courtesan in the Late Qing." *Nan Nu* no. 1 (1): 107ff.

Zhang, Everett Yuehong. 2001. "*Guodui* and the State: Constructing Entrepreneurial Masculinity in Two Cosmopolitan Areas of Post-Socialist China." In *Gendered Modernities: Ethnographic Perspectives*, edited by Dorothy Hodgson. New York: Palgrave.

———. 2011. "China's Sexual Revolution." In *Deep China: The Moral Life of the Person, What Anthropology and Psychiatry Tell Us about China Today*, edited by Yunxiang Yan Arthur Kleinman, Jing Jun, Sing Lee, Everett Zhang, Pan Tianshu, and Guo Jinhua. Berkeley: University of California Press.

Zhang, Hong. 2006. "Making Light of the Dark Side: SARS Jokes and Humor in China." In *SARS in China: Prelude to Pandemic*, edited by Arthur Kleinman and James L. Watson, 149–170. Stanford: Stanford University Press.

Zheng, Tiantian. 2003. "From Rural Migrants to Bar Hostesses: Gender and Sex Industry in a Post-Mao City." Diss., Yale University, New Haven.

———. 2009. *Red Lights: The Lives of Sex Workers in Postsocialist China.* Minneapolis: University of Minnesota Press.

Zheng, Yangwen. 2005. *The Social Life of Opium in China.* New York: Cambridge University Press.

Zhong, Xueping. 2000. *Masculinity Besieged? Issues of Modernity and Male Subjectivity in Chinese Literature of the Late Twentieth Century.* Durham, NC: Duke University Press.

Zhou, Yongming. 1999. *Anti-Drug Crusades in Twentieth Century China: Nationalism, History, and State Building.* New York: Rowman & Littlefield.

Zhuang, Kongshao. 2002. *Huri: Xiao Liangshan minjian jiedu shijian* (Tiger Day: A Popular Method for Drug Detoxificaiton in Lesser Liangshan). Institute for Anthropology, Renmin University.

Index